Your
Boxer's
Life

Also Available from PRIMA PETS™

Your Beagle's Life by Kim Campbell Thornton

Your Boxer's Life by Kim D.R. Dearth

Your Cat's Life by Joanne Howl, D.V.M.

Your Chihuahua's Life by Kim Campbell Thornton

Your Dog's Life by Tracy Acosta, D.V.M.

Your German Shepherd's Life by Audrey Pavia

Your Golden Retriever's Life by Betsy Sikora Siino

Your Lab's Life by Virginia Parker Guidry

Your Rottweiler's Life by Kim D.R. Dearth

KIM D.R. DEARTH

Joanne Howl, D.V.M., Series Editor

Your
BOXER'S
Life

Your Complete Guide to Raising Your Pet from Puppy to Companion

PRIMA PETS

An Imprint of Prima Publishing

3000 Lava Ridge Court • Roseville, California 95661
(800) 632-8676 • www.primalifestyles.com

YOUR PET'S LIFE and PRIMA PETS are trademarks of Prima Communications, Inc. The Prima colophon is a trademark of Prima Communications, Inc., registered in the United States Patent and Trademark Office.

Interior photos by Kent Lacin Media Services
Color insert photos © Isabelle Français
Chapter 6 illustrations by Pam Tanzey © 2000 Prima Publishing
Boxers and their people: U-Bet Vihabra's Gold Fanfare ("Fanny") and Joan Ingram of U-Bet Boxers; Vihabra's U-Bet Sabra ("Sabra") and Joan Ingram, Pat Ingram, and Virginia Beadley of U-Bet Boxers; Ch. Random Lane's Texas Tornado ("Tori") and Ch. High Crest's Chances Are ("Lovie") and Maggie Johnson; Ch. Doggone Boom Box ("Hank") and Mary Ann Potts of Maywood Boxers; Ch. Gentry's King of Hearts ("Robo") and "Petie" and Paula Duncan of Gentry Boxers; and "Kelsey" and Wendy Mello. Thanks also to the Sacramento Valley Boxer Club.

Library of Congress Cataloging-in-Publication Data
Dearth, Kim.
    Your boxer's life : your complete guide to raising your pet from puppy to companion /
Kim D.R. Dearth
        p.   cm. — (Your pet's life)
    ISBN 0-7615-2048-1
    1.Boxer (Dog breed) I. Title. II. Series
SF429.B75 D33 2000
636.73—dc21
                                                                                    00-022036

00 01 02 03 DD 10 9 8 7 6 5 4 3 2 1
Printed in the United States of America

How to Order

Single copies may be ordered from Prima Publishing, 3000 Lava Ridge Court, Roseville, CA, 95661; telephone (800) 632-8676. Quantity discounts are also available. On your letterhead, include information concerning the intended use of the books and the number of books you wish to purchase.

Visit us online at www.primalifestyles.com

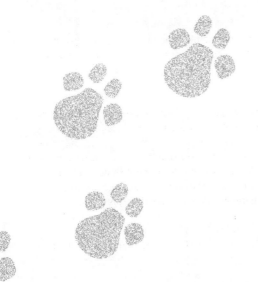

This book is dedicated to my husband, Dave,
who not only tolerates my dog obsession,
but actually encourages it,
and to Rio, Gorby, and Tux,
my furry buddies who provide daily inspiration.

Contents

Acknowledgments

I would like to express my deepest gratitude to the many people who contributed to this book, from my husband and family, who have always encouraged me in every endeavor, to the many Boxer owners whose comical, heartwarming, and poignant tales truly capture the spirit of this amazing breed.

Thank you all!

Introduction

If you are a Boxer owner, you already know the love, joy, and constant adventure this breed brings to his family. If, on the other hand, you have picked up this book because you are contemplating adding a Boxer to your life, you are in for quite a ride. There are many reasons why people are attracted to the Boxer. Maybe your neighbor has one, and you are enchanted by this dog's charming playfulness. Perhaps you have a family and have heard of the breed's unparalleled love of children. Maybe you've never actually met a Boxer, but love the strong, noble pictures you've seen in books.

Boxers are strong, courageous, sensitive, loyal, fun loving, and more. However, as with all breeds, there are negatives to consider along with the positives. If you are looking for a calm, docile pet, the Boxer is probably not for you. Boxers are strong willed, sometimes stubborn fountains of perpetual energy. Before you rush out to find yourself a Boxer, you'll need to understand all aspects of the breed's character and make sure this is indeed the dog for you.

An Overview of Boxer Ownership

If you own a Boxer, you will never be lonely. Boxers live to be with their people. They are extremely sensitive to their owners' moods, and adjust their demeanor accordingly. When you are happy, your Boxer will play the clown and entertain you with his playful antics. When you are down, your Boxer will approach you with concern in his eyes and a healing kiss. If you are ever in danger, your Boxer will defend you against any foe. And, if you have children, your dog's traits will only intensify around them—he will be a gentle playmate and watchful guardian all rolled into one.

Some of the traits that at first seem attractive in the Boxer may not conform well to your lifestyle, however. Playfulness can turn into hyperactivity or even destructiveness if a Boxer doesn't receive adequate exercise. The Boxer's need to be with people means he must truly be a part of the family. Boxers cannot be relegated to a kennel in the yard, or they will become distraught. In addition, the same self-confidence that makes the Boxer appear so noble can turn this dog into a tyrant if he isn't taught his proper place in the household. Boxers need strong leadership, or they will be more than happy to take advantage of your kindness by taking over the living-room couch, jumping on guests, or displaying other misbehavior.

What It Means to Have a Boxer in Your Life

Are you the right owner for a Boxer? Are you capable of being strong, yet fair and consistent with your dog? Do you have the time to devote to exercising, training, and playing with this dog, who is as strong minded as he is strong bodied?

Although Boxers love to race around the yard, don't think this is all the exercise your dog will require. You will need to take long walks, jog, or bike with your Boxer to provide him with sufficient exercise. Also realize that the Boxer's mind is as nimble as his body. Sports such as agility (an obstacle course for dogs) or flyball (a type of canine relay race) can work your dog's brain while giving his body a workout.

Your Boxer must be taught proper manners. He must learn that while greeting visitors with a friendly butt wiggle and perhaps a lick on the hand is acceptable, leaps into a newcomer's lap will not be appreciated. Your muscular pet must learn to walk on a leash properly or you will find your neighbors asking who is walking whom. And, although he may love children, he must learn not to get too excited around little ones or a toddler could easily get knocked to the ground.

How Much Thought Have You Given to Having a Boxer?

Some people want a Boxer because they think the dog looks tough. They don't understand that, although the Boxer will courageously protect her loved ones should the need arise, the Boxer is first and foremost a loving companion. This dog cannot be left out in the yard or in a kennel or, even worse, chained up, which will only teach this fundamentally friendly animal to be aggressive.

Some people have heard of the Boxer's uncanny love of children and think they will actually acquire a built-in baby-sitter. Although there are many amazing stories of Boxers keeping children from danger with no adult supervision, remember the Boxer is still a dog, not a human. No dog should be left alone with small children. The children could hurt the dog, intentionally or not, and, although rare in the case of the Boxer, the dog may react. Accept the Boxer for the loving pet she is, but don't expect her to be a nanny for your family.

Some people underestimate this breed's need for exercise and companionship. If you put in much overtime at a demanding job or travel frequently, choose another breed. The Boxer will not thrive without daily human-canine interaction.

Dog Ownership:
The Many Sacrifices, the Many Joys

Nothing is more heartwarming than being greeted by big, soulful eyes and joyous kisses after a hard day at work. There's no doubt about it—having a dog in your life is a wonderful experience. They are always ecstatic to see you, never judge, and have a knack for chasing away your blues when you are feeling down. They are always up for anything you suggest, from cuddling in front of the fire on a stormy night to racing waves at the beach on a crisp sunny day. If you're shy, a dog is a wonderful conversation piece, introducing you to new friends around your neighborhood or at the park. Dogs can make you laugh, they can help you cry— they are the best of companions.

While many people can't imagine life without pets, it's only fair to the animal to be realistic about the commitment needed before you bring home a puppy or adopt an older dog. How much time do you have to devote to your dog? While your pet will be grateful for every minute he spends with you, it isn't fair to get a dog if you don't have the time between work, school, or outside activities to give him the companionship he craves. If you are getting a puppy, you'll need to spend extra time house-training, socializing, and obedience training your little Boxer.

Are you willing to give your dog the proper exercise? Many people acquire a dog, put up a fence, and think their job is done. But, as much as your Boxer may like to do laps on his own, you need to be prepared to walk, jog, bicycle, swim, play fetch, or engage in canine sports with your dog to provide companionship and extra exercise. Once you've experienced the boundless energy of a Boxer, you'll be happy to take part in some of these activities to help wear your dog out!

You also must be dedicated to obedience-training your Boxer from the moment you bring him home. He will not hesitate to push his boundaries if proper household manners are not taught and enforced. If you don't want your dog pushing you out of your own bed at night, you'll need to be a strong leader.

Is everyone in the household excited about obtaining a Boxer? It's not fair to bring a dog home when the dog is not truly wanted by one or more members of the family. In order to understand and obey the rules you set up, your dog will need consistent direction from each and every member of the family. This is impossible if someone is intimidated by or simply not interested in a Boxer. If this is the case, discuss with your family whether another breed might be better suited to all your lifestyles and expectations, or if your family may not be right for a dog after all.

Finally, have you thought about cost? Many people are perfectly willing to shell out the cost of buying a dog but forget to take into consideration the money needed to keep him healthy and happy. While grooming costs are minimal for a Boxer, feeding your dog a nutritious diet, taking him in for annual veterinary checkups and vaccinations plus office visits should he become sick or hurt, buying the necessary equipment (crate, bowls, collars, leash, fencing, etc.), and paying for training classes, boarding, and/or pet-sitting services add up to a substantial investment. Figure out these costs spread over the life of your dog and you will see you can end up paying a small fortune for your Boxer.

If, however, after carefully and realistically considering all the above sacrifices involved in dog ownership, you still feel your life is incomplete without a willful, loving, enthusiastic bundle of canine energy at your side, you are ready for a Boxer! As you read on, you'll not only share the personal experiences of many people who have opened their hearts and homes to this breed, you'll also learn everything you need to know about dog ownership, from choosing a puppy to selecting the best food to exercise and health care. So sit back and get ready to explore the world of the Boxer.

So, You Want a Boxer

In This Chapter

○ What Makes a Boxer Special?
○ Keys to Your Boxer's Happiness
○ Where Do I Find the Perfect Boxer for Me?

W hen first meeting a Boxer, you will be struck by the sheer nobility of this charismatic dog. He exudes confidence, strength, and an air of watchfulness. This is a dog who fears nothing, and will protect his family against foes of any size should the need arise.

After spending some time with the Boxer, however, you'll also discover the many other attributes of this multi-faceted canine. There is the sensitive partner, who has an uncanny ability to read your mood, whether joyful or down, and react accordingly. There is the goofy clown, who will bound in the air and wag his entire body with pure joy when you come home. There is the unparalleled children's companion, both gentle and playful with human charges from infants to teenagers.

Then, there is the strong-willed, independent Boxer who will dominate the household if he is not taught his proper place within the family structure. The Boxer is no remote-controlled pet—if you expect him to behave in a certain way, you will need to make him understand why it is in his best interests to comply. Boxers are extremely intelligent, but this doesn't always equal obedience. Their intelligence leads them to bore easily, so you'll need to be creative when teaching a Boxer commands.

Before acquiring this breed, not only must you educate yourself about all aspects of the Boxer's temperament, you also must understand what your Boxer will need from you in order for him to remain happy. Does your lifestyle allow for the exercise, training, and attention this type of dog requires? If you believe you are a strong enough match for the loving but boisterous Boxer, your next step is to learn how and where to find that perfect pup or adult dog.

What Makes a Boxer Special?

What makes a Boxer such a unique and charming breed? All dogs are believed to be descended from wolves, which is more apparent in certain breeds, such as the Alaskan Malamute, than in others, such as the diminutive Chihuahua. Many years ago, man befriended the wolf and decided to harness this animal's considerable talents to suit human needs. Our ancestors then molded dogs into certain breeds to perform specific jobs, from hunting and herding to guarding and companionship.

What's the American Kennel Club?

Founded in 1884, the American Kennel Club (AKC) is a non-profit organization dedicated to the protection and advancement of purebred dogs. Composed of over 500 dog clubs from across the nation, the AKC's objectives include maintaining a registry of purebred dogs, promoting responsible dog ownership, and sponsoring events, such as breed shows and field trials, that promote interest in and appreciation of the purebred dog.

To be eligible for AKC registration, a puppy must be the offspring of individually registered AKC parents, and the breeder must obtain the proper paperwork before the puppy's sale. Once registered, a dog is eligible to compete in AKC-sanctioned events and, if bred with another AKC-registered dog, to have his/her offspring registered.

The AKC approves an official breed standard for each of the 147 breeds currently eligible for registration. The standard is written and maintained by each individual breed club. An attempt to describe the "perfect" dog of each breed, the breed standard is the model responsible breeders use in their efforts to produce better dogs. Judges of AKC-sponsored events and competitions use the breed standards as the basis of their evaluations.

Because of the AKC's emphasis on excellence and high standards, it is a common misconception that "AKC registered" or "AKC registrable" is synonymous with quality. However, while a registration certificate identifies a dog and its progenitors as purebreds, it does not necessarily guarantee the health or quality of a dog. Some breeders breed for show quality, but others breed for profit, with little concern for breed standards. Thus, a potential buyer should not view AKC registration as an indication of a dog's quality.

A Bit of History

The Boxer is an ancient breed. It is believed to have originated from the Mollosser, a large, powerful, aggressive type of dog found in Europe and Asia that later spawned most of the working breeds of today. The Mollosser evolved into several different strains, including one with a somewhat lighter frame and better agility, combined with a heavy, short head. This strain eventually became breeds such as the Bulldog and Boxer.

The dogs of this type that were living in Germany from the twelfth to fourteenth centuries were distinguished by the job they performed for their masters. The Bullenbeisser, or bull biters, did simply that: They were used to fight and bring down bulls by hanging on to the nose of the bull to avoid personal injury, not letting go until the hunter came and finished the kill. Function definitely came before form; these early dogs were no beauties. However, their short snouts enabled them to breathe while they were hanging on to their tough opponents, and their massive heads and muscular bodies allowed them to hang on. These dogs also possessed extreme courage and dedication to their master's will.

As large game hunting began to wane, the Bullenbeisser was bred smaller and even more agile. They were used as guardians and even herders. Sadly, although game hunting was diminishing, bullbaiting as a sport continued into the nineteenth century. It finally was banned due to its cruelty, but not before it had brought about the horrible demise of many a dog and bull.

In the 1830s, an English Bulldog was imported into Germany and introduced into the Boxer breeding program. More of a Mastiff type, this Bulldog was much different than the breed we know today. Until this point, the Bullenbeisser only came in colors of brindle or fawn, with black masks, but this dog added the white markings seen in the modern Boxer. Flocki, the result of one of these matings, became the first Boxer registered in the German Stud Book.

In 1896, the Deutscher Boxer Club was formed in Munich, and the first German breed standard, which described the club's vision of the ideal Boxer, was adopted in 1902. Boxers gained steadily in popularity in their home country. The advent of

World War I, however, proved very difficult on the breed. Many dogs were shipped to the front lines, where they were used to guard prisoners and German camps, as well as to take down the occasional enemy soldier and sniper. Only the best champion Boxers were chosen, since to become a champion in Germany, a dog not only had to be attractive, he also had to show proven working ability. Sadly, many dogs lost their lives in battle.

After the war, the Germans tried to regroup and get back to the business of breeding the best Boxers possible. Boxers began to be utilized as police and service dogs, although they weren't officially recognized as police dogs until 1925. Around 1930, the Boxer standard in Germany was changed, disqualifying white as a registerable color. Black, a rare color to begin with, had been disallowed in 1904. There are several theories as to why white was disqualified. Some say it was because white Boxer police dogs were too easy to see at night, while others said it was to distinguish them from English Bulldogs. Regardless of the reason, the disqualification stuck.

During World War I, a number of distinguished war dogs had come from the kennels of Frau Stockmann, a pioneer in the breed. After the war, Boxers from her breeding found their way to the United States, where they, along with other imports from German breeders, founded the breed in America.

The American Boxer Club was founded in 1935, and the breed enjoyed moderate popularity from 1946 to 1956, which has been called the "Golden Age of the Boxer." The Boxer began to prove his worth in the show ring, taking his first Best in Show at the famous Westminster Kennel Club Dog Show in 1947. People took notice of this handsome breed that

Did You Know?

The wolf, from which dogs are descended, was the first animal to be domesticated.

not only was a joy to look at, but also combined the enviable traits of supreme watchdog and gentle family friend. Indiscriminate breeding to satisfy the public's demand took its toll for a while, leading to unhealthy dogs with poor temperaments. Thankfully, as the breed's popularity leveled off, its health and good-natured temperament returned.

> The American Boxer Club was founded in 1935, and the breed enjoyed moderate popularity from 1946 to 1956, which has been called the "Golden Age of the Boxer."

Interpreting the Standard

In the United States, the American Kennel Club standard is the most commonly used guideline to define the perfect Boxer. While the standard at first glance may seem to be merely a blueprint for a handsome dog, it is actually much more than that. It takes into account not only proper conformation in performing a specific job, but also balanced movement, and, most importantly, a correct temperament. (Visit www.akc.org for the official breed standard.)

The Boxer was bred as a hunter of large game, and the standard reflects that goal throughout. The Boxer is a medium-sized, square-built dog. While both males and females should be well muscled, males are slightly larger and heavier boned, ranging from 22½ to 25 inches at the withers (shoulders) while females are 21 to 23½ inches tall. While there is no disqualification due to size, a much taller Boxer would need to be larger overall to keep his square appearance, which would lead to a heavier, more cumbersome dog than called for by the standard.

The head of the Boxer makes the breed. The strong, undershot jaws were designed to allow the breed to hang on to its prey indefinitely, while the slightly upturned nose allowed the Boxer to

How Did the Boxer Get His Name?

There are a number of theories as to how the breed became known as the Boxer. Some claim the name developed from the breed's curious manner of punching with his paws when playing or even fighting. Others say it is because these dogs sometimes box with their heads. One interpretation even claims the boxlike shape of the breed's head is the reason for the Boxer moniker. And finally, since the German word "Boxer" translates as "prizefighter" in English, proponents of this theory claim the breed's excellent fighting ability is the true force behind its name. Whichever of these theories is correct, the name Boxer truly defines the breed.

breathe during this death grip. As the breed became more of a companion and less of a hunter, expression became extremely important. The Boxer appears intelligent and alert. His dark brown eyes combined with his wrinkled brow give him an amazing range of expression, making him seem almost human. Long, tapered ears cap the show Boxer's magnificent head. The ears do not grow this way naturally, however, and must be cropped when the Boxer is 6 to 12 weeks old. Many pet owners choose to let the ears grow naturally, and indeed many countries in Europe frown on cropping. Understand, however, that this cosmetic adjustment also had a utilitarian purpose in Boxers of old, since long, flapping ears were easy targets during a fight.

The body of the Boxer, being both muscular and agile, is that of a true athlete. The high-set tail is usually docked to prevent injury. Of course, docking protects knick-knacks, vases, and any other fragile household items located at dog-height from a Boxer tail's energetic enthusiasm as well! The Boxer's coat is short, shiny, and smooth and comes in fawn and brindle. Fawn ranges from light tan to deep mahogany. Brindle ranges from sparse, but clearly defined black stripes on a fawn background to such heavy striping that the fawn color barely shows through, giving an appearance of reverse brindling. The face always has a black mask, although some white may intrude on the black. White markings should merely accent the coat, and, according to the standard, may not exceed one-third of the entire body. White on the flanks or back are considered faults, and, as in Germany, totally white Boxers are disqualified in the show ring.

Keeping with his athleticism, the Boxer exhibits a smooth, far-reaching gait. A stilted gait would have been a severe hindrance to the hunting Boxer.

Finally, but most importantly, the standard addresses the character of the Boxer. This hearing guard dog is alert, dignified, and confident. While he should be somewhat restrained in the show ring, with his family and friends the true Boxer is the eternal puppy, ever playful and animated. While he will certainly play with children, he will adjust that play to the size of the child and show unfailing patience with children's antics if properly trained. When meeting a stranger, the Boxer will first evaluate the person, then respond if the newcomer is friendly. If he perceives a threat, however, the Boxer is fearless.

As temperament and personality are such vital characteristics in a pet, let's examine these areas more closely.

Personality

Like all dogs and all people, Boxers are individuals. Not all Boxers are guaranteed to have the same personality. That being said, in general, the Boxer is a fun-loving, people-oriented breed with boundless energy.

Til Bagby of Jacksonville, Florida, has this to say about the Boxers' need to be loved by all: "No Boxer I have known can stand being ignored. Those people who dislike dogs in general usually end up at least liking our Boxer. Those dogs are smart enough to know when they are being ignored and are curious enough to want to know why. We have learned that being ignored simply gives a Boxer a project to work on. They will sit and stare at the offending person until he or she breaks down and looks back. They will nuzzle the offender's hand, lay their heads in the offender's lap, bring a toy, or resort to climbing in the offender's lap. Without fail, the Boxer will wear down anyone's dislike or distrust of dogs—at least of Boxers."

Boxers also love to play the clown. Some owners who attend obedience trials with their dogs experience difficulty when their Boxer discovers that misbehaving actually gets more audience re-action than behaving, and who can deny an audience?

Often Boxers seem to think they are doing a good deed and do not quite understand their owners' odd reactions. Tina Starr of East Hartford, Connecticut, tells of her Boxer, Ivy, who has an interesting way of "protecting" her owner.

"Ivy has a tendency to attack undergarments and then look at me as if to say, 'Look Mom, the socks in the laundry were talking about strangling you in your sleep so I killed them all! Aren't you happy with me?' Wiggle, wiggle, slurp, slurp."

Unfortunately, Ivy's protection work doesn't stop there. "Often, Ivy will then take all those mommy-killing socks and underwear out to the trampoline in the yard and bounce them until they are definitely dead. Then of course she has to show all the neighbors, 'Look, I killed Mommy's under-wear!' I guess it's my fault for putting in a doggie door."

Joyce and Bryce Peckham of Topeka, Kansas, had to refine their Easter tradition of hiding eggs in the yard when their Boxer, Phaedra, became too enthusiastic a participant.

"Phaedra was a very funny girl, one of the 'kids.' On Easter one year, I hid the eggs in the yard and provided three baskets. Phaedra soon got the hang of finding eggs and putting them in her basket. The girls finally said, 'Mom, make Phaedra go inside! She's finding all the eggs first.'"

Easter eggs weren't the only things Phaedra collected. "If we left her home alone, she would go into each bedroom and get people's things, make a mountain of our personal belongings in the living room, and lay on them, so when we came home we knew how much she missed us."

This intense love of their special people is one of the most endearing qualities of the Boxer. Although the Boxer may look tough, this is not a dog suited for outdoor life. Not only does the Boxer's thin coat make him vulnerable to both heat and cold, he also craves human affection.

Judy Schrimpf of Port Jefferson Station, New York, says her Boxer, Brandy, is never far from her family. "When you sit down, she'll put her head on your lap and just squirm up until she's practically in your lap. She doesn't realize how big she is!" When Judy's husband, Doug, lounges on the floor while watching TV, Brandy wiggles her way into the "cave" between Doug's back and the couch and settles in for the night.

Chewbaka, owned by Kim Monroe of Scottsdale, Arizona, made sure Kim set aside special "together" time every morning. "I would be standing in the bathroom drying my hair and Chewey would come running in the minute he heard the hair dryer. He would lean against me and almost beg for the warm air of the dryer to blow on him. He would close his eyes and I would move the air up and down on him. He loved it, and it made me laugh every time."

Boxers also are meticulously clean and will actually lick their paws and groom themselves like cats. Joyce Peckham says Phaedra's cleanliness almost let her get away with executing the Great Blueberry Pie Caper.

"My two girls were seven years old, and it was bake sale time at the grade school. I baked two blueberry pies and had just pulled out the oven rack for them to cool. I came back a little later and there were two empty pie shells sitting there, with not a blueberry in sight. 'Okay,' I hollered, 'Who ate the blueberry pies?' 'Not me,' replied daughter one. 'I don't know,' replied daughter two. Then I spied Phaedra, sitting in the corner of the dining room with her back toward the room. Her head was frantically bobbing up and down. When I got to her I made her lift her head so I could see her face. It was dyed blue from her eyes to her chest—she had been trying to wash it off as fast as she could. She was blue for a week!"

Even old age doesn't usually slow a Boxer down; he will remain playful and puppylike well into his senior years. Boxers will turn anything into a toy, from legitimate dog toys to children's stuffed animals to wastebasket trash, so it is essential that Boxer-prohibited objects be kept up high or behind closed doors. Boxers are game for anything their master asks of them, from a romp in the park to hide-and-seek in the backyard to a snooze on the couch—after that boundless energy has been exhausted, that is.

Temperament

Boxers are hearing guard dogs. Despite their guarding vocation, they are relatively

Did You Know?

The word for "dog" in the Australian aboriginal language Mbabaran happens to be "dog."

quiet and won't bark at every passerby. However, they are quick to alert owners to any sound that may indicate danger. The gruff "woof" of a Boxer on alert is usually enough to deter anyone who was even contemplating trespassing on a Boxer's territory.

Judy Schrimpf says Brandy is lackadaisical about most of the comings and goings on her street. However, she instantly gives the alert if someone's actions seem odd. "The only time she will bark is if a delivery truck sits idling without the driver getting out. For example, if the UPS man is delivering a package across the street and he stays in his truck to fill out forms, she barks. She doesn't like him just sitting there."

Although protective by nature, the Boxer is quick to make friends once he knows a stranger means no harm. While a Boxer living with a single owner will bond intensely with that person, a Boxer living in a family environment will be happy to share his love and affection equally among all family members.

While some breeds are good with kids, Boxers revel in them. They have an innate sense that they must be gentle with these miniature humans, and also seem to realize that children don't mean to hurt when they tug on an ear or try to teethe on a tail. Still, no dog should be required to put up with abuse of any kind even if it is not intentional; parents must teach their children how to properly relate to the family Boxer. And, as with all dogs, never leave a child and a dog alone. Even the most stoic dog may react negatively when pushed too far.

> Never leave a child and a dog alone. Even the most stoic dog may react negatively when pushed too far.

Donna Murphy of Baldwinsville, New York, experienced firsthand the Boxer's instinctual adoration of children. "When my girlfriend was pregnant with her first child, my male Boxer, Paris, would sniff her stomach and then sit there and wag his butt. Once the baby was born, she and her husband came over to visit. She placed the newborn on a blanket on the living room carpet among my three Boxers—much to her husband's horror. The Boxers were so gentle and just couldn't get over this small addition to their 'pack.' When the baby was sleeping on my bed, Paris stationed himself outside the bedroom door and would come to get us if the baby cried. He also didn't want my friends to leave the house with the baby, much to my frustration. He never growled, but paced the whole time they tried to leave. What a great baby-sitter!"

As Boxers are happy to take over the duty of watching the children, they also will gladly take over the entire household if given the chance. Boxers are very willful and very strong, which is a bad combination if you are not capable of asserting yourself as the alpha, or leader, of the family pack. A Boxer who is allowed to dominate the household will come to think he is the king, sprawling on furniture and refusing to move aside for family members. While a Boxer's dominance will rarely turn into aggression, they still must be taught that they are subordinate members of the pack.

If you clearly and consistently establish yourself as leader, your dog will happily settle into a lower ranking in the pack. He will allow you to greet strangers first and take cues from you as to whether this person is friend or foe. He will get down immediately from furniture, or at least move over enough to allow his owner to sit down! A Boxer who knows his place in the pack will gladly permit his owner to remove a biscuit from the Boxer's mouth, trusting that his fair leader will soon return the treat to him.

A Tale of Two White Boxers

White has been banned as an acceptable color in the Boxer for many years, both in the breed's native Germany and in the United States. White Boxers are born when both parents possess the gene that causes flashy white markings, such as substantial white on the feet and face. These markings are valued in the show ring, and many of the pair's puppies will be of the proper coloring, also with flashy markings. However, a certain percentage will likely be white.

Deafness, as well as a higher incidence of blindness, is believed to run in white Boxers. Historically, white Boxers were disposed of immediately to keep them from passing their genes on to future generations. Today, although members of the American Boxer Club are forbidden to breed or sell white Boxers, they are allowed to place them in homes for adoption as long as they are spayed or neutered.

Mary Moore of St. Paul, Minnesota, knows firsthand that a white Boxer makes just as wonderful a pet as a fawn or brindle Boxer. She rescued Gus, otherwise known as Moore's All Flash, from a backyard breeder who performed no health testing and didn't understand why so many Boxers in the breeding program were turning out white.

"We have two other Boxers and really weren't looking for a third," says Mary of herself and her husband. "But we knew he was deaf and we wanted to give him a chance."

Gus quickly settled into the household. "My husband and I made a list so we would use the same signals for Gus. Some came from American Sign Language, some came from the Utility level of dog obedience—in which you can't use verbal commands—and some we made up." Mary says Gus has actually proven to be more focused on her than her other two Boxers. "Boxers are hearing guard dogs and are always alert to what's going on. Gus has to constantly watch me to know what I'm going to ask of him next." Gus also is very fo-

Life Expectancy

Sadly for Boxer owners, this is not a long-lived breed. Although the Boxer's exuberance into his senior years may make his life ap-

cused on his surroundings, and learned where the doggie door was and how to avoid the backyard pool much faster than Mary's two hearing Boxers.

Gus has learned a number of obedience commands and has even picked up flyball, a canine relay race using hurdles and tennis balls, and agility, a doggie obstacle course, proving that with plenty of patience and lots of love, deafness doesn't have to be a handicap.

Jeni Mellott of Parker, Colorado, has also experienced the special qualities of a white Boxer. When she and her husband decided to add a second Boxer to their home, they contacted their first dog's breeder to inquire if there were any puppies available. The only pup the breeder had was a white female with the same father as the Mellott's first Boxer, who had been returned to the breeder at seven months old for being "unmanageable, aggressive and growling at the owners." The breeder discovered the dog had been chained to a tree and given no attention during the critical first months of her life.

At first, Matilda didn't even know how to walk on a leash and would flinch if anyone raised his or her voice or even innocently gestured with a hand. With structure, obedience classes and lots of attention, however, Matilda is now a loving, sweet family pet. She and her brother also are certified therapy dogs who bring joy to countless residents at hospitals and nursing homes.

"I'm also trying to find a program for abused children to share Matilda and her story with," says Mellott. "Matilda had surgery before her first birthday to have two tumors removed, which left large scars on her shoulder and elbow. This puts children who have been through surgeries at ease with her. I tell them about her battles with the tumors, being tossed out of her house and the stigma of being a white Boxer, and it makes them forget about their own troubles for a short time."

As Gus and Matilda prove, a Boxer by any other color still can prove just as sweet.

pear longer, many Boxers leave this Earth far too soon, living only an average of 10 years. You can do your best to help your dog live the longest life possible by feeding him a nutritious diet, keeping him in shape, and taking him to the vet for regular checkups.

Keys to Your Boxer's Happiness

Before bringing a Boxer home, you need to analyze your lifestyle. Will it complement the needs of your dog? The Boxer is a highly energetic, demanding breed, often seeming more like a Tazmanian devil than a dog. To keep your Boxer happy, you will need to provide lots of exercise, training, and attention.

How Much Space Does a Boxer Need?

Although Boxers can adjust to city life, they do best with a large fenced yard in the suburbs or the country. Boxers need enormous amounts of exercise, more than many owners have time for. If you live in the city, you must be willing to take your dog for several long walks each and every day. Many cities provide fenced dog parks where canines can romp off-leash with their friends, which provides another outlet. If you have a fenced yard, your Boxer will be happy to tear around to work off excess energy. However, he will still enjoy, and indeed, need, walks and other exercise for variety and greater energy expenditure.

How Much Exercise?

If the preceding paragraph didn't get the point across about how much exercise Boxers need, the answer is: a lot! Boxers were bred to have the stamina of a hunter. While they may no longer hunt, their stamina remains intact. Frequent short walks are perfect for puppies and older dogs who can't take the strain of extended jaunts, but adults need more intense exercise to stay in shape. Jogging, swimming, and joining you as you bicycle are all excellent options that really give your dog a workout. Remember, though, to always condition your dog slowly and keep an eye on your Boxer for breathing difficulties. The Boxer's short snout makes her susceptible to heat stroke in warmer weather. For variety in your Boxer's exercise regime, try a canine sport such as agility or flyball. These activities help your dog keep off extra pounds, stay mentally fit, and make her a calmer, healthier pet all around.

> Always condition your dog slowly and keep an eye on your Boxer for breathing difficulties. The Boxer's short snout makes her susceptible to heat stroke in warmer weather.

How Much Training?

As sweet, adorable, and innocent as a Boxer pup may appear, he will need some basic obedience training if he is to grow up to be a well-mannered canine citizen. As mentioned above, Boxers need strong leadership in their lives or they will happily assume the role of leader themselves. As far removed as they may seem from their ancestors, domestic dogs still think like wolves. They live by the code of pack leadership. Every pack has an alpha, and all the other wolves fall into place in the hierarchy from this "top dog" down to the bottom-ranking wolf. In your dog's new human-canine pack, you must function as the alpha. As a matter of fact, every human in your household, including the tiniest infant, must rank above the Boxer. Although Boxers are wonderful with children, they must not believe that they are dominant over them or pack order will be disrupted.

Til Bagby learned firsthand the possible dominant nature of Boxers when she got married. Although her husband had grown up with the breed, Twister was the first Boxer Til had ever lived with. "Every night, Twister would trap me in a corner and not let me go to bed. He wasn't aggressive and I think he thought it was all a game. I quickly learned that in order to live with a Boxer you can't let them intimidate you."

Although not aggressive, the Boxer is by nature a willful breed. For you to establish yourself as alpha, or pack leader, you must firmly and consistently set your household rules from the start. From the moment you bring home your eight-week-old puppy, you must let him know what you expect. Teach him not to jump on people or grab food off the table. Teach him that mouthing and nipping are not acceptable. Teach him to enjoy being touched all over to prepare him for later grooming sessions and veterinary visits. It is important that you teach your Boxer to comply with your wishes while he is still young. If you wait until he is six months or older to begin training, you may find yourself in a power struggle with a very muscular, strong adolescent.

Take your puppy to a puppy preschool or kindergarten class, where he will receive socialization with other puppies and people in a safe environment. Invite friends and neighbors of all ages to come visit and play with your puppy. The more you socialize your puppy now, the more willingly he will accept people and animals of all types when he is full grown.

Boxers also have been known to train their owners when the opportunity arises! Til Bagby explains that her Boxer, Trapper, has taught her and her husband his own language. "I know he is developing his own language, because he has adopted behaviors that always mean the same thing and that always get a response from us. The unique thing is that these are behaviors that we have not taught him. Sometimes we wonder who is training whom!

"Trapper always asks permission to jump onto the furniture. He puts one paw on the furniture and looks at us. He will not get on the furniture unless he gets permission. Later, he began to put both front paws on the furniture while he looked at us. Every time he did that, he jumped onto the furniture and then curled into our laps. We have been taught that one paw means the couch, and two paws means the lap."

When training your Boxer, keep in mind that they are extremely intelligent dogs who were bred to be independent thinkers in their vocations as hunters and guardians. Although they may not take to obedience lessons as quickly as Golden Retrievers or Shetland Sheepdogs, this lack of enthusiasm for learning by rote should not be confused with a lack of intelligence.

Juli Bechard of Jacksonville, Florida, says, "The hardest part of training Corey has been learning how different he is from the other breeds I've had. Boxers are such a sensitive, goofy breed. I can't raise my voice and am not allowed to be upset around him. He's a natural clown and often fools people into thinking he's stupid. Unfortunately, they underestimate him. I can't keep him in a cage if he wants out. He can open any door unless it's locked. He also does numerous tricks, including a few he picked up from my other dog."

Boxers bore easily if asked to do the same exercise over and over, so it is important to be creative and spontaneous when training. Above all else, Boxers love to have fun. Keep training light and interesting and you'll end up with a dog who loves to please you.

Did You Know?

The fastest dog in the world is the Cape Hunting Dog, which can reach speeds of 45 mph. The Greyhound is second at 39.65 mph and the Whippet is third at 35.50 mph.

Can My Boxer Stay Home All Day Without Me?

Boxers certainly are people-oriented dogs who need human companionship. But what if you work or go to school? Will your Boxer be content to stay home alone without damaging your house or, worse, hurting himself?

The answer is yes, with some help on your part. If you leave your dog at home alone all day while you work and also consistently leave him at home all evening while you go out with friends, you shouldn't get a dog in the first place. However, if you are willing to come straight home after work and devote several hours to exercising and playing with your dog at night, then yes, your dog can stay alone during the day.

There's an old saying that a tired dog is a good dog, and this couldn't be truer of the Boxer. If you wear out your dog when you're home, she'll be more likely to happily sleep away the day while you're gone. But if you constantly push aside your dog in favor of the other commitments in your life, she is bound to use up her energy with such unacceptable pursuits as chewing, digging, and other destruction. It's also important that you give her something productive to do while you're gone, such as chewing on a Kong, a hard, hollow rubber toy that can be stuffed with treats. Adding a second Boxer for companionship also can help keep your dog content, as long as you have the time and resources for another canine companion.

Although an adult Boxer should experience no difficulty in waiting until you get home to relieve herself, a puppy is a different matter. Whether your pup stays in a crate or in a blocked-off room, such as a kitchen or laundry room, someone will need to let her out every few hours to do her business. If you can't get home during lunchtime to give your Boxer a potty break, ask a neighbor or hire a pet-sitter to drop by.

Surefire Ways to Make Your Boxer's Life Unpleasant

We've looked at the things a Boxer needs to stay happy. Now, let's look at what is intolerable to the breed.

Things a Boxer Simply Cannot Live With

Boxers can't live with an owner who lacks a sense of humor. These dogs are natural comedians and are bound to display some antics that seem funnier to your Boxer than they are to you. You must learn to put disobedience in perspective. If your dog consistently knocks you off your feet when you come in the door, he must learn to control his exuberance. If you come home every day to shredded used tissues deposited throughout the house, the best action is a good-natured sigh and a vow to keep all wastebaskets behind latched cabinet doors.

Boxers cannot live with harsh treatment. Although willful, Boxers love their owners and cannot tolerate abuse of any kind. While they need a leader who is consistent and firm, they also need a leader who understands and respects their sensitivity. Cruel punishment will simply shut a Boxer down emotionally.

> Boxers can't live with an owner who lacks a sense of humor.

Boxers can't live with owners who don't desire a true companion. A Boxer needs to be with his people. Boxers don't do well in kennel situations, and your pet will feel isolated and neglected if you leave him alone out in the yard and away from your side.

Boxers can't live with owners who are couch potatoes. They need daily, energetic exercise. When you feel your Boxer has gotten enough exercise, he likely is just getting started. This is not a dog who will be content to lounge by your feet for hours on end. Your Boxer will love to cuddle with you, but only after his tremendous energy has been spent. A workaholic also makes a poor candidate for Boxer ownership. Anyone who doesn't have the time and energy to devote to the physical and emotional needs of the Boxer should not get one in the first place.

Maybe a Boxer Isn't the Dog for Me

What if you are buying this book after the fact and already have a Boxer? What if you either neglected to research the breed or ignored some of the negatives of the breed, and just focused on the positives? What if you now realize that getting a Boxer wasn't the best choice for you?

If the problem is that your Boxer is asserting himself and taking over the house, don't give up. Chances are you feel intimidated by your muscular adolescent or adult Boxer, and he is using this to his advantage. Enroll in an obedience class now. Training is the best way for you to regain control and to bond with your dog. If you feel the problem is too out of control to handle in a group setting, find a trainer who offers private lessons or will even come to your home to teach you how to work with your dog. It is imperative that you and your entire family become your Boxer's leader.

If the problem is that you didn't realize a Boxer would be so energetic, you have some decisions to make. Your first option is to admit your mistake and vow to change your lifestyle to meet your dog's needs. Trying to keep up with an athletic dog will actually prove beneficial to your own health. You may find you enjoy your newly active lifestyle and reap the physical and mental rewards of such a change. On the other hand, you may decide you are not ready to make such a commitment.

If you decide that you just don't have the fortitude to own a Boxer, give your dog the best chance possible to find a new home. Don't turn in your dog to a shelter, where you can't guarantee he will find a home in time, and he may be destroyed. First, contact your dog's breeder to see if he or she will take your dog back. If this is not an option, or you didn't get your dog from a breeder, call a local rescue organization and turn your dog over to it. (You can find a Boxer rescue group through the national breed club; see the resource listings in the appendix.) These organizations are experienced in dealing with the breed and will undertake any rehabilitation necessary before placing your dog with a new family.

Next time, make sure you know all the facts about a breed before you bring one home.

Where Do I Find the Perfect Boxer for Me?

If you've decided that the Boxer is indeed the breed for you, don't make the mistake of rushing out and buying the first Boxer you see. Searching for a dog is an emotional experience. Too often, we fall head over heels in love and let our hearts govern our actions without consulting our level-headed brains. Of course, you want to find a dog with whom you click, but you also must ensure that the dog you pick is truly one you can live with long-term. For example, you may like a certain dog's looks and not take the time to ask questions about his and his parents' health, or you may be so charmed by a certain dog's exuberant personality that you do not realistically consider your ability to handle such a high-energy dog.

Puppies Versus Older Dogs

It might seem that the first step in obtaining a dog consists of finding the right place to purchase one. However, before you decide where to get your Boxer, you need to decide whether you want to buy a puppy or adopt an adult dog. Both options have their pros and cons.

Just as parents find it magical to watch their children grow from helpless infants to awkward teenagers and successful adults, so, too, do dog owners' hearts proudly witness their pets' progression from sweet but bumbling puppies to gangly adolescents and self-assured, agile adult Boxers. If you choose to get a puppy, you'll have the chance to mold that pup from an early age into the dog you would like him to be. You can socialize him with people of all shapes and sizes as well as with other animals, and know that you are helping him develop into a calm, confident adult. You can feed him the right food from day one and ensure he gets the proper health care and training.

However, along with the joys of puppyhood also come the demands. You may spend at least a few sleepless nights trying to ignore a howling puppy who hasn't yet decided to make the crate his home. You'll at least find yourself sleepwalking out into the yard once or several times a night to let your Boxer relieve himself. You also will likely become an expert carpet and floor cleaner, and you may find a few household items ripped to unrecognizable shreds, because you weren't keeping an eye on your little darling. Puppies, as cute and loving as they are, also are draining and need lots and lots of attention.

Perhaps you feel you don't have the time and energy to devote to puppy rearing, but you believe you can provide the ideal home for an older dog. An older dog may already be house-trained, and may know basic obedience commands as well. Although Boxers are quite puppylike even into old age, an adult Boxer will possess a somewhat calmer disposition and will more willingly spend some quiet time relaxing at your feet after proper exercise than would a puppy who is in overdrive and always on the go. Think of the difference between a finely tuned sports car that needs frequent spins on the open road and an out-of-control Mack truck, and you'll have some idea of what I mean! Plus, if you obtain a mature Boxer from a rescue group or a humane society, you'll also secure the added bonus of knowing you are providing a home for a dog who has been given up or abandoned.

Before you decide to adopt, however, you should understand some of the negatives of bringing a grown dog into your home. An adult Boxer will already have established certain behaviors, both good and bad. You definitely can teach an old dog new tricks, but it may take more time and effort to reshape an older pet's ingrained behaviors than it would to teach a puppy what you expect of him. Also, although some dogs are given up through no fault of their own—perhaps

Did You Know?

The United States and France have the highest rates of dog ownership in the world (for countries in which such statistics are available), with almost one dog for every three families. Germany and Switzerland have the lowest rates, with just one dog for every ten families.

because their owners didn't realize what they were getting into or someone in the family developed an allergy—other dogs end up in shelters or rescue organizations because of serious behavioral problems. Rescue groups and shelters try to evaluate their dogs and to place them in suitable homes; however, a dog's behavioral peculiarities may not fully surface until the dog has settled into his new home.

> Rescue groups and shelters try to evaluate their dogs and to place them in suitable homes; however, a dog's behavioral peculiarities may not fully surface until the dog has settled into his new home.

When purchasing an adult dog, try to find out as much as possible about his previous owners and the reason they gave him up. If possible, also try to find out the type of environment in which he was reared, because the first few weeks of a puppy's life play a large part in his personality development and health. Your Boxer should also be well socialized with people and other dogs so that he will know the proper way to interact in all situations.

Pet Shops—Pros and Cons

Now, where should you get your pet? Pet stores rarely have older dogs for sale, but some do sell puppies. For the novice buyer, a pet store may seem like the perfect place to find the puppy of your dreams. A pet store is, after all, the home of instant gratification. An eager potential owner can walk in at any time during business hours, choose the puppy who appeals to him or her, pay a fee, and take the pup home, expending a minimum of time and effort. Rarely will a pet store ask you questions to determine if the puppy cradled in your arms is right for you or, just as important, if you are right for the puppy. Sounds tempting, doesn't it? But wait! Don't devote a significant amount of your time and energy to researching the Boxer breed only to choose your puppy in such a haphazard manner.

Although a few pet stores do everything in their power to socialize their dogs and to care for both their mental and physical needs, many do not. The majority of puppies that end up in pet stores have been taken from their mothers and littermates at too young an age and have suffered the stresses of being shipped to a retail outlet. If they came from a large commercial kennel, they may not have received important socialization and human attention in their early formative weeks.

The pet store may supply you with proof of vaccinations and worming, but it is unlikely to give any information on the puppy's genetics. Boxers are susceptible to a number of genetic conditions, and all breeding stock should receive tests for these diseases. Rarely can a pet store produce the documentation of genetic testing that is vital in determining a puppy's health. Although most pet stores offer some sort of health guarantee, often that guarantee is good only until a veterinarian checks the dog, usually within 24 to 48 hours of purchase. Many genetic diseases do not produce symptoms for several years. Finally, pet stores seldom provide ongoing support on house-training, behavioral problems, and other aspects of raising a healthy, well-adjusted Boxer.

Breeders—Pros and Cons

Breeders actually comprise several different types of people who breed dogs. The breeder umbrella encompasses commercial breeders, backyard breeders, and hobbyist breeders. Each type of breeder has its own set of pros and cons.

Commercial Breeders—Some large-scale breeding operations produce a number of different breeds and generate large quantities of dogs. If you encounter someone who breeds such diverse dogs as Boxers, Great Danes, and Poodles, you very likely are dealing with a puppy mill. When a single facility produces many different breeds and an enormous number of dogs, it is unlikely to provide proper genetic screening and health care.

In the interest of making money quickly, many of these breeders sell to pet stores rather than taking the time to place their puppies individually. Again, these puppies often are separated from their mothers too early in their lives and are stressed by the shipping process. Even if you buy directly from them, puppy mill breeders probably won't provide any ongoing support for owners with questions. They will rarely take back a dog past a short window of opportunity.

Even an extremely large kennel that breeds only Boxers may not provide the ideal environment for a puppy's formative first few weeks. Excessively large operations are less likely to give puppies the socialization they need to develop into calm, stable, and well-adjusted adults who will make good family pets.

Backyard Breeders—This category of breeder includes people who breed their dog with the neighbor's, because "They will make such cute puppies" or so that their children can experience the miracle of birth. Then, they offer the puppies for a discounted price or even "free to a good home." Backyard breeders, like pet stores, may seem like convenient sources for Boxer puppies. After all, you may think, why should you pay more money for a dog who has a fancy pedigree or whose parents have all kinds of bizarre titles you can't even understand, when all you want is a pet.

Once again, the question of genetic health comes into play. Most people who breed once or even occasionally to "recoup the money they paid for their dog" know nothing about the complex genetics of purebred dogs and do not test the mother or father Boxer for inherited diseases. A backyard breeder typically offers no guarantee of health nor any support to the new owner should questions about the dog's care arise later. These breeders generally live by the credo "Let the buyer beware." Most backyard breeders will refuse to take back a dog who later develops a genetic malady, and few will help the owner find a new home for the pet if the dog needs to be given up for some unforeseen reason at some point in the dog's life.

> A backyard breeder typically offers no guarantee of health nor any support to the new owner should questions about the dog's care arise later.

Don't be fooled by the "but-he's-AKC-registered" sales pitch. AKC registration means only that a purebred Boxer mother and a purebred Boxer father reproduced purebred Boxer puppies. It does not guarantee good health or temperament.

Hobbyist Breeders—People who breed dogs as a hobby or on a limited basis are generally the best sources for purebred puppies. They may only breed one litter a year, but they usually devote much time and energy to ensuring the health and well-being of those puppies. Most hobbyist breeders know the genetic problems that are specific to Boxers, and they will perform all the necessary tests on breeding stock. Most also test puppies for soundness and give them all the proper vaccinations.

Good hobbyist breeders raise each and every Boxer as a member of the family and take great care in finding the right homes for their charges. They can serve as lifelong sources of information on everything from training and nutrition to grooming. In fact, these breeders often pride themselves on the friendships they have developed with their puppy buyers. Most also will take back a dog into their home at any time during his life if the original owner can no longer care for him.

Puppies from hobbyist breeders usually cost the same or less than those found in pet stores. And, keep in mind, that the price of a pup bought from a hobbyist breeder typically includes genetic testing, socialization, and future support.

Although most people think of buying young puppies from breeders, some breeders occasionally offer older puppies for sale as well. This usually occurs when a show prospect developed some type of fault as he grew that, although it posed a problem in the show ring, does nothing to detract from his quality as a wonderful pet. This type of situation provides the advantage of getting a relatively young dog who is probably already house-trained and may also know basic commands, such as Sit and Come.

Of course, even though hobbyist breeders are usually the best possible source for puppies, you still need to thoroughly investigate each breeder to ensure he or she lives up to your standards. Make sure you get references from each potential breeder, and ask these references if they were satisfied with their puppies and what type of ongoing support they received from the breeder.

Next, make an appointment to visit the breeder's facilities to personally check them out. The breeder ideally should keep the Boxers in the house as pets. If a breeder keeps his or her dogs in kennel runs, each dog should receive "house time" every day. The puppies should be whelped (birthed) and brought up in the home, which is important in acclimating puppies from an early age to the hustle and bustle of family life. Puppies raised in kennels often grow up fearful of normal household noises, such as vacuum cleaners and dishwashers. A breeder also should start to house-train and crate-train the puppies before releasing them to their new homes, which is impossible to do if a puppy is living in a kennel. In addition, puppies should receive daily handling by humans while they're living at the breeder's. Pups who are raised in the house are much more likely to receive this special one-on-one attention than those raised in a kennel.

A breeder should gladly let you see all of his or her dogs, especially the puppies' mother. Although the mom may not run up and lick you in greeting, she should appear friendly and allow you to pet her. Don't believe a breeder who explains away an aggressive Boxer mom by saying, "She's just being protective of her puppies" or "She takes a while to warm up to people." A hostile mother is contrary to the breed and is likely to produce hostile puppies.

If the puppies' dad is on the premises, make sure you meet him as well. However, don't be surprised if he is not present; in order to make the best match for their bitch, breeders often use dogs from across the country as studs. If the breeder you are visiting does not own the father, get the name and phone number of the male dog's owner and conduct a phone interview to learn about the dad's personality and health. Ask his owner to ship you a picture or video of the stud and any pertinent health records. The father's photo may even appear on the owner's Web site advertising stud services.

When visiting a breeder, you can expect to answer as many questions as you ask. In fact, if the breeder doesn't ask you any questions at all, don't buy your dog there! A reputable breeder will place a puppy as if he or she is finding an adoptive family for an infant. The owner will ask whether you have ever owned a dog before and, if so, what happened to him. If you have a history of abandoning dogs, it is unlikely a good breeder will allow you to take home a new pup. The breeder also will ask whether you work and how much time you will devote to exercising and socializing your dog. Do you have a fenced yard? Why do you want a

Boxer? What type of training experience do you have? Don't feel insulted or that the breeder is nosy. He or she is simply trying to guarantee that both you and the puppy find the perfect match.

By the same token, you should have plenty of questions for the breeder. Find out whether both parents have received health clearances for the genetic diseases common in the Boxer and request to see the documentation. Ask for the puppies' pedigrees. Although dogs with titles aren't guaranteed to produce sound puppies, breeders who bother to title their dogs usually strive to breed the best Boxers possible. Also inquire as to what type of training, socialization, and veterinary care the puppies have received.

Finally, ask at what age the puppies will be ready for their new homes. Around eight weeks of age is the ideal time for a pup to bond with his new owner. Don't buy a puppy from anyone who lets puppies go at six weeks or earlier. Pups who are separated from their mothers and littermates at too young an age miss out on important canine socialization and, as adults, may have difficulty reading canine body language and getting along with other dogs. Conversely, puppies left with their littermates for a longer period of time may bond more with other dogs than they will with their owners. This is why it is unwise to bring home two puppies at the same time. If you would like to eventually own two dogs, wait until you have fully bonded with the first pup before introducing a new one. Another important factor to consider is that the few weeks after the eighth week are considered the puppy's fear imprint period. If you bring home a puppy during these weeks, you must take extra care to ensure the experience is a pleasant one for your new Boxer. Anything that frightens the puppy during these weeks will remain in-

> *Around eight weeks of age is the ideal time for a pup to bond with his new owner.*

grained for a longer period of time than if the puppy were to encounter the same situation at a younger or older age.

A negative of buying from a hobbyist breeder is that you may have to wait longer than you would like to get a puppy. Hobbyist breeders may produce litters infrequently, and demand for their pups is often high. If the breeder places you on a waiting list, keep in mind that six months or a year is well worth the wait for a healthy and even-tempered dog with whom you will live for a decade or more.

Signing the Contract Now, let's address puppy-buying paperwork. A puppy sales contract provides protection for both you and the breeder. It should spell out terms of the sale and any conditions. For example, most breeders require that the owners of pet-quality dogs spay or neuter them. Again, don't take offense at this and feel it is intrusive. The breeder is looking out for the health of your dog and is trying to prevent unwanted puppies from being born in the future.

Another condition frequently included in puppy contracts is the first right of refusal, which means you agree to return your Boxer to the breeder if you can no longer keep him for any reason during his lifetime. Usually, one condition to avoid is a showing or breeding clause or a co-ownership clause. Some breeders will sell a potential show puppy to a family with the condition that if the puppy grows into a show-quality dog, the breeder retains showing and breeding rights to the dog. Unless you truly want to get involved in the world of dog shows, avoid this situation. If showing your dog intrigues you and seems like fun, make sure the contract spells out all aspects of the partnership. These specifications should include: where the dog will reside when he is not being shown; who is responsible for show entry fees and stud fees; where a female Boxer will reside during her pregnancy; and who will raise the puppies. As you can see, owning a show dog involves much more than just collecting ribbons and trophies!

Animal Shelters—Pros and Cons

Although it is remotely possible to find a purebred Boxer puppy at an animal shelter, it is highly unlikely. Your chances of finding an adult Boxer at a shelter are much better, however. Boxer owners sometimes take their pets to shelters when they discover the dog is more than they bargained for or when extenuating circumstances, such as a family move or illness, force them to give up their pets.

Most shelters do their best to evaluate their dogs and to release them only to homes that are prepared for the responsibility. Some organizations attempt to retrain dogs before placing them in the hopes of preventing the dogs from being returned in the future. Others offer post-adoption classes for new owners and their dogs. Some shelters, however, are so inundated with homeless dogs and cats that they lack the time and resources to screen the animals as well as they should. If you find a Boxer that you would like to adopt in a shelter, find out as much as possible about the dog before making a decision. Ask why he was given up and how he has behaved since arriving at the shelter. Also inquire whether he has any health problems and, if so, how they are being treated. If possible, spend some time alone with the dog in a getting-to-know-you room or take him for a walk around the shelter's grounds.

Like a hobbyist breeder, a shelter will ask questions of you to determine if you are a good fit for the dog you are considering. Shelters also require that you spay or neuter the dog you adopt, if they have not already performed the operation.

Shelters offer many wonderful animals for adoption. If you adopt a Boxer from a humane society, know that you have saved a life.

Rescue Groups—Pros and Cons

If you are looking for an older Boxer, rescue groups are excellent sources. Rescue groups are organizations that take in dogs of a specific breed and try to find another home for them. Like the dogs that end up in animal shelters, dogs at rescue groups may have been given up for a variety of reasons, some of which are not their fault. The advantages of rescue groups are that the people who run them are extremely knowledgeable about the Boxer breed and take the time to retrain Boxers who are given up because of behavioral problems. Rescue organizations also thoroughly check each Boxer's health and treat any medical problems.

Before allowing an adoption, rescue workers will ask as many questions of you as you will of them, and may even request an in-home interview to check out your home situation personally. Like the hobbyist breeder, rescue organizations encourage ongoing contact and make themselves available for follow-up calls or even visits if you encounter any problems after you take your Boxer home.

Most rescue groups charge a donation for adopting a dog. This fee typically is much less than the cost of buying a purebred Boxer pup from a breeder.

One potential disadvantage of rescue groups is that they rarely have puppies to place. If you are looking for a puppy, you can try a rescue group, but you will probably end up having to go to a hobbyist breeder. Even if you are willing to take in an older dog, you may have to wait for quite a while before the rescue organization has a dog with whom you will be compatible. Another potential negative is that no rescue group may exist in your area. If you can locate a rescue group within driving distance, however, it may offer your best bet for finding an older Boxer who is right for you.

How Do I Choose the Pick of the Litter?

Let's say you've decided to purchase a Boxer puppy. You have interviewed breeders, checked their references, and visited their homes. You've finally settled on a breeder you feel will provide the ideal puppy for you. Now, you're confronted with a wriggling, licking mass of adorable puppies. How do you choose one?

A good breeder will offer lots of expert advice and will help you pick the puppy with whom you are most compatible. He or she not only will encourage you to visit several times to get to know the puppies before settling on a specific Boxer, but also will ask you what type of companion you are looking for. Do you want a Boxer strictly for a pet? Do you want your pet to compete in sports, such as obedience or agility? Perhaps you are an experienced dog owner looking for a dog to join a search and rescue team. Each of these scenarios calls for a dog with a specific personality type. The breeder knows these puppies inside and out and can guide you toward the pup who will best suit your lifestyle. We will address temperament tests in a moment, but first let's learn how to tell whether a puppy is healthy.

Signs of Good Health

Although it is tempting to take home the runt of the litter or the scrawny pup being bullied by her siblings, you should consider the pup's health before allowing your heart to choose for you. The smallest puppy may be diminutive but generally healthy, or she may be sickly. You don't want to set yourself up for years of expensive veterinary bills and the possible early demise of your beloved pet.

A healthy puppy will have bright, clear eyes. A little clear eye discharge usually is fine, but anything more than that may indicate a health problem. The pup should appear energetic and playful. If the puppy you are interested in seems to want only to sleep, come back and visit at another time to see whether she's perked up. Sleepiness may mean the puppy is merely exhausted from an extended romp with her littermates, or that she is sick. Only a second visit (and an honest evaluation by the breeder) will help you determine which is the case.

Common knowledge has dictated that you should pick a plump puppy. However, we now know excessive weight, even in a pup, is unhealthy. With light pressure, you should be able to feel a puppy's ribs—they should neither protrude nor hide under layers of fat. A protruding belly could also indicate the presence of internal parasites.

Other signs of good health include: a clean, soft, and sweet-smelling coat with no signs of fleas; smooth skin that is free of scabs and growths; clean and sweet-smelling ears; strong, white teeth; light-pink gums; and a cool, moist nose free of discharge.

Temperament Tests

If conducted a number of times by an expert, temperament tests can reveal much about a puppy's personality. A novice who runs a single temperament test on a litter may misinterpret the results or not fully understand the behavior he or she is seeing. To ensure the accuracy of the readings, therefore, the breeder should test the puppies' temperaments a number of times in different locations. The breeder also should gladly allow you to test the puppies while he or she is present and can help you put the results in perspective.

What are temperament tests? They are a series of tests that measure a puppy's responses to certain situations and stimuli and that determine her level of dominance, her trainability, and her interest in people. Most owners will fare well in taking home a puppy who scores in the middle range on her temperament tests. A more dominant, strong-willed dog may provide the perfect match for someone who needs a working dog or wishes to compete in an intense canine sport, but will probably prove too much for the average dog owner to handle. Likewise, the extremely shy, hesitant puppy does not make a good prospect for a pet, since puppies with extremely passive personalities can grow into defensive dogs or even fear biters.

When conducting a temperament test, bring the puppies one at a time to a location with which they are unfamiliar. Tie a different colored ribbon around each puppy's neck to keep track of who is who. Take notes, so you will remember how each puppy scored. Although temperament tests do vary, the following basic tests and interpretation guidelines will give you an idea of how these tests work.

○ **Following.** Place the puppy on the ground and take a few steps back, then clap softly and call the puppy. A puppy who follows you right away is people oriented and will train more easily. She will also grow into a more sociable family pet. Avoid the independent puppy who walks away and the fearful pup who runs and hides.

○ **Restraint.** Place the puppy on his back and gently hold her in that position for 30 seconds. The best future family pet will struggle briefly, then relax. A puppy who remains frozen in fear or who growls or tries to bite will make a poor pet choice for the average owner. Pay attention as well to the puppy's eye contact. A polite, easier-to-train puppy will look away. Beware of the dominant puppy who tries to stare you down, even while she's on her back. After you release the puppy, she should recover immediately and may try to lick you or climb in your lap. You should avoid any puppy who runs away and hides or who comes up fighting.

Next, place your hands under the puppy's chest and lift her off the ground for 30 seconds. Once again, the most trainable puppy will briefly struggle, then relax.

○ **Pain Sensitivity.** Take the puppy's paw and firmly press between her toes until she reacts. A puppy who immediately yelps or bites at your hand will not adapt well to a household with small children, where she will inevitably get stomped and pulled on now and then. A puppy who responds after several seconds and gently mouths your hand will train with relative ease. Puppies who do not respond have a high pain threshold. These dogs don't respond well during training to gentle physical corrections, such as short, light tugs on the leash when the dog is pulling. Rather, you will need to entice your dog to follow your commands by using positive reinforcement, and if your dog still won't comply, by applying stronger corrections, such as a training collar.

○ **Noise Sensitivity.** Stand behind the puppy and throw keys or drop a book. The noise will not startle the ideal family pet, who instead will calmly turn to investigate. An extremely fright-ened puppy will have a hard time adjusting to the normal chaos of a household. The puppy who doesn't react at all may have a hearing problem, as is the case with some white Boxers. If the puppy appears not to hear, try clapping and calling the puppy from behind her to see whether she is, indeed, deaf. Deaf dogs can make wonderful pets, but they do require extra training.

A Boy or a Girl?

Many people hold preconceived notions about male and female dogs. They may contend that males are more protective and females are more affectionate, that males are more aloof, while females are better with children. The myths go on and on but, in reality, every dog is an individual, and these sex-based generalizations about dogs' dispositions are simply false.

Before you purchase your dog, however, you should know about some differences between female and male dogs.

Unneutered males tend to mark their property, whether it's the backyard fence, trees, telephone poles, or your living-room couch. Intact males who smell a female in heat will do anything to get to her, including scaling or digging under the fence you thought was impassable. They also may display a willingness to fight anything and everything that gets in their path.

Females go into heat once or twice a year, which can make quite a mess. Their disposition can change to extremely anxious and restless until they mate or their heat cycle ends. If you breed your female, you must deal with her pregnancy as well as the raising and placing of puppies.

If you spay or neuter your Boxer, you won't have to deal with any of these things. (The advantages of spaying and neutering are discussed further in Chapter 4, Medical Care Every Boxer Needs.)

Appearancewise, the male Boxer in general is larger and more substantial looking than the female. He also is heavier and stronger, which can be exhausting to the ill-prepared owner who attempts to take a boisterous male for a walk. The female is lighter and more feminine looking overall, although many female Boxers are just as energetic as males. With training, however, any Boxer can be taught to behave properly.

Males can be just as affectionate as females, and females can be just as protective as males. The only time gender really comes into play is if you add a second dog to your household. Typically, Boxers of the opposite sex get along the best. This is not to say, however, that dogs of the same sex can never live in the same family. If you provide strong leadership, your dogs will be less likely to vie for a higher position in the pack. There are plenty of households filled with a number of peace-loving, content Boxers. Remember that individual personalities are at the heart of dog-dog relationships.

○ **Curiosity and Retrieving.** Throw a ball across the puppy's path. Does she run after it to investigate and possibly even retrieve the ball? If so, this puppy will be easiest to train. Next, tie a rag to a long piece of string. Toss it in front of the puppy and then pull it toward you. Once the puppy chases and catches the rag, let go. A good family pet will seem curious and will follow the moving rag, but will quickly lose interest once the rag stops moving. A puppy who attacks the rag and continues to bite and shake it after the rag stops moving possesses a strong prey drive and may make an excellent working or competitive dog, but will be less suited as a family pet. Once again, you should avoid a dog who runs away and hides.

○ **Energy Level.** The average owner should seek a puppy who is neither high-strung nor extremely lethargic.

Your breeder may perform different versions of these temperament checks or may add other tests to the mix. The important thing is to trust the breeder's interpretation of the results and to remember that you are only witnessing the puppy's reactions on this particular day and at this particular moment. A puppy who has been playing all morning or who is feeling slightly under the weather may not react in her usual manner.

2

Welcome Home!

In This Chapter

❍ Preparing for Your Boxer's Arrival
❍ Boxer-Proofing Your House
❍ What Equipment Do I Really Need?
❍ Homecoming Day for Your Boxer Puppy

So, you've decided that the Boxer is indeed the dog for you. Congratulations! There's nothing quite as special as the love and companionship of your very own dog. You'll soon be bringing home a new best friend to share your laughter, tears, long walks, and snuggles by the fire after a long, hard day. But first, you've got work to do!

Preparing for Your Boxer's Arrival

Before you bring your new puppy or adopted older dog home, you have decisions to make and shopping to do. You and your family need to discuss and assign dog-care duties, establish physical and behavioral boundaries your dog will adhere to, dog-proof your home and yard, and buy all manner of doggie supplies. You may be tempted to rush your new pet home and work out the details later. But trust me, putting forethought into your Boxer's physical and emotional needs will ease the adjustment period for both of you and start your relationship out on the right paw!

Setting Boundaries

Just as people need laws to understand how to interact in a society, your dog will need household rules to fit into your family life. These rules must encompass clear-cut behavioral boundaries, as well as indoor and outdoor physical boundaries. In order for these rules to work, everyone in the household must agree on the rules and vow to stick to them. If one family member allows the Boxer on the couch and another yells at him for the same behavior, your dog will have no idea what is expected of him.

> Putting forethought into your Boxer's physical and emotional needs will ease the adjustment period for both of you and start your relationship out on the right paw!

Where will your Boxer sleep? Where will he stay during the day? Will you limit his access to only certain rooms or areas when you are home, or will you allow him free reign of the house? These questions all require careful consideration and resolution before your dog arrives.

Indoor Boundaries   A crate is an indispensable tool for setting and enforcing your Boxer's indoor boundaries. Although some people mistakenly believe that crating is cruel and harshly confines an animal, nothing could be further from the truth. Like their wild cousin, the wolf, dogs instinctively seek dens. If you don't provide a crate for your dog, he'll actually look for denlike areas in your house, such as in corners, behind chairs, or under tables. While these areas provide some escape, they still leave your dog exposed to the normal chaos of everyday family life. A crate provides much more security, and is a place he can really call his own. Once your dog is introduced to his crate, he'll seek it out whenever he needs a break.

A crate not only "protects" your dog from the household, it also protects the household from your dog! When your puppy is in his crate, you know he's not chewing table legs, piddling on the carpet, or creating other Boxer mischief. Crating your dog also facilitates the house-training process, since dogs instinctively do not want to soil their dens. (House-training is discussed further in Chapter 6, Basic Training for Boxers.)

> A crate not only "protects" your dog from the household, it also protects the household from your dog!

Whether you are bringing home a puppy or an adult dog, do not give in to the temptation to immediately give him free run of the house. Remember, your new dog will not know the rules of the household until you teach them to him. And how can you teach your dog if you are not right there with him to correct mistakes and praise him when he is behaving? Picture this scenario. You are watching television in the family room and your Boxer is contentedly gnawing away on a dining-room-table leg. Suddenly, you realize you haven't seen your Boxer puppy in a while. You call him to you, and he joyously bounds into the room. You praise him for coming when called and curl up with him on the floor for some more TV watching. An hour later, you get up to get a glass of water. As you wander through the dining room, you discover puppy's disastrous attempts at architecture. Can you punish your Boxer for this crime against wooden humanity? No! Punish yourself for not keeping a better eye on your puppy.

At this point, you may be wondering how you are going to keep a constant watch on this fur-clad bundle of energy. This is where the crate comes in. When you can't watch your puppy, simply place him in his crate. The crate should be located in an area where your Boxer can be alone yet still be around his family. A corner of the kitchen is often a good option, since families tend to congregate there. When you can devote your attention to your Boxer, let him out to explore the house. Hang back at a discreet distance, but be ready to correct any bad behavior with a firm "No!" Don't forget that praise is as important as correction. When puppy is being good, let him know. These rules also apply to a newly adopted adult dog. Don't assume because a dog is full grown that he automatically knows proper household manners. Take your time, and clearly and consistently teach him the behavior you expect.

As your dog masters the house rules, slowly grant him more freedom. For best results, increase his freedom incrementally. For example, start by gating off the kitchen where your dog's crate is, then perhaps add a hallway, then the family room. Remember to take these steps slowly; wait until you're sure your Boxer understands how to behave before increasing his roaming space.

In the evening, it's a good idea to either move your dog's crate into your bedroom or have a second crate for this purpose. There is no better way to begin bonding with your Boxer than to allow him to sleep in your bedroom, where he can take comfort in knowing you are right beside him all night long. There will be a lot of new sights, sounds, smells, and noises in your dog's new home. He will feel much calmer and settle in much more quickly if he knows you are nearby. Having a puppy sleep in your room also will aid in house-training by allowing you to hear your pup if he needs to go out to relieve himself during the night. Again, the same goes for older dogs—your adult Boxer will settle in much more quickly if he can be with you as much as possible.

Crates are truly wonderful tools. When you are home and can't keep an eye on your new dog, or if you need to leave him alone in the house, a crate provides safety and security for your pet and peace of mind for you. However, while crates are indispensable, do not overuse or misuse them. No dog, especially a puppy, should be left in a crate for hours on end. You or a helper, such as a neighbor or pet-sitter, should let the dog out every few hours for exercise and to relieve himself.

> There is no better way to begin bonding with your Boxer than to allow him to sleep in your bedroom, where he can take comfort in knowing you are right beside him all night long.

As your dog becomes more reliable and you wish to grant more freedom when you are gone, again, take your time. Don't rush from crate to unrestricted freedom, but use gates to confine your dog to a specific room, such as the kitchen. If you are leaving your dog alone in any room, you first must make sure all hazards are put away. (See Boxer-Proofing Your House, to follow.)

Outdoor Boundaries Never give your Boxer unrestricted access to an unfenced area. Your dog may roam off your property, which can result in some harrowing consequences. He could get lost, picked up by the animal welfare department, or hit by a car. He could be stolen, especially if he is very friendly. Plus, you are liable for any mischief your pet may get into, such as digging in a neighbor's garden. The bottom line is, don't allow your dog to run loose!

Some misinformed owners believe chaining their dog in the yard is a solution to keep their Boxer from straying. No dog should ever be tied up. Tying a dog in the yard can promote aggression in the unlikeliest candidates. I once knew a diminutive Shetland Sheepdog who was a sweet, friendly dog when she was out for a walk or in her home, but who turned into a snarling, frothing fur ball of fury when chained in her front yard. Although most Boxers are eager to make friends with passersby, being chained can quickly end that desire. When people and animals walk by your yard, your Boxer will naturally advance towards them. When he reaches the end of his chain, he will experience a sharp jerk on his neck, which he will associate with the intruders on the sidewalk. The dog will respond by lunging again more vigorously, resulting in him being jerked back more harshly and further increasing his aggressive behavior.

The best way to keep your Boxer in your yard and out of trouble is to put up a tall (six-foot-high) fence. Your Boxer will love to run and play in his own safe domain.

Some dog owners opt for invisible fencing. These increasingly popular fences consist of a signal-emitting electrical wire that runs through the ground bordering your property and a corresponding receiver on a collar worn by your dog. If the dog tries to cross the border, he receives an electrical shock, which usually corrects him from leaving the property. This type of containment system presents some problems, however. For one thing, while invisible fences may keep your dog in, they will do nothing to keep intruders out, whether those intruders are friend or foe. A stray dog could come on your property and attack your dog, or a thief could sneak on your property, remove your dog's collar, and steal your pet. Another problem with most invisible fences is that the correction, or electrical jolt, occurs only at the periphery of your property. If your dog is intensely focused on a person or animal walking on the other side of the street, he could break through his boundaries only to find the correction stops once he has cleared the underground wire. The only way to ensure your dog will stay in your yard is to build a sturdy, conventional fence.

Behavioral Boundaries As important as physical boundaries are to your Boxer's well-being and your relationship with him, behavioral boundaries are just as important. Once again, establish rules and stick to them from day one. If you institute one set of rules when your puppy is an adorable, cuddly eight-week-old, then change the rules as he grows into a muscular, agile adolescent and adult, he will have no idea what is expected of him. For example, Boxers are known for jumping. While you may think it is cute for your puppy to jump up to greet you when you come home, picture that behavior in a full-grown adult. If you will not appreciate a certain behavior in an adult Boxer, don't allow it in your puppy. Discourage all undesirable behaviors now or they will be very difficult to break in the future.

If you are bringing home an adult dog who was rescued, don't allow him to do things you wouldn't otherwise dream of in an effort to make up for his neglectful or abusive past. Your dog will appreciate clear-cut rules and a strong show of leadership by you, his new alpha.

Setting behavioral boundaries actually reinforces your position as leader.

Did You Know?

According to the American Animal Hospital Association, over half of all dog and cat owners give their pets human names.

What Do You Mean It's My Turn?

Divvying Up Dog-Care Responsibilities

Often, parents buy a dog "for the kids" and end up taking on all the responsibilities of caring for the pet themselves. Even couples have been known to purchase a puppy with the understanding that they'll share dog-care duties, only to find one spouse doing the majority of the work once the pup arrives. When family members shirk their responsibilities, it not only can cause resentment, it also can prove detrimental to the puppy's care. To avoid these problems, call a family meeting before bringing your new dog home and divide all dog-care duties among family members. Keep in mind that, although children should be given some responsibilities related to puppy care, other jobs, such as obedience-training an adolescent or adult Boxer, must be taken on by an adult in the household. Also, during the meeting, clearly spell out the boundaries you expect the dog to follow, so all family members will be consistent in their dealings with your new pet.

Questions you should answer include:

○ Who will feed and walk the dog?

○ Who will clean up after the dog?

○ Who will groom the dog?

○ Who will house-train the dog?

○ Who will obedience-train the dog?

○ Who will play with the dog to ensure he gets to release his energy and doesn't become bored?

○ What kind of games are okay to play with the new dog and what kind of games should be avoided?

○ Who will take the dog to the veterinarian for his regular checkups and shots, as well as if he becomes sick?

○ Where will the dog sleep at night?

○ Once he has learned the rules of the household, will he have free run of the house or will he be confined to a crate or certain rooms?

○ Where will the dog stay during the day when no one is at home?

○ Will the dog be allowed on the furniture?

○ How will the dog be contained in the yard?

○ Will the dog be given people food occasionally, or never?

○ How will the dog be corrected when he makes a mistake?

Since the Boxer can be quite an independent, headstrong breed, strong leadership is a must. If your dog is especially dominant, you may need to institute certain rules, such as no lying on the furniture, that a more submissive dog may not require. Since in dog culture, height directly relates to dominance (a dominant dog will stand over a submissive one), taking such simple steps as requiring your dog to sleep on the floor will automatically tell your dog you are the head of his new pack.

Boxer-Proofing Your House

Before bringing your new Boxer home, you will need to dog-proof every inch of your home, garage, and property. Puppies, and even adult dogs, have an instinctual need to investigate their surroundings. Just like human toddlers, puppies investigate by placing everything enticing in their mouths. It is your job to make sure there is nothing hazardous within teeth-range of your pet. While you can't barricade your pup from everything in your home unless she is in her crate, you can use some simple precautions. Get on your hands and knees and investigate your house from a dog's-eye view.

Kitchens are filled with many tempting sights and smells. Keep all food items behind closed cupboard doors, to the backs of countertops, atop the refrigerator, or on high shelves. If you have an adult Boxer, you'll need to be especially diligent. Sandwiches have a habit of disappearing from the kitchen table or countertop when a Boxer is around. Boxers also are very creative and incredibly dexterous. "Baby latches" installed on cabinets are essential to keep out these canine Houdinis.

While a stolen sandwich is merely a nuisance and probably won't harm your pet, the garbage can pose some real danger. Keep all garbage cans, even those with lids, behind closed doors. A flimsy plastic garbage lid is no match for a foraging Boxer. Although some garbage is innocuous, other trash, such as tinfoil or poultry bones, can seriously harm your dog. Place a short trash can under the sink or keep a taller garbage container in the garage or an adjoining room with a door you can shut.

> There are supplies to be bought, decisions to be made concerning dog-care responsibilities and lots of dog-proofing to be done around your home and yard.

Treat your bathrooms in a similar fashion. Cleaning agents may not seem exciting to us, but their smell and very existence are enough to intrigue a puppy, and many of these supplies are toxic. Keep all cleaning supplies locked up or on high shelves. If you don't want half-chewed cotton swabs, tissue paper, and other doggie delicacies strewn throughout your house, keep your bathroom wastebasket under the sink as well. Keep all makeup, hair products, deodorants, and medications in latched drawers or cabinets. Don't mistakenly assume that bottles and metal or plastic containers will halt a Boxer onslaught. A determined dog can easily crush a pill vial or hair spray canister in her teeth and ingest the contents, which may be toxic.

Fluffy bathroom rugs and toilet seat covers may look like the ultimate chew toys to your Boxer. If ingested by your pet, decorative rugs and linens can cause intestinal blockage. You may need to store these until your pup has gotten past the chewing stage or, if you've adopted an older dog, until you're sure she can be trusted around household accessories. Also, remember to keep the toilet seat down. Although drinking plain toilet water is just a disgusting habit, drinking toilet water that has been treated with a chemical cleaner could be fatal to your Boxer. A final temptation in the bathroom is the toilet paper roll. While toilet paper won't harm your puppy, you may find it wasteful to have it papering your house, thanks to some creative Boxer redecorating!

In the laundry room, store laundry detergent, dryer sheets, and toxins such as bleach on high shelves or behind locked cabinets. Keep all your clean and dirty laundry off the ground or you may need to wash clean laundry again, and/or replace a few shredded socks and undergarments. If you iron in the laundry room, make sure you don't leave the cord from the iron dangling off the side of the ironing board. Not only could your Boxer chew on the cord, she also could accidentally pull the iron down on herself.

Carefully examine the room or areas of the house where you sew and store your sewing supplies. Store all needles, pins, thread, scissors, buttons, and other sewing items in locked cabinets or keep sewing kits well out of your dog's reach.

In bedrooms, keep closet doors closed to protect your clothing and shoes from chewing disasters. Keep perfumes and colognes to the backs of dresser tops and shoe polish on a high shelf in the closet. Anything on a nightstand is probably within Boxer reach, so be careful what you store there.

Home offices, which are becoming more prevalent, present their own dangers. Printer toner can be toxic, and staples, paper clips, thumbtacks, and other office supplies can cause intestinal blockage and possibly bleeding if eaten. Books stored on the bottom of bookshelves can pique a puppy's curiosity. Keep bottom shelves empty of books until you are sure your Boxer won't devour them.

In the home office and throughout the house, electrical cords and outlets pose a serious threat to a curious dog's health. Insert plastic caps into all outlets not in use, and unplug electrical cords before leaving a puppy in a room alone. If wires especially intrigue your pup, cover them with electrical tape, bury them under the carpet along the baseboards, or spray them with a "dog-off" product, such as Bitter Apple spray, or even Tabasco sauce. Also check child-safety stores or Web sites for an extension cord that shuts off when cut or chewed—instantaneously. Never leave cords dangling; your puppy could get tangled and hurt himself.

Houseplants add beauty to your home, but may cause harm to your pup. Consult plant books or speak with someone at your local garden supply store to ensure that none of the plants in your home or yard are poisonous. If your Boxer loves to dig in dirt, try using large rocks to cover the soil in your indoor planters.

> Home offices, which are becoming more prevalent, present their own dangers.

If your basement is a storage disaster, it's probably best to keep your Boxer out by means of a closed door or doggie gate. If your dog is allowed in the basement, keep all hazards in locked cabinets or on high shelves. It's also a good idea to keep storage boxes up high, since a curious Boxer may view a cardboard box as an enticing chew toy. Better yet, invest in durable plastic tubs for storing holiday decorations, old photos, and important papers.

If you have cats, you'll need to keep your Boxer from getting to the litter box and taste-testing some "kitty crunchies." If you keep the litter box in the bathroom, invest in a litter pan cover to discourage your Boxer from sampling these unapproved snacks. However, a determined Boxer may still poke his head in the opening and help himself. Another option is to keep the cat box in the basement and block it off with a doggie gate. Your cat will still have access by leaping the gate, but your Boxer will be kept at bay.

Throughout the rest of the house, you and your family will need to be diligent about cleaning up. Dirty dishes or glasses left on coffee tables or TV trays are bound to be licked clean if left there for long. Cigarettes can look like tempting chew toys to puppies, but they can cause nicotine/tobacco poisoning. The same goes for cigarette butts left in ashtrays. If you have a party, don't think you can leave the cleanup until morning. It is especially dangerous to leave out glasses with alcohol in them. Your dog not only could get sick from drinking the alcohol, she also could knock the glass to the floor and get cut. If you have put candy and nuts in bowls on your tables for guests, take them up immediately after your guests go home. Chocolate, especially, is toxic to dogs, sometimes fatally so. Make sure your guests understand the dangers of feeding your dog candy as well. If there are young children present, you may want to keep candy off the coffee table altogether, since they may not understand the grave consequences of giving your Boxer a nibble.

If you have children yourself, make sure toys are picked up and stored in toy boxes or in closets behind closed doors. A dog can choke or experience intestinal blockage from ingesting tiny toy cars, game pieces, or even bitten-off parts of larger toys. Whether or not you have children now, if you plan to have them in the future, consider not introducing your pup to doggie fleece toys. While the difference between a child's stuffed animal and a dog toy may be obvious to us, it's too vague a distinction for most dogs to make. If your Boxer loves to chew her stuffed toys to unrecognizable shreds, you can be sure she'll do the same to a child's cherished stuffed pal.

When cleaning your house, you may opt to place your Boxer in her crate, unless another family member can keep an eye on her. Your puppy may decide to take a sip from a bucket filled with your cleaning supply cocktail, and wind up a very sick dog. In fact, most cleaning supplies are hazardous to dogs. Take extra care to keep your puppy away from any type of pest control products, such as ant bait, rat poison, flypaper, and mousetraps.

While holidays bring joy and festive celebrations to your home, they present their own dangers to your dog. Chocolate and rich foods, for example, can be detrimental to your dog. Your pet might chew, swallow, or choke on ornaments, tinsel, and other decorations. Chewing on a Christmas tree itself or drinking out of the tree stand can make your Boxer extremely sick as well. After opening gifts, throw away or otherwise remove all ribbons and bows since these, too, can cause intestinal blockage. In the spring, grass from an Easter basket can pose the same danger. And when the chill of autumn arrives once again, protect your pet from Halloween hazards. Don't let your children share their Halloween haul, or you may find yourself making an unplanned trip to the veterinarian.

> While holidays bring joy and festive celebrations to your home, they present their own dangers to your dog. Chocolate and rich foods, for example, can be detrimental to your dog.

Boxer-Proofing Your Yard

Now that you've Boxer-proofed the inside of your home, it's time to take a look at the outside. Keep your yard clear of anything that could harm your dog, such as rusty old rakes, nails, wire, and broken glass. Inspect all wooden lawn furniture to make sure no nails protrude and no large splinters are breaking off. If you ever catch your Boxer chewing on wooden furniture or see telltale teeth marks, spray the wood with a bitter dog-off product from a pet supply store. If you use a clothesline in your yard, hang it high enough to prevent your dog from getting entangled.

Patrol your fence line regularly to ensure that there are no weak spots where your dog could break through or areas where your dog has been digging and might escape. Repair or replace any loose pieces of chain link, since they can hook your dog's collar and choke him. Always securely latch and/or lock the gate to your yard, and make sure neighborhood children understand that they must never open the gate to "let your Boxer come out and play."

Examine all the plant life in your yard. If you find a plant that could be toxic to your dog, either dig it up and dispose of it or block your Boxer's access to it with fencing. You'll also need to block him from compost piles. The smell of the rotting organic matter will likely attract your dog, and the bacteria that break it down produce toxins. If you occasionally treat your lawn, keep your dog off it for 24 to 72 hours after application, until the area is fully dry. Carefully read the labels of any lawn-care products to see if they are hazardous, and keep the labels after you throw away the container, in case your pet becomes poisoned and you need to tell your veterinarian the product's ingredients.

Block your Boxer's access to swimming pools and hot tubs; your Boxer may decide to take a dip one day only to find that he can't get out of the pool or Jacuzzi. It's a good idea to teach your dog how to climb the ladder out of the pool in case of an emergency. Also block access to old wells and other potentially dangerous holes in the ground.

Although your Boxer will enjoy time outside, it is a myth that dogs need to spend hours outside every day. If your dog will be spending any substantial amount of time outdoors, however, make sure he has access to shade and lots of cool water to drink. Although he may enjoy a romp in the snow, the Boxer's relatively thin coat keeps these forays short. Never leave your Boxer outside for prolonged periods of time in extreme heat or cold. While outdoor exercise is important, your Boxer wants, and needs, to spend the majority of his time indoors with you, his family.

Safeguarding Your Yard

While it is essential to protect your dog from any hazards lurking in your yard, you also need to protect your yard from your dog. While pristine rose bushes and succulent tomato gardens may be the picture of perfection to us, they seem incomplete to our dogs. To the canine mind, those roses petals and ripe vegetables would look much better strewn around the yard, and a few potholes and stool piles would surely spruce up the place! The question is, how can you bring your Boxer around to your point of view?

Even if your dog never agrees with your sense of aesthetics, you can train him to keep your yard relatively destruction free. If you want certain areas of your yard, such as a flower bed or vegetable garden, to remain intact, block your dog's access to them. Either use interior fences to block off certain areas or keep your dog in a kennel run when you can't supervise him. Teach your dog to defecate in one area of the yard by taking him there on a leash and praising him when he does his business. Since dogs tend to use the same spot over and over for elimination, this should be relatively easy to do, and will keep your yard free of doggie land mines.

Although digging is a natural behavior for dogs, you can curb this behavior through training. First of all, realize that digging can be a symptom of boredom and excess energy. Dogs that are left unsupervised for hours on end in the backyard often dig out of frustration. A dog that participates in plenty of interactive exercise and play with his family will be less likely to dig, bark, or otherwise misbehave. If your dog gets lots of exercise and social time with his family but still is working on an excavation project in your yard, you'll need to teach him that this behavior is inappropriate. Watch him discreetly from inside the house whenever you let him out and immediately interrupt any attempt at digging by rushing outside and sternly telling him "No!" When he stops, praise him. This may take some time, but remember to be consistent and your dog will learn what is expected of him.

> A dog that participates in plenty of interactive exercise and play with his family will be less likely to dig, bark, or otherwise misbehave.

Boxer-Proofing Your Garage

Garages and outbuildings usually contain numerous items capable of making your Boxer sick or even killing him. Many car products, including windshield-washer, brake, transmission, and engine fluids, are poisonous to dogs. Due to its sweet taste, antifreeze is especially tempting to dogs and can be fatal. Some new types of antifreeze are safer for pets, but it is still wise to keep your pet away from antifreeze spills and containers.

Due to these potential dangers, puppies should never be left alone in a garage. Even if you are going to be in the garage with your Boxer, store lawn chemicals, car-care products, paint, batteries, gasoline, kerosene, and other hazards on high shelves or in locked cabinets. Make sure that you understand the properties of any chemicals you are dealing with before placing them behind closed doors, however. Some chemicals cannot be safely stored in

Common Hazards for Dogs

- ○ Household cleaners, laundry detergents, bleach, furniture polish
- ○ Medication
- ○ Suntan lotion
- ○ Poisons (such as ant poison)
- ○ Mousetraps
- ○ Human trash (poultry bones, spoiled food)
- ○ Pins, needles, buttons, and other sewing accessories
- ○ Ribbons or string that can get lodged in the throat or intestines
- ○ Plastic
- ○ Rubber bands, paper clips, twist ties, thumbtacks
- ○ Shoe polish
- ○ Alcohol
- ○ Cigarettes and other tobacco products
- ○ Matches
- ○ Antifreeze, motor oil, brake fluid, windshield-washer fluid
- ○ Paint and paint remover
- ○ Nails, screws, saws, and other sharp objects
- ○ Chocolate

closed places, especially in hot climates or during the summer, or near hot water tanks and furnaces, and should be placed up high and out of reach. If your garage contains a workshop, store nails, screws, tools, and other sharp objects in a toolbox or on a high shelf, and cover or hang saw blades where your dog cannot get them. Keep rodenticides, pesticides, and insecticides, all of which can be toxic, high enough that your dog can't reach them when standing on his hind legs.

What Equipment Do I Really Need?

Now that you've Boxer-proofed your house, yard, and garage, it's time to purchase all the essentials your new dog will need to make

Common Poisonous Plants

This list contains some, but not all, common plants that can harm your dog. Consult a plant book or a nursery if you have any doubts about a plant in your home or yard.

Alfalfa

Amaryllis

Asparagus (Sperengeri) fern

Azalea

Beech tree

Belladonna

Bird of paradise

Black locust tree

Caladium

Castor bean

Chinaberry

Coriaria

Crown of thorns

Daffodil

Daphne

Datura

Dieffenbachia

Elephant's ear

Euonymus

Foxglove

Henbane

Honeysuckle

Hydrangea

Iris

Ivy (especially English, heart, needlepoint, and ripple)

Jack-in-the-pulpit

Jerusalem cherry

Jessamine

Jimsonweed

Larkspur

Lily of the valley

Mistletoe berries

Monkshood

Moonseed

Morning glory

Mums (chrysanthemums—spider and pot)

Nightshades

Oak trees (acorns)

Oleander

Periwinkle

Philodendron

Plant bulbs (most)

Potato (green parts and eyes)

Poinsettia

Precatory bean (rosary pea)

Rhododendron

Rhubarb (leaves, upper stem)

Skunk cabbage

Tobacco

Tomato vines

Tulip

Umbrella plant

Water hemlock

Wisteria

Yew tree (Japanese, English, Western, American)

your house her home. In addition to basic supplies, such as a food bowl and collar, there are many other fun accessories to be had, from luxurious bedding to fanciful ID tags to myriad doggie toys.

Feeding/Water Dishes

Bowls come in all shapes, sizes, and materials. Although plastic bowls may seem like a bargain, they won't be in the long run. For one thing, plastic bowls look like odd-shaped chew toys to many dogs. Not only are plastic feeders easy to chew, the food smells and flavors that become embedded in the plastic also make them especially tempting. A plastic bowl is no match for a Boxer's teeth, even a puppy's, and you'll find you have to replace the bowl often. For small puppies, pieces of plastic that have been bitten off and swallowed can be harmful. Another problem with plastic bowls is that teeth marks and scratches in the plastic become a perfect breeding ground for bacteria from your dog's mouth, un-eaten food, and other contaminants.

Ceramic bowls are durable and come in a variety of colors and designs. They also are heavy, which will keep them from getting knocked across the kitchen floor by a boisterous Boxer. Although some must be washed by hand, others are dishwasher safe. Stainless steel bowls are also a good choice. They are virtually indestructible and sterilize easily in the dishwasher. Whichever type of bowl you buy, consider buying an elevated bowl stand that raises the bowls to your dog's chest level, which is believed to help prevent certain digestive problems.

> A plastic bowl is no match for a Boxer's teeth, even a puppy's, and you'll find you have to replace the bowl often.

How Much Is This Going to Cost Me?

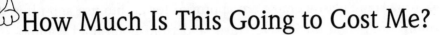

The basic supplies for your new dog can come with a hefty price tag depending on size and quality, and often it's a price you'll be paying more than once. Remember to factor in these costs when making the decision to get a dog. Prices likely will vary depending on where you live, but the following should give you a good idea of what to expect.

Item	Low Price	High Price
Crate	$20.00	$200.00
Food and Water Bowls	3.00	60.00
Collar	4.00	40.00
Leash	4.00	50.00
ID Tag	3.00	15.00
Pet Stain/Odor Remover	4.00	10.00
Brush	4.00	20.00
Toys	1.00	40.00
Food (eight lb. bag)	4.00	9.00
Bed	10.00	200.00
TOTAL	$57.00	$644.00

Crate/Bedding

As mentioned previously, a crate serves many purposes. In addition to keeping your Boxer secure and out of mischief when you can't watch her and aiding in house-training, a crate also provides your dog with "a room of her own." Crates come in two basic varieties: plastic and heavy-duty wire. Both have their advantages and disadvantages. Plastic crates, which are more enclosed and therefore look and feel more like a den, may seem homier to your Boxer. Many plastic crates are approved for airline use and offer more protection during car travel and from household commotion than do open wire crates. Wire crates, on the other hand, provide better circulation than the plastic variety, which tend to retain more of your pet's body heat. During summer months or in close quarters, the trapped heat of a plastic crate may prove uncomfortable for your pet. If you decide on a wire crate but want to give your dog more privacy, drape a sheet or lightweight towel over the top and partially down the sides.

You may decide to invest in one of each. You can use the wire crate for the house and the plastic crate for travel, or keep one crate in the kitchen and one in your bedroom. If you are bringing home a small puppy, you can choose to buy a crate just big enough for the puppy to stand up, turn around, and lie down in comfortably. You will find yourself upgrading quickly to a larger crate as your pup grows, however. To avoid buying a succession of crates, buy one big enough for an adult Boxer, then section it off with a solid, thick piece of wood to make it puppy sized. The wood can be shifted incrementally as your Boxer grows. Remember to spray the wood with a dog-safe repellent to discourage chewing.

Until your puppy is house-trained and past her chewing stage, it is best to leave the floor of the crate bare. If your puppy has an accident in her crate and buries it with a towel, she won't be as bothered by her mess and she may be more likely to soil in her crate again. Also, it may take you longer to discover this slip in house-training. As the puppy gains more control, you can throw in a towel or mat for comfort, but only if you're certain your puppy won't chew on it. If your Boxer does begin to tear up the towel, remove it until she has gotten past the teething stage, since she could choke on threads or pieces of towel or, worse, experience intestinal blockage. As your puppy becomes more reliable, or if you have adopted an older Boxer, you may want to invest in a dog pillow or cushion, or even use old blankets or quilts to soften the floor of the crate. This bedding can be removed from the crate later on and placed beside your own bed once your dog is allowed more freedom in the house.

Doggie Gates/Puppy Pens

As you give your pet more freedom, you may still want to block your puppy or adult Boxer from certain rooms. A doggie gate, or a child's baby gate, works well to keep pets in, or out of, certain areas. If your Boxer is a voracious chewer, spray the gate with Bitter Apple. A determined Boxer can easily chew her way through a plastic gate; wooden gates generally are sturdier. You can also try wire exercise pens to contain your puppy either in the house or in a certain part of the yard. These aren't as vulnerable to doggie teeth as plastic or wood.

Outdoor Shelter

Once again, I want to stress that no dog should be relegated to live outside. Dogs are pack animals. They need to be with their people, and react to isolation with frustration and loneliness.

Dogs are pack animals. They need to be with their people, and react to isolation with frustration and loneliness.

Also, Boxers are not equipped to handle extremes in weather conditions. That being said, if your dog is going to spend any substantial time outside unsupervised, she will need some type of shelter outdoors.

If you purchase a kennel run, make sure it has some type of covering to protect your dog from precipitation and sun. You also may want to buy or build a doghouse. Choosing the size of a doghouse is much like choosing the size of a dog's crate; it should be big enough for your pet to stand up and turn around, but not so roomy as to lose its denlike quality. A properly sized and constructed doghouse will stay comfortably warm, but not too warm, from your dog's body heat. Make sure the entrance to the house is off-center and is covered with a flap to allow your Boxer to escape drafts. In addition, you'll want a house with a removable roof to make it easier to clean.

Collars/Leashes

Your dog, whether a puppy or adult, will need a flat buckle collar to hold his ID tags. (Training collars are discussed in Chapter 6, Basic Training for Boxers.) Nylon or leather works well, but leather will last longer. If you are getting a puppy, you will definitely want to purchase an adjustable collar that will grow with your pet. For the first collar, you may want to go with the less-expensive nylon, since you'll probably replace it several times. For a grown Boxer, a sturdy leather collar is a good investment. Whether your dog is a pup or an adult, the collar should be tightened so that you can only fit two fingers between the collar and your dog's neck. If the collar is too loose, it can get caught on something and choke your pet. Check the size of your Boxer's collar frequently during his first year.

Leashes, too, come in a variety of materials. Nylon and leather leashes are the most common; as with collars, both work well, but a leather leash is more durable.

One type of leash to avoid is the chain-link leash, because they are difficult to grasp and can hurt you if they become wrapped around your hand. Another type of leash not well suited for Boxers is the flexible, retractable leash. Until your dog is extremely well trained, this type of leash does not exert the control you will need to walk an energetic, muscular Boxer. What is more, flexible leashes actually encourage dogs to pull, a behavior that the Boxer needs no encouragement to try! A six-foot leather leash is ideal for training and taking walks. It is easy to grasp, strong, and durable. Unfortunately, to your puppy it may look and smell like something good to chew. If your puppy insists on trying to walk herself, with leash in teeth, apply a bitter dog-safe repellent or Tabasco sauce to the lead.

Identification Tags

Your dog will require tags, including an identification tag, rabies tag, and possibly a local license tag. An ID tag should, at the least, state your phone number and possibly your name. Some people include their pet's name, while others do not, because they believe that knowing this information may give a potential thief an advantage. Every dog must receive a rabies vaccination at around four months of age and must wear a corresponding rabies tag. Some towns and cities also require ownership licenses for dogs and issue a licensing tag that the dog must wear. If the jingle of dog tags isn't music to your ears, you can opt for plastic tag, tag covers, or an ID plate that attaches along the dog's collar. Then again, clinking tags are a great beacon to signal your scheming puppy's whereabouts!

Did You Know?

The average cost per year for owning and maintaining a dog in the United States is $1,220.

ID Tags and Beyond

Identification tags are your dog's first line of defense if he ever gets lost. Many a dog has been quickly reunited with his family because he was wearing a tag with his owner's phone number. But what if your dog's collar comes off or is removed? How will your Boxer find his way back home? Two other forms of identification can supplement the ID tag: tattooing and microchip implants.

With tattooing, a series of numbers or letters, or a combination of both, is imprinted onto your pet's body, and the code is then recorded in a database. If someone finds your Boxer, he or she can call the toll-free number of a tattoo registry, which maintains a database record with your name and phone number, corresponding to your dog's tattoo ID code. The toll-free number usually is provided on a tag that attaches to your dog's collar. Advantages to the tattoo are that it is a permanent and visible means of identification. One disadvantage is that, if your dog loses his collar, whoever finds your pet may not know whom to call. Also, if your dog won't let a stranger near him, the person who finds him may not be able to get close enough to read the tattoo. Finally, horror stories tell of stolen dogs who have had a tattooed ear removed to keep them from being identified. To prevent this, it is safer to tattoo your dog's inner thigh.

Like tattoos, microchips contain a unique code, which can be read by a hand-held scanner that is passed over the skin of the animal where the chip was inserted. The code corresponds to information in a database, such as the owner's name and phone number. An advantage to microchips is that they, too, are permanent. The microchip itself is composed of nontoxic components sealed in biocompatible glass. The chip, about the size of the lead tip of a pencil or a grain of rice, is fitted into a hypodermic needle and injected under the skin of the dog between his shoulder blades. A disadvantage is that not all scanners read all microchips. Humane societies usually have only enough money to invest in one scanner, at best, and if that scanner can't read the chip in your dog, it's useless. Again, if your dog is uncomfortable being handled by strangers, he may be difficult to scan.

Tattoos and microchips are gaining popularity as permanent means of identifying your pet. The standard ID tag that dangles from your pet's collar, however, remains an invaluable tool for helping return your lost pet to you.

Puppy Cleanup

Since you cannot avoid the inevitable, when your puppy relieves herself in the house, not just any cleaning solution will do. You'll need an enzyme-based urine cleaner to thoroughly remove the scent and stain. Many products superficially clean the offending area but, remember, your dog's sense of smell is much keener than yours. An enzyme-based cleaner, available at any pet store, will remove all traces of urine, feces, and vomit, which will help to keep your dog from returning to the same spot the next time she needs to relieve herself.

You'll also need some means of picking up your dog's waste on walks and around the yard. You can use anything from store-bought plastic bags to the bags your newspaper arrives in every morning. Since you are dealing with a larger dog with substantial stool-producing capabilities, however, you might want to invest in a pooper-scooper. This allows you to pick up doggie dung without a lot of bending over.

Grooming Equipment

While the Boxer is an easy breed to keep looking her best, you'll still need some basic grooming supplies. A currycomb made of hard rubber, a natural bristle brush, and/or a hound glove work well to remove dead fur and stimulate the skin to keep it healthy. Invest in a high-quality dog shampoo and conditioner for baths. Do not use human shampoos and conditioners because they have a different pH factor than do dog products. (Brushing and bathing are covered fully in Chapter 7, Grooming.)

You'll also need a dog toothbrush and some dog toothpaste to keep your Boxer's teeth clean. Never use human toothpaste, since their foaming agents can make your dog sick if he swallows them. Every dog needs her nails clipped, so you'll want to buy nail clippers, available in a scissors or guillotine style, and start using them on your dog when she's a puppy to get her used to the procedure. In addition, purchase cotton balls and ear-cleaning solution to keep your Boxer's ears free from infection.

Toys

Now, let the really fun shopping begin—it's time to buy toys! There are myriad toys available for pets, in every color, size, and shape imaginable. Some of these toys are fine to leave with your Boxer when she is alone, and some should only be given to your dog when you are around to supervise.

If you are giving your dog a toy to play with while you are gone, stick with hard toys that can't be chewed apart. Hollow, hard rubber toys such as Kongs are excellent because they can be stuffed with treats to keep your dog occupied for hours. The Buster Cube works on the same principle: You fill it with kibble and, as your dog noses or bats it around, the kibble gradually dribbles out, one piece at a time. Toys like these not only work off some of your dog's energy, they also give her brain a workout. Hard synthetic bones such as Nylabones are good options as well. These bones keep your Boxer occupied and also scrape her teeth, which reduces tartar buildup.

> If you are giving your dog a toy to play with while you are gone, stick with hard toys that can't be chewed apart.

Rawhide, however, is not a terribly healthy toy/treat for puppies, since they tend to bite off and swallow pieces that then expand in their stomachs. If you insist on giving your puppy or adult Boxer rawhide, limit the amount she gets, especially if she seems to be obsessed with the treat, and don't leave her alone with rawhide, or she could eat a small piece and choke on it. Some dogs can devour an entire rawhide chew in a matter of minutes and come back looking for more. If your dog is given unlimited access to rawhide, that makes for a lot of soggy, expanding pulp in her stomach. Take away the rawhide when it has been whittled down near to the end, so your dog doesn't choke on it. If you are going to buy rawhide, read the package carefully to confirm it was made in the United States. Rawhide from other countries often is preserved with chemicals that are unhealthy for your pet. Even some rawhide manufactured in the United States contains harmful preservatives, so if your dog becomes ill after chewing a treat, discontinue using that brand.

Soft rubber toys are fine for when you are playing with your dog, but they are too easy for your dog to rip apart and swallow when he plays alone with them. The same caution applies to fleece toys; many dogs love to destroy these fake-fur balls and eat the insides, which can block their intestines. Never leave a dog alone with a toy that has a squeaker inside; again, your dog can chew a hole in the toy and then swallow the squeaker.

Rope, rubber, or fleece tug toys can be lots of fun for a Boxer who loves to toss toys in the air and catch them. They also are great for puppies playing together with canine friends. You must be careful how you use these toys when interacting with your Boxer, however. If your dog shows any signs of being dominant, playing tug-of-war with her will only encourage dominant behavior. Tug-of-war promotes a show of strength on the part of your dog. While you may be able to wrestle away a tug toy while your Boxer is a puppy, this is

Removing Doggie Stains and Odors

If you have purchased a puppy, you must accept the fact that you will encounter a house-training accident or two, no matter how diligent you are, until your dog is fully trained. Even if you have adopted an adult dog, there may come a time when you find a mess on your carpet, whether that mess is urine, feces, or vomit. Even the best-trained dog may not be able to control himself when he is sick.

Not only must you remove the stain and odor you can smell, but more important, you also need to remove the odor your dog can smell. Remember, a dog's sense of smell is much more acute than ours. Therefore, you'll need to use a product designed specifically for pet-odor removal. Never use an ammonia-based product. Since ammonia is present in urine, your dog will actually be more attracted to urinate there again.

If your dog has an accident, first clean up any solid waste that is present. Next, apply an enzyme-based stain and odor remover. A number of products are available at any pet supply store. Follow the directions carefully to ensure that the cleaner does its job. If you are applying the cleaner to a carpeted area, test it in an inconspicuous spot first to make sure it won't change the color of your rug.

unlikely when she becomes a powerful adolescent and adult. For tug-of-war to be played correctly, the human must always win. Otherwise, your dog will be put in a position in which she is stronger than you and she is controlling the game. If you have any dominance issues with your dog, avoid playing tug-of-war.

Fleece or other fabric toys are poor choices for a dog that has a penchant for destructive chewing. A Boxer who is allowed to tear apart a soft, stuffed dog toy is every bit as likely to shred a child's stuffed animal or the accent pillows on your living-room couch. In the same vein, never give your Boxer an old shoe to chew on; otherwise, you'll need to keep your good shoes under lock and key for the rest of your dog's life.

Supply Checklist

○ Food and water bowls (ceramic or stainless steel)

○ Crate (plastic, wire, or both)

○ Dog bed or crate cushion

○ Doggie/baby gates

○ Outdoor kennel and/or doghouse and/or secure perimeter fencing

○ Collar

○ Leash

○ ID tag

○ Enzyme cleaner

○ Grooming supplies (currycomb, hound glove, shampoo, dental and ear-cleaning supplies)

○ Safe toys

Homecoming Day for Your Boxer Puppy

The day has finally arrived! It's time to bring home your new puppy and introduce him to his new home and family. If you work outside the home full time, arrange to take off at least a few days to help your puppy adjust. If possible, schedule his arrival for early in the day to give him time to fully investigate his new environment before bedtime.

If you are picking up your puppy, rather than having him delivered to you, prepare for a less-than-smooth ride home. Unless the breeder has already taken your puppy for short trips, this may be his first car ride. Bring along several old towels in case your pup drools excessively or vomits. The most important thing to do if your puppy whines or cries is to act as though nothing is wrong. Don't ooh and ahh over your nervous pup—you'll just reinforce his fear of car rides. Instead, act calm, even businesslike. Sing along with the radio, or talk to your puppy in a matter-of-fact tone. The best way to introduce your dog to car rides is discussed further in Chapter 8, Family Life, but for now, you'll just want to get through this first car ride as quickly as possible!

As soon as you get home, take your puppy outside to the area you want him to use as his bathroom. Chances are, after his exciting ride, he will need to go right away. Pick a phrase such as "go potty" or "hurry up" and use it when your dog starts to eliminate. Timing is extremely important. If you issue the command before your dog goes, in your dog's mind it may take on the meaning of something else that is going on with your dog at the moment, such as "sniff the tree" or "chew on grass." Once your dog understands the command by associating it with the action, you can use the command to elicit the behavior. Each time your puppy eliminates outside, remember to praise, praise, and then praise some more! You must help the puppy realize from the beginning that pottying outdoors is the goal. If he doesn't go right away, take him inside and put him in his crate for half an hour, then take him out to the designated spot again. Once he has relieved himself, you can take him inside and let him explore the house. Remember, you'll need to keep a close eye on your pup so that you can correct any mistakes he may make.

Resist the temptation to have all your friends and relatives over to see your new addition; too many people on the first day can be overwhelming for your new dog, whether he's a puppy or an adult. Instead, enjoy a private, getting-to-know-you first day with your pet. Although puppies do need lots of rest, you may want to try to wear your Boxer out on his first day home to help him sleep through the night! This doesn't mean going on marathon runs around the neighborhood; simply playing with your pup and letting him explore your house and yard should do the trick.

When it is bedtime, take your puppy outside to empty his bladder. Then take him to his nighttime crate in your room and turn off the lights. Some puppies cry all night during their first night in their new home, while others sleep "like babies" from the beginning. If your puppy begins to cry immediately after you have put him in his crate and you know he doesn't need to relieve himself, ignore him. It may be tough to do, but he will eventually settle down. If the puppy wakes up whining during the night, take him outside and make the trip as quick and businesslike as possible. If you play with your puppy and make the "potty trip" too fun, you'll find your Boxer waking you up every few hours to "party!" As your puppy gains more control, nightly trips outside will become fewer and farther between and eventually stop all together.

After the first few days, when life has settled back to normal and you return to work, either come home at lunch to let your puppy out or have a neighbor or friend drop in. Remember, a crate is a wonderful tool that shouldn't be abused. It's a good idea to pick a certain indestructible toy, such as a Kong stuffed with treats, that the puppy gets only when he is crated. This will give your Boxer something to look forward to when you leave and will help keep him from feeling bored and lonely.

Making an Older Boxer Feel Welcome

Before you bring an older Boxer into your home, make sure he has met all the members of your family. Although rescue groups and shelters try to match the right dog with the right family, it is best

Did You Know?

A dog named Saur served as king of Norway for three days in the eleventh century.

that you personally ensure that everyone clicks with the older Boxer before you adopt him. If you already have a dog at home, you may want to take her to meet the potential adoptee as well. Once you feel comfortable that all your loved ones will get along, it's time to bring your Boxer to his new home.

If you have another dog, the initial interaction between the two animals is critical. Have a friend or neighbor meet you at a local park or around the block and leave your new dog with him or her while you go home to get your other dog. Let the dogs meet and sniff on neutral territory, and then go for a walk together, all the while acting calm and positive about the introductions. Bring them into your backyard and watch carefully to be sure that your first dog does not become territorial. Once the dogs seem relaxed, you can unleash them.

It is important for you to realize that some tense moments may pass as the dogs establish rank. Do not interfere unless an actual fight breaks out. If a fight does occur, never get in the middle, or you could be bitten. Instead, spray the dogs with a hose to break them apart or throw a blanket over them and try to remove the less-aggressive dog. Once your pets have established who's top dog, things will settle down. While it is understandable to feel protective of your original dog, it is vital that you don't interfere with this process. If your new dog is the natural leader and you keep backing up your first dog, you are merely disrupting pack order and keeping both dogs in a constant state of stress.

Boxers can get along well with cats if introduced carefully. Begin by letting them sniff each other under a closed door. Next let them in the same room, but keep your Boxer on leash so you can pull him back if he lunges at your cat. Practice obedience commands with your dog while you talk to your cat in a soothing voice. Make sure your cat always has areas to escape to and that she has privacy when she eats and uses the litter box.

If you are bringing home an older Boxer, you may or may not know much about his past. Just as in the case of a puppy, you must limit his freedom in your home until you have learned his habits. If he is not reliably house-trained, you'll also want to keep him crated when you can't keep an eye on him. If you want to give him a little more freedom than his crate, block off the kitchen or laundry room with a baby gate. Make sure you still keep your dog's opened crate in the room with him, so he will have a cozy place to rest.

> If your Boxer is a rescued dog, making him feel secure in his new home is crucial.

If your Boxer is a rescued dog, making him feel secure in his new home is crucial. Don't think that just because he is an older dog, he would be happier sleeping in the kitchen or laundry room. Make up a special bed in your room. In the beginning, you'll probably want to crate him until you know he can make it through the night without any accidents. After that, a dog bed placed next to your own bed will help your Boxer bond with you, since he will sense your presence and feel more at ease. This is especially important if you are away from your dog for hours at a time during the day while you work.

If you have taken in a rescue dog, you will want to start with as clean a slate as possible. If you know your pet was abused, resist the temptation to baby him. Providing lots of praise, love, and firm, consistent leadership will benefit your dog more than anything else will. Grooming and training your dog are excellent ways to bond with your new pet. Obedience practice will also help you establish from the beginning that you are the alpha of the pack, and enable your dog to feel secure.

As with a puppy, you will want to establish physical and behavioral boundaries from the beginning.

As mentioned earlier, don't fall into the trap of thinking that you can right the wrongs done to your dog by allowing him liberties you wouldn't dream of otherwise. Again, firm leadership and lots of love are what your dog craves most of all.

3

Food for Thought

In This Chapter

○ What Is the Best Food for My Boxer?
○ How Often and How Much Do I Feed My Boxer?
○ Is It Okay to Share My Food?
○ What's All the Fuss About Supplements?

So, you've chosen bowls, beds, collars, leashes, toys, and other basic doggie necessities. Now, we come to perhaps the toughest, and most important, decision of all when buying essentials for your new pet: What are you going to feed him? Today's dog owner is bombarded with a vast array of dog-food options, ranging from convenient grocery-store brands to premium foods at your local pet supply store to homemade recipes. Then there's the choice of dry versus canned, and the perplexing question—to supplement or not to supplement? Words of advice from well-meaning fellow dog owners are as limitless as the dog food options themselves. How can you make the best choice?

Why Nutrition Matters

First, you need to understand how vital good nutrition is for the health of your Boxer. Proper nutrition will boost your dog's immune system and help her fight infections. It will keep her bones and teeth strong, her coat glossy, and her skin smooth and supple. Not so long ago, people didn't really worry about what they were feeding their dogs. They would feed their pet whatever brand was on sale, or just give her some leftovers, including bones, from the evening meal. As consumers became more savvy about the importance of their own diet, however, they began to be more concerned about what they were feeding their dogs as well.

> **P**roper nutrition will boost your dog's immune system and help her fight infections.

Many learned that the old way has its dangers. Changing dog food randomly because a different brand is on sale can give dogs diarrhea or other digestive problems. Feeding trimmed fat or other unhealthy portions of the family meal doesn't give dogs the proper nutritional balance they need for a healthy coat and stable weight. Plus, veterinarians have gotten the word out that bones are dangerous to a dog's health, and can even be lethal if they are swallowed, since they can puncture internal organs. To help you determine the best food for your Boxer, you need to understand what nutrients she needs to stay healthy and happy.

First, I'd like to dispel a common myth about the dog: She is not a carnivore (strictly a meat eater). Instead, she is an omnivore, which means she needs a small amount of plant material as well as meat for a complete, balanced diet. This stems from the eating habits of her ancestor, the wolf, who consumed her prey's last plant meal as well as the meat of the prey itself. Therefore, while your Boxer in most cases shouldn't have a purely vegetarian diet (there are vegetarian diets available, but they are very difficult for most dogs to digest), some plant material is important for the proper nutritional balance.

What nutrients does your dog need, and which ingredients supply them?

Proteins form the major building blocks of your dog's blood, bone, muscle, and immune system agents. Proteins are made up of amino acids, which are essential in the formation of DNA, growth, metabolism, the development and repair of body tissues, the digestive system, hormone production, sexual development, the functioning of the immune system, and the transmission of nerve impulses. Of the 22 amino acids, 10 of them must be supplied in food since they can't be manufactured in the dog's own body. These 10 essential amino acids are arginine, histidine, isoleucine, leucine, lysine, methionine, phenylalanine, threonine, tryptophan, and valine. Different food sources supply different amounts of these amino acids, as indicated by a chemical score for the protein source. For example, eggs, which supply 100 percent of the essential amino acids, have a chemical score of 100, making them an excellent protein source. Proteins are found in meat and meat by-products, including beef, chicken, turkey, lamb, fish, eggs, meat and fish meal, and milk and milk products (whey and cheese). They are also found in plant sources, such as wheat, corn, rice, soy, and barley.

Carbohydrates serve primarily as a source of energy, and also aid in the digestion of other foods. Although extra protein can provide the necessary nutrients if your dog's food is lacking in carbohydrates, carbos are included in most dog foods for taste, added energy, and fiber to aid in digestion. If your Boxer doesn't get enough energy, her body will turn to its own tissues for fuel. An excess of energy supply, on the other hand, leads to increased body fat. Carbohydrates are also protein sparing, which means they relieve proteins of some of their duties. When the body takes in enough carbohydrates, it doesn't rely as heavily on proteins to supply energy, freeing those nutrients to perform other necessary functions. Carbohydrates are present in plant sources such as corn, rice, oatmeal, beet pulp, and wheat.

Fats provide about twice the energy per gram than do proteins or carbohydrates. Fats also are extremely efficient, with more than 90 percent digestibility. They supply the body with the essential linoleic, alpha-linolenic, and arachidonic fatty acids, which are needed on the base cellular level to make up cell walls, and also are necessary for healthy skin and coat. Fatty acids also carry fat-soluble vitamins through the body. Finally, fats make food taste better.

Although fats are extremely beneficial, keep in mind that feeding the proper amount of fat is important. Too little fat can result in a dull coat or dry, flaky skin, or it can even slow your dog's growth if the deficiency is extreme. Too much fat can lead to an overweight dog and all the problems that come with obesity. The right amount of fat in your dog's diet, on the other hand, will provide benefits you can see—an energetic dog with a glossy, healthy-looking coat. Fats are supplied in animal products, such as chicken or turkey fat, or may be added to the diet via cold-pressed oil, such as linseed, wheat germ, or soybean oil.

Unfortunately, fats are fragile. Heat, light, and oxygen can destroy the essential fatty acids, so it's important to protect them during the dog food manufacturing process. Since fats can easily turn rancid, preservatives must be added to dog food to keep it fresh. There are two main types of preservatives or antioxidants—chemical and natural. The chemical preservatives of ethoxyquin, BHA, and BHT have been used since the early 1900s to preserve dog food, and even appear in some human food (ethoxyquin is approved for use in paprika and chili powder, and BHA and BHT are present in bread, for example). There has been some concern over their safety, however. Anecdotal testimonials have blamed these chemicals for everything from allergies and immune system problems to cancer. Yet, to date, no study has proven that these preservatives are harmful in the levels approved for dog food. Still, consumers' concerns about the long-term effects of these chemicals has led many manufacturers to switch to natural antioxidants, including vitamins C and E, as preservatives. Although no health concerns are associated with these natural antioxidants, they are much less efficient preservatives than their chemical cousins, and dog food preserved in this way has a much shorter shelf life. It's critical that you always check the expiration date stamped on dog-food bags or cans and don't feed your Boxer any food that has expired. If you open a bag that hasn't expired but it smells rancid, trust your nose and throw it away.

Next, we come to vitamins. Vitamins help the body fight disease and maintain the critical balance between constructive and destructive cellular changes. Vitamins themselves must be properly balanced since excesses or deficiencies of vitamins, or interference between vitamins, can cause serious health problems. The fat-soluble vitamins A, D, K, and E are stored in the liver and fatty tissues. Since they can be maintained in the body, an excess intake of these vitamins can easily become

Did You Know?

Veterinarians estimate that between 30 percent and 50 percent of today's dog population is overweight.

The Importance of Water

Water is important to every living creature, and your Boxer is no exception.

Water makes up around 65 percent of your adult dog's body and even more of your puppy's constitution. Dogs need water to help their cells function properly and to aid in proper digestion. Basically, dogs need water to live. Without water, a dog will die within only a few days.

The water in your dog's body needs to be replenished on a regular basis, since it is routinely lost through respiration, digestion, and urination. On hot days or when exercising heavily, your dog needs even more water to keep his body running smoothly.

To keep your Boxer at optimum health, provide him with constant access to plenty of cool, fresh water.

toxic. Water-soluble vitamins, on the other hand, are flushed from the body daily and must constantly be replaced. Both plant and meat sources contain vitamins, plus manufacturers often add vitamins to dog food during processing.

Minerals are needed for the body's metabolic processes and to keep the proper level of salts in the bloodstream. They also are an essential part of your dog's bones and teeth. Canines need seven major minerals and 15 trace minerals. Like vitamins, all minerals, and especially trace minerals, need to be properly balanced or they can be toxic. And, like vitamins, deficiencies or excesses can contribute to myriad health problems, from anemia to hip dysplasia. Minerals also are present in both vegetable matter and animal tissues, or are added by the manufacturer during processing.

Now we come to the most essential nutrient of them all—water. Water is necessary for the proper function of every living cell in your pet's body. Since water is constantly being used up or excreted through normal body function, dogs need to continually replenish their supply. The best way to keep your dog fully hydrated at all times is to always give her access to plenty of clean, fresh water.

What Is the Best Food for My Boxer?

Now you understand the nutrients your Boxer needs to keep him healthy. But that doesn't do much to narrow down all the choices bombarding you from the dog-food aisle. First, let's address whether a more expensive dog food is really better for your pet.

Premium Foods Versus Grocery Store Foods— Is There a Difference?

Perhaps the dog you grew up with was fed grocery store food, and he seemed perfectly healthy. You recognize the big-name manufacturers you find at the grocery store, and who can beat the convenience of buying your dog food while you shop for your own food? Why should you make a special trip to a pet supply store to buy a premium food that's going to end up costing more money?

First, we need to figure out what makes a food premium. Start by looking at the label. Dog food labels are actually made up of two parts: the main display label and the information panel. The main display label states the brand name, flavor of the food, life stage for which the food is meant (puppy or senior, for example), and weight of contents. The information panel is the more instructive part of the label. It lists a number of items, including the guaranteed analysis (the minimum levels of crude protein and fat and the maximum levels of fiber and water), the ingredient list (listed in descending order by weight), and a statement verifying that the food has undergone feeding trials by the Association of American Feed Control Officials (AAFCO) and provides complete and balanced nutrition. If the label doesn't include this statement, do not buy the dog food, no matter how highly your breeder or neighbor down the street recommends it.

In general, the ingredient list will give you a hint as to whether you are dealing with a premium or lower-quality food. Premium foods tend to list chicken, lamb, turkey, and meat by-products as their first ingredients, while lower-quality foods often have plant sources such as corn as their top ingredient. However, you also must read closely to see if any ingredients were split in their listing. For example, a bag that lists several different types of corn scattered throughout its ingredient list may actually contain as high a portion of corn as the "honest" bag that lists corn first and only once. Corn is corn, no matter how you describe it.

> Premium foods tend to list chicken, lamb, turkey, and meat by-products as their first ingredients, while lower-quality foods often have plant sources such as corn as their top ingredient.

This may seem easy—read the ingredient list and choose the one with the better-sounding ingredients near the top. It gets more complicated when you know that the simple statement of an ingredient doesn't verify its quality. Bioavailability, or the ability of a nutrient to be absorbed and used by the body once it's been eaten, is extremely important. This is the main difference between premium and lower-quality dog food. Premium foods are more expensive precisely because they use higher-quality ingredients with greater bioavailability, so nutrients reach your dog's organs and tissues more quickly.

Another quality that sets premium foods apart is that they are manufactured using a fixed recipe, meaning the same exact ingredients are always used and the nutritional quality is consistent.

Lower-priced food is often formulated with a variable recipe that uses the least expensive ingredients available at the time of manufacture. These foods may always list the same ingredients, but the exact nature and actual quality of those ingredients may vary dramatically from bag to bag. This change in ingredients could cause digestive problems in your dog, or in extreme cases, could even hinder the proper development of a puppy.

The use of consistent, higher-quality ingredients in premium foods leads to their higher price. The truth is, though, that feeding a premium food may not cost any more money than a lower-quality, lower-priced brand in the long run, and in some cases may even save you money. How can this be? Since premium foods are more bioavailable, your dog can eat less and get the same amount of nutrients he would receive from consuming a greater amount of a lesser brand. Premium foods also tend to contain less filler. So, although you're spending more money per bag on a premium brand, you might actually spend no more or even less per amount actually consumed by your dog. Another advantage of greater bioavailability is that, as your dog eats less food and absorbs more nutrients from it, he'll produce fewer, and in most cases, firmer, stools. Every owner of a Boxer can appreciate that added bonus!

The bottom line when choosing a dog food is to look for a brand from a company with a good reputation that lists better ingredients at the top of its ingredient list and that has undergone AAFCO feeding trials.

Canned Versus Dry

Now that you've chosen a brand, you'll need to decide which formula of the brand you want to feed your dog. Most brands of food come in two forms—dry and canned. Both types have their pros and cons.

Dry food is the more popular type, accounting for 80 to 90 percent of the dog food market in the United States. Proponents argue that dry food aids in dental health by scraping away tartar during the chewing process and by helping to maintain healthy gums. Chewing dry food, as opposed to gulping canned, also stimulates salivation and assists in digestion. Dry food stays fresh longer when left out than canned food, which can turn rancid quickly. Finally, dry food usually is less expensive.

Canned food has the advantage of generally being more palatable. Owners usually view canned food as a more exciting meal for their pets. On the downside, canned food tends to be more expensive and can't be left out or it will go bad. If your dog doesn't finish his portion, refrigerate the leftovers. You can warm them for a few seconds in the microwave before the next meal to make them more enticing, but make sure there aren't any "hot pockets" before feeding them to your dog. Unfortunately, some dogs refuse to eat leftovers regardless of whether they are heated, adding to the expense of canned food.

Some people like to mix canned and dry food for variety. If you are going to do this, make sure you are mixing varieties of the same brand so the nutritional value will be consistent. Also, if you are feeding a senior-formula dry food, for example, don't mix it with an adult-maintenance canned food or you negate the effects of the dry food. If you want to spice up your dog's dry food but don't want to spend the money on canned, you also can try adding a little water and microwaving briefly to make a warm doggie stew. Once again, make sure the food is a safe temperature before giving it to your hungry Boxer.

A third category of dog food that isn't as well known as canned or dry is semi-moist food. This type usually comes in individual bags and is colored and shaped to look like real meat. While this food may look more appealing than dry or canned, this is for your benefit, not your dog's. Don't be fooled by its outward appearance—these foods typically contain high amounts of corn syrup or other sweeteners that are unhealthy for your pet.

In general, dry food is easier to feed, better for your dog's teeth, and less expensive than canned products (or the to-be-avoided semi-moist variety). If your dog likes his kibble, don't mess with a good thing!

> In general, dry food is easier to feed, better for your dog's teeth, and less expensive than canned products. If your dog likes his kibble, don't mess with a good thing!

All-Natural Foods

Many people, wanting the best for their pet, go beyond the grocery store versus premium food debate and search for a natural dog food. Unfortunately, there are no standards at the moment to verify what "natural" is. Manufacturers of "natural foods" criticize the general pet food industry, saying that dog food processing depletes ingredients of their nutritional value. Most of these manufacturers advocate using whole grains, whole fresh meats, and organic ingredients. They often sell their food in smaller-portion bags so less food will be exposed to oxidation when opened. Finally, many also offer a line of supplements to be used with their foods. If you want to feed a natural food, make sure you are buying from a proven company with a good reputation. Read the ingredient list carefully and ask the manufacturer any questions you have about the content.

Natural prepared foods can be a healthy choice for your pet, as long as you research them carefully. Many all-natural foods have not undergone AAFCO feeding trials and certification, however, and instead are supported only by customer testimonials. Don't buy food from an unknown manufacturer based purely on its "all-natural" claims, or your dog's nutritional health could suffer.

Preparing Your Boxer's Meals Yourself

Some owners take the concept of a natural diet even further, by cooking their dogs' food themselves or even feeding them a raw diet. While in theory this may sound attractive, be aware that it is very difficult to maintain a healthy dog on a home-prepared diet. You will need to find a proven recipe and stick to it 100 percent of the time, or your dog can miss out on essential nutrients. Never begin feeding a homemade diet without first consulting your veterinarian. He or she may even refer you to a canine nutritionist to ensure that you are giving your dog the proper nutrients in the proper amounts. Remember, too much of a certain nutrient can be as dangerous to your dog as too little.

A raw diet presents its own perils if not used cautiously. Suddenly switching your dog to a raw diet will expose him to the many disease-causing organisms present in raw meat, which could lead to serious digestive problems. You also must handle raw meat carefully so you don't get sick as well.

If preparing your Boxer's meals yourself still intrigues you, dedicate yourself to finding the best, well-balanced recipes available and carefully monitor your pet's weight and overall health. Cooking for your dog on a whim could spell nutritional disaster for your pet.

Hypoallergenic Diets

Is your dog scratching a lot or chewing at his fur? If he is free of fleas, the problem might be a food allergy. But, you say, he's been eating the same food for years. Surprisingly, food allergies take an average of two years to develop. This is because allergies develop due to repeated exposure to a certain substance or ingredient. Mild food allergies can even show up seasonally when a mild inhalant allergy combines forces with the food allergy.

Your dog can develop allergies to any food or ingredient, although protein—chicken, beef, lamb, or other sources—is the most common. Lamb used to be regarded as a hypoallergenic ingredient because most dogs had never been exposed to lamb-based food before. Now that lamb and rice foods are increasingly popular, dogs are developing allergies to lamb about as often as they are reacting to the old standbys of chicken and beef.

Your veterinarian may try an elimination diet of specially formulated foods made of unusual ingredients such as catfish and rice, or rabbit and potatoes, or may prescribe a homemade diet. As I mentioned in the above section, however, home-prepared diets are time-consuming and can be expensive. A veterinarian must carefully monitor elimination diets, since they often are lacking in certain nutrients. Another option is to switch to a different commercial diet and hope that eliminates the problem. Unfortunately, preservatives, flavoring, or other additives, which show up in many commercial foods, may be the culprit.

Did You Know?

The world's heaviest, as well as longest, dog ever recorded was an Old English Mastiff named Zorba. In 1989, Zorba weighed 343 pounds and was 8 feet 3 inches long from nose to tail.

Food allergies are frustrating to decipher, and only become more frustrating if you change foods randomly without a plan. Work closely with your veterinarian to discover the source of your dog's allergy so you can relieve the problem.

Prescription Diets

A relative newcomer to dog-food options is the prescription diet. These diets should be used only on the advice of a veterinarian. There are a variety of brands and formulas for use with a number of canine conditions, including liver disease, chronic renal failure, diabetes, and congestive heart failure.

How Often and How Much Do I Feed My Boxer?

Your dog requires different amounts of food during the different stages of her life. It is up to you to regulate the amount of food your Boxer gets each day. But before we look at how much you are going to feed your dog, let's determine *how* you'll feed her.

There are three methods of feeding: free-choice, timed, and portion feeding. Free-choice feeding is exactly what it sounds like—you fill your dog's bowl to the rim and leave it down all day, allowing your pet to eat whenever and how much she wants. There are several problems with this type of feeding. For one, while some dogs adjust their intake to the amount of food their body requires, many do not, and gorge themselves day after day until they become obese. In addition, leaving down an imprecise amount of food all day long makes it difficult to monitor your dog's eating habits. Chances are, it will take you longer to notice a decrease in appetite in your dog if you are feeding free-choice than if you choose another method. Finally, only dry food can be left down all day without spoiling, so feeding canned or even mixing canned with dry is not an option.

The second type of feeding is timed feeding, in which you fill your dog's bowl and put it down for 15 to 20 minutes per feeding, then take up any leftovers. With this method, it will be easy to see if your dog's appetite is decreased, plus you have the freedom to add canned food if you want. You also can add to your pet's food any medication she may need and watch to see that she actually eats it. If you have a dog that tends to overeat, however, you may again have a problem with this type of feeding. These dogs quickly learn to wolf down their food before it disappears, leading to overeating and also increasing their chances of developing bloat. This is a potentially lethal syndrome in which gases suddenly accumulate in the stomach, often causing the stomach to twist over on itself. (As a side note, never allow your dog to eat or to drink a large amount of water right before or after exercising, as this is another suspected cause of bloat.)

The method of feeding I prefer is the third choice, portion feeding. For this, you determine the amount of food your dog needs per day based on age, weight, and recommended feeding guidelines printed on the dog-food bag, and divide that amount by the number of times a day you are feeding. If you are feeding dry food, each portion can be left down until the next feeding or can be picked up after 15 minutes or so. This still allows you to see if your

Did You Know?

Dogs and cats in the United States consume almost $7 billion worth of pet food a year.

dog's appetite is up to par, but also gives you greater control over the total amount of food your Boxer is consuming each day.

Puppy Feeding Schedules and Amounts

From the moment you bring home your puppy, you'll want to establish a feeding routine. First, pick a place in your house where your dog can eat undisturbed, but still be close to her "people." The kitchen is usually a good option, and placing your dog's bowl in her kitchen crate can help her feel secure while still being a part of the family goings-on. This also helps your Boxer associate being in her crate with good things. Secluding your dog in another part of the house to eat, such as the laundry room, can cause him to become overly protective of her food.

> Watching your dog's overall health and appearance is the best way to determine whether she is on the right food.

In the beginning, feed your dog the food she has been eating at her breeder's home. If she seems to thrive on that brand, don't feel you need to try different foods. Many people mistakenly believe their dogs need variety in their diet, when in fact the opposite is true. Changing your puppy's food too frequently or too quickly can result in digestive problems such as diarrhea. Watching your dog's overall health and appearance is the best way to determine whether she is on the right food. Look for clear shining eyes, a glistening coat, and an alert, playful personality. Chances are, if she's wearing you out, she's probably eating a well-balanced, nutritious diet!

If you feel your Boxer would do better on a different food, make sure you make the switch gradually. The first week, mix 75 percent of the old food with 25 percent of the new. Make it a 50/50 mix the second week. The third week, decrease the old food to 25 percent and increase the new to 75 percent of the mix. By the fourth week, you should be able to feed your pup 100 percent of the new food without any digestive problems.

Now, what about amount? To determine the amount of food to give your puppy each day, start by consulting the feeding panel on the dog-food bag. These instructions usually give an average range of cups to feed per day, based on the weight of your dog. In general, Boxer puppies between eight and sixteen weeks of age need between three and four cups of dry food per day. As your puppy gets older, monitor her weight and body condition, and adjust her food accordingly.

It's important to remember that the guidelines on dog-food bags are simply that—guidelines. Some puppies need more food, while some need less. In fact, these guidelines often run on the high end for most dogs, so you need to watch your Boxer's waistline to determine how much food she really needs.

People used to think that the pudgy puppy was the healthiest in the litter, but now we know better. In fact, you should be able to feel your puppy's ribs when you run your fingers along his sides. If you stand over your dog and look down, he should have a visible waistline. When you check out your puppy from the side, her abdomen should "tuck up" from the ribs to the pelvis. Signs of an overweight puppy include fat rolls around her neck or the base of her tail and shortness of breath or a lack of energy when playing. On the opposite end of the spectrum, protruding ribs are signs of a seriously underweight pup. If your puppy seems too fat or too thin, adjust her food accordingly. Don't feel bullied into following the dog-food bag recommendations religiously—your dog's appearance is the best indicator of how much food she needs.

Puppies generally should be fed three to four times a day until they are five or six months old, at which point they can be cut to two meals a day. Puppies need to eat several meals a day for a number of reasons. Since they carry little fat for energy reserves, they need to eat more often. Also, if they don't eat every few hours, their blood sugar levels can drop to a dangerously low level, which can lead to hypo- glycemic seizures.

> **D**ogs, being social animals, really enjoy mealtime around their families.

Always try to feed your puppy at the same time each day. Not only does such a rou- tine ease your dog's mind (she'll know exactly when her next meal is coming), it also helps the house-training process run more smoothly. Since puppies tend to eliminate soon after each meal, feeding your puppy on a schedule helps you time your trips out- side and keep indoor accidents from occurring.

Feeding Your Adult Boxer

Adult dogs also thrive on routine. While some people feed adult dogs one meal a day, I recommend sticking with the two-meal-a- day regimen throughout the life of your Boxer. Not only will spreading out meals lessen your dog's chances of getting bloat, it also will give her something extra to look forward to. Dogs, being social animals, really enjoy mealtime around their families. If you've recently adopted an older Boxer, feeding her on a set schedule in her kitchen crate will help her feel secure and a part of the family, as well as aid in any house-training problems.

Is It Okay to Share My Food?

Some people live by the rule that a dog is a dog, a person is a person, and their food never shall meet. These folks say feeding table food upsets the balance of the dog's own nutritionally complete dog food. Plus, who wants a dog who begs every time you open the refrigerator door or the snack cupboard?

On the flip side are those owners who acknowledge that, being human, many of us will have an unconquerable desire to occasionally give our dog a treat. If you are one of this latter category, it's important that you learn which treats are healthy and which can be dangerous to your dog.

Healthy Treats

The first thing you need to realize is that no matter how healthy treats are, they should never make up more than 5 to 10 percent of your dog's food. The last thing you want is a dog who skips his meals because he is filled up on treats!

There are a number of healthy treat options. Commercial treats range from baked biscuits (which often use the same ingredients as dry dog food but come in fun shapes and color) to semi-moist treats (which are popular with dogs but tend to be high in sugar and preservatives) to super-creative treats, including a doggie substitute for ice cream. Read the labels of these treats to determine just how nutritious they are and whether you can indulge your dog frequently or give them only on special occasions.

Then there's people food. While some people foods are reasonably healthy for dogs, others are downright dangerous. In general, if you know a treat

Toxic Treats—
Dangerous Foods for Dogs

Certain treats, while they are all right for human consumption, can be dangerous, or even lethal, for your pet.

Certain high-fat meats are difficult for dogs to digest. Also, meats doused in rich sauces, rich gravy, or spices can wreak havoc on your dog's digestive system.

Bones pose a serious danger to your dog. Never feed your dog bones left over from your meal, particularly poultry, fish, and pork bones. Pieces can break off and cause constipation, intestinal punctures, or blockage of your dog's digestive tract.

Never be tempted to ease your dog's thirst with anything other than water. Soda contains sugar or artificial sweeteners and unhealthy additives, and alcohol can be harmful, or even fatal, if consumed in large quantities.

Avoid salty, calorie-laden snacks, such as potato chips. Excessive salt can dehydrate your pet, and extra fat calories will only translate into extra pounds.

Sugary snacks, such as candy and cookies, also are bad for your Boxer. At the least, they'll fill him up with empty calories and leave him less interested in his own food, which can result in poor nutrition. At the worst, they can make your dog sick, causing diarrhea and/or vomiting.

Chocolate is especially dangerous for a dog; it can even be deadly. Different types of chocolate pose varying risks. While milk chocolate will probably make your Boxer very ill, baking chocolate could possibly kill him. Be safe and never feed your dog chocolate of any kind.

isn't terribly nutritious for you, it most certainly won't be for your dog. For example, candy, which is a questionable snack for us, is very unhealthy for dogs and, in the case of chocolate, can even be deadly. Table food, such as well-cooked meat or unseasoned vegetables, are all right for your Boxer in moderation, but table scraps, such as the fat you trimmed off your meat, shouldn't be pawned off on your dog. And please, don't feed any people food to a dog with a medical condition that requires him to be on a restricted diet.

Healthy people food for dogs includes: pasta (without the sauce); carrots, celery, and other vegetables; bananas; plain or air-popped popcorn; and well-cooked meat. Some owners use cheese or hot dogs for occasional treats, such as for rewards while training, but again, practice moderation.

Actually, training is an ideal time to dispense treats. Make your dog earn his treats by first requiring him to respond to an obedience command, such as Sit or Down. This way you take control of when and why your dog gets a treat, instead of the other way around. The last thing you want is a pushy Boxer who insists you supply treats on his demand!

What's All the Fuss About Supplements?

Many owners are unsure whether or not to give their dog supplements. Advocates of supplements reason that if human diets are lacking in certain nutrients, dogs' diets must also be deficient. We take pills to give us added vitamins, minerals, and herbal supplements, so why not do the same for our beloved pets? Dog food manufacturers, however, argue that their foods are formulated to provide complete and balanced nutrition without the need for supplementation. They stress that excesses of certain nutrients, such as calcium, can actually cause harmful conditions in growing dogs. Many canine nutritionists agree.

Yet, other experts say that the varying metabolisms and dietary needs of individual dogs, as well as the range in actual nutrient content in some dog foods, make supplementation necessary. Also, certain nutrients can be cooked out of dog food during the manufacturing process or may lose potency over time or when exposed to air.

Some people choose to supplement to achieve certain results, such as a glossier coat or an improved immune system. Others give supplements to dogs that take part in high-energy pursuits, such as canine sports or police work. Finally, dogs with certain diseases may need supplements to improve or maintain their health.

The key is never to supplement haphazardly and always consult your veterinarian first. He or she will be able to tell you whether your dog really does need supplements and, if so, guide you toward the right formula for your Boxer.

Does My Puppy Need Supplements?

You should especially never give supplements to puppies unless it is on the advice of a veterinarian. If your puppy is eating balanced, nutritious food, she is receiving all the vitamins and minerals she needs. It can be dangerous to give your pup an overabundance of calcium or other vitamins or minerals. Adding supplements to your pup's food can cause serious, irreversible nutritional problems. The only exception to this is a puppy who is ill or undergoing extreme stress—but again, only give supplements under your veterinarian's supervision.

What About My Older Dog?

As your dog gets older, she will need more vitamins and minerals than she did when she was young. Dogs with reduced kidney function lose B vitamins in their urine. Old age also decreases the ability to absorb vitamins in general. Softening bones may benefit from added calcium and phosphorus. Thus, a Boxer who never took a supplement before may need one in her sunset years. But again, never add any supplementation to your dog's diet without first consulting your veterinarian.

Some senior-formula foods provide the balanced nutrition for this life stage. In most cases, you won't need to supplement these senior foods unless your dog has a specific medical condition. Whatever your reason for wanting to supplement your Boxer's food, make sure to first discuss it with your veterinarian and to monitor your dog's health carefully. If your pet seems to have a bad reaction to a supplement, stop using it and take her to the veterinarian.

4

Medical Care
Every Boxer Needs

In This Chapter

❍ Your Boxer's Veterinary Care
❍ Preventive Medicine
❍ Sick Calls and Emergencies

I deally, you will select a veterinarian for your Boxer before you even bring your new dog home. Finding the
right vet for your pet is just as important as finding the best
doctor for your family. If you wait until your Boxer is sick
or hurt to choose a veterinarian, you may choose one based
on close proximity or convenient hours, not necessarily on
his or her expertise, compassion, or rapport with animals.

Your Boxer's Veterinary Care

To choose the right veterinarian from the start, you'll need
to learn what to expect from a vet and what type of medical

care your dog needs to maintain his health and to treat any illnesses he might develop.

Selecting the Right Vet

Referrals are a great starting point when choosing a vet. If you live near your dog's breeder, ask him or her for recommendations. With all the hazards of puppy rearing, most breeders put a lot of research into finding a dependable vet. If your dog's breeder lives a distance away, ask other dog owners, such as friends and neighbors, for their recommendations. If you don't get any good leads, page through the phone book. It will list most, if not all, vets in the area, and the display ads can give you some information on each vet's practice, such as services offered and affiliation with professional organizations, including the American Animal Hospital Association (AAHA). But remember, no matter who recommends a vet to you, you'll want to check out him or her personally to ensure this veterinarian is the right one for you and your Boxer.

First, make a list of the things you feel are important in a vet and a vet clinic. What are the veterinarian's credentials? Just as a diploma from a well-known, accredited medical school is important when finding a doctor, you'll want to choose a vet with a distinguished academic background. Are the vet and the facility members of the AAHA? Although this isn't necessarily a requirement, AAHA members are held to certain standards for medical procedures and hospital management.

Does the vet seem to genuinely like animals? And, just as important, does the vet genuinely like people? While there are many wonderful vets out there who have a special way with animals, a vet also must be able to communicate with owners. It is important that you feel comfortable with your Boxer's vet and that the vet is able to explain complex medical information in layman's terms.

Is the facility small, with just one or two vets, or is it a large multi-doctor practice or even a teaching hospital? Many people want a vet who will get to know them and their dog personally. Seeing the same vet each visit allows him or her to intimately know the dog's medical history, which can be advantageous when diagnosing ailments. A negative of smaller facilities is that they often lack some of the high-tech equipment found in larger establishments. This may mean you'll be referred to a larger clinic or a hospital for certain procedures during your dog's lifetime. Large practices, on the other hand, frequently offer doctors specializing in certain areas of veterinary medicine as well as modern equipment and laboratories on hand to conduct tests and interpret the results. You may end up seeing a different vet each time you visit, however, making it difficult to establish an ongoing relationship.

Is someone on call 24 hours a day? If not, does the clinic recommend an after-hours facility for emergencies? If so, you'll want to check out that facility as well.

Where is the clinic located? If you live in a busy household, you may need to choose a clinic close to home. You'll also want a vet who is convenient to get to during an emergency. At the same time, it may be worthwhile to choose a vet who is located a few miles farther away rather than settle for a closer clinic that doesn't meet your other requirements.

For most owners, a clinic's hours are also an important factor. Choose a facility whose hours of operation coincide

Did You Know?

Shelters in the United States take in nearly 11 million cats and dogs each year. Nearly 75 percent of those animals have to be euthanized.

with your schedule. Most clinics have evening hours at least one night a week, and/or are open on Saturdays. Although rare, some vets still make house calls; such a vet may offer the convenience you're seeking.

What kind of services does the vet offer? If you are only looking for medical care from a vet, then a traditional practice may be right for you. Some clinics now offer add-on services—such as grooming, boarding, training, pet supplies, and food—for the owner who wants "one-stop shopping." Some vets are even located in pet supply stores or obedience schools to offer convenience to busy owners.

How much do services cost? Although most vets charge fees comparable to other vets in the area, some clinics offer wellness programs or multi-pet discounts that can help you save money. Don't be enticed, however, by a vet who charges considerably less than the going rate for veterinary care. A vet who charges so little for services may not have the credentials or expertise you are looking for. Quality vet care can be expensive—never skimp on your dog's health just to save a few dollars.

> Quality vet care can be expensive—never skimp on your dog's health just to save a few dollars.

Once you've prepared your list of questions, start calling the vets who have been recommended to you or who seem qualified from their phone book ads. Evaluate the call from start to finish. Was the phone picked up quickly or did it ring 10 times before someone answered? Was the receptionist friendly and helpful? Even if the person at the front desk doesn't deal directly with the animals, he or she most likely reflects the overall atmosphere of the clinic. Explain that you are looking for a vet and would like to ask a few questions. Don't be put off if no one can talk to you right at that moment;

the clinic might be very busy, and sick animals should be their top priority. The receptionist should gladly take down your name and number, however, and someone should get back to you in a timely manner. If no one returns your call, take your business elsewhere.

Once you've asked your list of questions and have narrowed down your search, set up a time to personally visit the clinic. Again, you should be treated courteously. Ask to see examination rooms, kennel runs, and cages where dogs are kept. Every area, from the waiting room to the kenneling area in the back, should be neat and clean. You'll detect a slight animal odor in any clinic, but other than that, the facility should smell fresh and clean. Make sure you meet at least one of the vets, even if you have to pay a consultation fee. He or she should be friendly and a good communicator. The most knowledgeable vet in the world won't be of much help to you if he or she can't explain in plain, simple language how to care for your pet. Pay attention, as well, to how the staff treats the other clients. A good veterinary clinic will treat all clients—human and canine—with courtesy and compassion, whether it is their first visit or they have been coming for years.

> The most knowledgeable vet in the world won't be of much help to you if he or she can't explain in plain, simple language how to care for your pet.

When you get home, write down your impressions. Next, contact your state's veterinary medical board. The board can verify whether the vet in question has a license to practice in your state and can tell you if the vet holds any special certifications. The board also can tell you if any formal disciplinary action has ever been taken against that veterinarian.

If you feel you have clicked with the perfect vet, great. But, if you're still not sure, by all means check out another facility. Keep all your notes on each facility in case your first choice doesn't work out.

Your Boxer's First Visit

From the very first time your Boxer steps foot (or paw!) in the veterinarian's office, make sure the experience is as pleasant as possible. Believe it or not, some dogs actually look forward to vet visits. Tell your dog in an upbeat tone of voice, "We're going to go visit your buddy, Dr. Bones!" Remain calm and cheerful throughout the car ride and as you enter the clinic. If you are nervous or apprehensive, your dog is sure to pick up on your emotions and act the same. Also, don't baby your dog. If you ooh and aah over him each time he goes to the vet, he'll be convinced a vet visit is a bad thing, or else you wouldn't be fussing over him! If your Boxer acts nervous, tell him in an even, businesslike tone of voice that he's being silly. When he calms down, offer him lots of praise and perhaps a treat. You'll want to praise every positive step, from being quiet during the car ride to sitting calmly in the waiting room to standing patiently while he is examined.

If you've adopted an older Boxer who seems unduly afraid of the vet, don't worry that all is lost. Again, be upbeat and positive and don't indulge inappropriate behavior. With time, patience, and lots of positive reinforcement, even the most fearful dog can learn to tolerate trips to the veterinarian's office.

Make sure you arrive early for your first appointment so you can fill out any necessary paperwork. Bring a list of questions and concerns so you'll remember them, as well as records of your dog's previous vaccinations and dewormings. To protect your Boxer, keep him from licking the floor or getting too close to other dogs in the waiting room. Not only could your pet pick up an infection, he also could get bitten if he intrudes into another dog's space. It's best to keep a puppy on your lap or in his travel crate to keep him out of trouble.

What can you expect from your Boxer's first veterinary visit? First, the vet will examine your dog from nose to tail to make sure he is sound. He or she will check for indications of good health, such as: clear, bright eyes; clean-smelling, light-pink skin inside the ears; healthy, white teeth and pink gums; a shiny coat and smooth, healthy skin; and a normal temperature and heart rate. The vet will palpate, or feel, your dog's internal organs to ensure that they are the proper size and shape, and will listen to your dog's lungs. If your Boxer is a male, your vet will check that both testes are fully visible. Sometimes one testicle or both are retained inside the body, which can cause health problems later and means your dog must be neutered. If your Boxer is a female, the vet will check her vaginal area for discharge or other signs of infection. Other general problems the vet will look for during the exam include: watery eyes; infected ears or evidence of ear mites; teeth that do not meet properly; lumps underneath the skin or patches of missing fur; a fever; or symptoms of congenital problems such as a heart murmur.

Remember to bring a fresh fecal sample, which the clinic will check for intestinal parasites. If you collect the sample several hours before your appointment, wrap it well and store it in your refrigerator until you are ready to go. Puppies especially are susceptible to such parasites, so don't be upset if your Boxer needs to be dewormed.

Did You Know?

Tests conducted at the Institute for the Study of Animal Problems in Washington, D.C., revealed that dogs and cats, like humans, are either right- or left-handed.

Questions to Ask Your Vet

Ask questions such as those listed below to evaluate whether a veterinarian is right for you and your dog.

○ What are the veterinarian(s)' credentials? Is the clinic affiliated with the AAHA?

○ How many vets work at the clinic? Can I request to see the same vet each time I visit or will I see whomever is available?

○ What type of equipment do you have on hand at the clinic? If you do not have certain equipment, where would you send my dog to receive treatment? What is that facility's reputation?

○ Do you have a lab onsite or do you send out for test results? How quickly are results available?

○ What are your clinic's hours and where are you located?

○ Do you offer any add-on services such as boarding or grooming?

○ What are the average fees for check-ups, spaying/neutering, vaccinations, etc.? Do you offer a wellness program or a multi-pet discount?

○ Do you treat any other Boxers in your practice? (While much canine medicine applies to all breeds, certain diseases and health concerns apply specifically to Boxers. You'll want to make sure your veterinarian is knowledgeable about genetic problems that run in the breed.)

The vet will weigh your dog to chart his future growth, or establish a base measurement for an adult dog. He or she also should address any questions you have about feeding, training, spaying/neutering, house-training, or other issues. Your vet also should discuss proper health care and may even demonstrate how to clip your dog's nails and/or how to brush his teeth.

Next, the vet will administer whatever vaccinations are due, and may start your pup on a heartworm preventive, depending on the time of year and whether you live in an area where heartworm is prevalent. He or she also should discuss fleas and ticks and how

Questions Your Vet May Ask You

○ Is this your first dog? Is this your first Boxer?

○ What are your feelings about spaying/neutering? (Dogs who are pet quality and are not going to be bred should be spayed or neutered. This helps prevent overpopulation and also is healthier for your dog.)

○ Have you located a training school for your new dog? (Your vet may offer recommendations, or the clinic itself may hold training classes.)

○ What type of food are you feeding your dog?

○ What types of toys does your dog play with? (Some toys should only be played with under supervision, such as toys with squeakers or toys that are easily chewed apart.)

○ Are you crate-training your dog?

○ Do you have any questions concerning house-training, obedience-training, nutrition, etc.?

to prevent them from infesting your dog. At the end of your visit, be sure to set up a schedule for follow-up visits and shots.

Preventive Medicine

Just as it is important for the human members of your family to have annual checkups, your Boxer needs to see the vet regularly for wellness exams. Many illnesses are easy to treat if caught early, but can be much more problematic if they are only discovered after serious symptoms begin. Don't wait until your dog is ill—preventive medicine is the best medicine.

Annual Visits

Each year your Boxer should visit the vet for a complete physical and any booster vaccinations that may be due. The vet will check your dog thoroughly, both internally and externally, to ensure that she is healthy. Examining your dog each year better enables your vet to catch health problems at an earlier stage than if you only take your pet in when she shows obvious symptoms. Also, seeing your vet on a regular basis will help you build a relationship with him or her and will keep you current with the latest information on pet care.

> Don't wait until your dog is ill—preventive medicine is the best medicine.

Vaccinations

Vaccines provide an important defense against a number of canine diseases. Since puppies' immune systems are still developing while they are young, they need extra help to prevent them from catching infectious diseases. Your puppy received some immunity from his mother during the first weeks of his life. Female dogs that have been vaccinated or have built immunity by being exposed to and surviving a disease pass on antibodies to their puppies in their first milk. These antibodies remain active in the puppies until they are 6 to 20 weeks old, depending on the disease. While active, antibodies not only protect a puppy against the disease, they also counter the vaccine, which contains a bit of inactivated or killed disease. Since it is difficult to know when a puppy's antibodies have declined enough to accept the vaccine, veterinarians usually recommend a series of vaccinations spaced at three- to four-week intervals during this critical time period.

Most vets give puppies their first vaccinations at eight weeks of age; a vaccine given earlier probably would fail, due to the antibodies in the mother's milk. The series of vaccines usually continues at weeks 12 and 16, and possibly longer, with each vaccine taking about two weeks to fully activate. (Note: Your vet may use a slightly different schedule.) Vaccines should be spaced no more than three or four weeks apart, because spacing the vaccines too far apart could leave the puppy vulnerable to the diseases themselves. Conversely, vaccinating more frequently can overload a puppy's immune system.

For your Boxer's health, you should keep your puppy confined to your yard and not let her interact with strange dogs until she is fully immune. For most dogs, this is week 17 or 18. Many of the diseases mentioned here are shed by infected dogs in their feces and saliva excretions, leaving the environment, such as the park or even your neighborhood, full of ticking time bombs.

Socialization is vital for young dogs, however. You may be thinking, how can I socialize my Boxer when she shouldn't go anywhere where she might come in contact with strange dogs? One option is to invite friends with vaccinated dogs for doggie parties at your house. The danger to your puppy is *infected* dogs, not all dogs in general, so those that you know have been vaccinated should present no health danger to your pet. Another option is to enroll your pup in a puppy preschool or kindergarten class that requires all owners to show proof that their puppies are being vaccinated. Puppy classes are wonderful, not only for the socialization they provide, but also for important early obedience-training.

After the first series of puppy shots, your dog will receive a rabies vaccination at about four months. After that, she will need annual vaccinations for all diseases except rabies, which can be boostered in intervals of one, two, or three years, depending on the law in your area.

Distemper, hepatitis (adenovirus), parvovirus, and parainfluenza are usually vaccinated against in a combination shot called DHPP. Leptospirosis vaccine may also be added, making a DHLPP vaccine.

> **P**uppy classes are wonderful, not only for the socialization they provide, but also for important early obedience-training.

Rabies, as mentioned before, is vaccinated against separately. Other vaccines your vet may recommend fight Lyme disease, coronavirus, and bordetella (kennel cough). Here is a brief explanation to help you better understand the diseases, their symptoms, and treatment, if any.

Distemper Distemper is a highly contagious virus that attacks the gastrointestinal, respiratory, and nervous systems. It causes symptoms that mimic a cold, such as a cough and eye and nasal discharge, as well as a loss of appetite, vomiting, and diarrhea. Advanced stages can bring weakness, muscle twitches, a lack of coordination, and even seizures. Dogs that develop distemper are treated with fluids and antibiotics to cure secondary infections. The prognosis is guarded. Some dogs that never develop neurological signs can get well. Others never fully recover, and for many dogs the disease is fatal.

Hepatitis This disease affects the kidneys, liver, pancreas, and blood-vessel lining. It can cause fever, lack of appetite, abdominal pain, vomiting, hemorrhaging, diarrhea, depression, and prolonged blood-clotting time. Dogs are treated with antibiotics and fluids, and animals with severe cases may require blood transfusions. The prognosis for this disease also is variable, with some dogs only experiencing a slight fever, and others succumbing to the disease. Young puppies are especially vulnerable and often die from a bout of hepatitis.

Parvovirus Parvovirus is also extremely dangerous for young puppies. It can cause intestinal inflammation (enteritis) or inflammation of the heart muscle (myocarditis). Symptoms include lack of appetite, lethargy, vomiting, fever, rapid dehydration, and bloody, foul-smelling diarrhea. Parvo is highly contagious. The virus not only is found in stool, but also can survive in the dirt after the feces have been cleaned up and last in the environment for months. Treatment includes antibiotics, fasting, intravenous fluid therapy, and isolation to prevent spreading the disease. While some puppies recover, the disease is fatal to many.

Parainfluenza Parainfluenza is a relatively mild virus that is evidenced by a hacking cough, sneezing, and eye and nasal discharge. Often, no treatment is necessary as this disease usually clears up on its own.

Rabies Rabies is perhaps the most feared of all diseases affecting the dog, and with good reason. This always-fatal disease not only is dangerous to canines, but also can infect almost all mammals, including humans. It is transmitted through saliva, usually by a bite. Early symptoms include personality changes—such as depression, aggression, and self-imposed isolation—as well as vomiting, fever, and diarrhea. In the final stages, the dog may become vicious and drool and foam at the mouth. Sadly, there is no treatment, and euthanasia is the only course of action.

Leptospirosis This disease, which can be caught from water contaminated with infected urine, affects the kidneys, liver, and urinary tract and can be transmitted to humans. Early symptoms include lack of appetite, vomiting, abdominal pain, fever, and weakness. As the disease progresses, the dog becomes extremely thirsty, and his temperature may fall below normal. Treatment with antibiotics and fluids can be effective if the disease is caught early. Fatal cases are usually due to kidney infection and failure. (Note: Some veterinarians do not recommend vaccinating against leptospirosis because of its high incidence of allergic reactions.)

Lyme Disease This tick-transmitted disease is most prevalent in wooded or grassy areas of Connecticut, Delaware, Maryland, Massachusetts, Michigan, Minnesota, New Jersey, New York, Pennsylvania, Rhode Island, and Wisconsin. Controversy exists over the effectiveness of Lyme disease vaccines, with some vets contending that the vaccine offers inadequate protection. These vets believe that tick-control products are more effective than vaccination. A dog infected with Lyme disease may exhibit sudden lameness, weakness, fever, and swollen joints. Most dogs fully recover after treatment with antibiotics and fluids, although lameness can last up to several months.

Coronavirus Coronavirus causes intestinal inflammation and is particularly severe in puppies. Many vets do not vaccinate against this disease, since they view it as not very prevalent. It occurs most often in dogs that are kenneled frequently or participate in dog shows. Since coronavirus is easily killed by most disinfectants, good sanitation should keep this disease in check. Symptoms of coronavirus include lack of appetite, vomiting, diarrhea, fever, and depression. Treatment consists of fluids and antibiotics to control secondary infections. The prognosis usually is good, although rare cases are fatal.

Kennel Cough (Bordetella) This extremely infectious but less serious disease tends to be picked up where large numbers of dogs come in contact with one another, such as at dog shows, boarding kennels, and dog parks. Dogs that will not be in these situations are usually not vaccinated. Often the only symptom is a dry, hacking cough that lasts for one to two weeks (but can last up to eight weeks). The cough usually disappears with or without treatment, which consists of general care and keeping your dog warm to prevent secondary infections, such as pneumonia.

The Vaccine Controversy Vaccines generally are accepted as the best way to prevent a number of serious illnesses in your dog. Some veterinarians, however, believe that dogs are being overvaccinated, causing immune problems. Some dogs also experience allergic reactions to vaccines, which can range from mild symptoms, such as lethargy and a low-grade fever, to shock, which requires emergency care. To prevent these problems, some practitioners recommend vaccinating against each disease individually instead of using combination vaccines. They also suggest vaccinating less, using safer "killed" versions of vaccines when possible, and even discontinuing regular boosters (except in the case of rabies, which must be vaccinated against by law).

Holistic vets believe boosting a dog's immune system through proper nutrition and exercise and avoiding chemicals, such as certain preservatives in commercial foods and chemically based flea treatments, benefit a dog more than vaccinations. This approach may leave your dog susceptible to some potentially dangerous diseases, however. The key is to work with your vet to decide which vaccines your dog needs and which may be unnecessary (such as Lyme disease vaccine, if you do not live in a tick-infested area).

Did You Know?

In 1957, Laika became the first dog in space, riding aboard the Soviet satellite Sputnik 2.

Spaying and Neutering

Some people are resistant to spaying or neutering their pet. Many fall in love with their dog, and reason that if they breed him or her, they will be able to produce another puppy just like their beloved Boxer. Some decide to breed to let their children witness the miracle of birth right in their home. Still others reason that having a litter or two will recoup some of the money they've spent on their first dog. None of these is a valid reason to breed your pet.

The truth is that millions of pets are put to death each year because not enough good homes are available to take them. Even if you produced a puppy similar to her mother or father (which is unlikely, since puppies are carbon copies of their parents about as often as human children are carbon copies of their moms and dads), can you guarantee you could find good homes for the rest of the puppies in the litter? Anyone who breeds a dog is morally responsible to find each and every puppy a home for life. Are you willing to take on that responsibility?

Teaching your children about reproduction is no excuse for producing puppies who may end up homeless or euthanized. Besides, it is not uncommon to lose a puppy during birth. Do you want to expose your children, or yourself, to that heartache? Whelping also can put the mother at risk. Could you ever forgive yourself if your pet died while giving birth?

Purebred dogs are prone to many genetic diseases (diseases particular to the Boxer are discussed in Chapter 5, Common Health Concerns). To limit these diseases and to ensure the reproduction of healthy dogs, only the best specimens of each breed should be mated. It takes years of studying pedigrees and genetics before a breeder is able to plan matings that will produce sound, healthy, and temperamentally stable puppies. You may have a beautiful female Boxer and your neighbor may have a handsome male, but together they may carry genes for some hidden defect that will show up in their puppies. Are you willing to take that chance?

As for making money by breeding dogs, you can pretty much forget it. With all the costs involved, most breeders just about break even. The mother will require various veterinary tests to ensure that she is healthy before she is bred and while she is pregnant, and the pups will need to be checked out once they are born. If complications arise during delivery, you may have to pay for emergency vet care. The mom will have special nutritional needs while she is pregnant and nursing, and once the puppies are weaned you will need to feed them until they go to their new homes. You also will need to take the puppies to the vet for their first shots, deworming and to obtain a health certificate for your legal protection. That's right: If your dog's puppies develop health problems down the road, their new owners could sue you for veterinary expenses. Then there's the cost of finding owners for the puppies, which most likely will require paying for advertising. The truth is, good breeders produce puppies in the hopes of achieving healthier, sweeter, happier Boxers, not to make money.

> The truth is, good breeders produce puppies in the hopes of achieving healthier, sweeter, happier Boxers, not to make money.

Spaying or neutering not only prevents unwanted puppies, it also actually helps your pet stay healthier. Spayed and neutered dogs are less likely to develop a number of health problems, including mammary tumors and pyometra (a disease of the uterus) in females, and testicular cancer, infected prostate glands, and

Breeding Myths—Common Misconceptions About Breeding Dogs

○ Females need to birth one litter to calm down.

○ "Mother" dogs are sweeter and gentler than females that never have puppies.

○ By breeding my dog, I'll produce a puppy just like him/her.

○ By selling puppies, I'll offset some of the money I've spent on my dog.

other urogenital diseases in males. Never allowing a dog to mate also protects both males and females from contracting sexually transmitted diseases.

Spaying or neutering can make your dog happier, as well. The desire to mate and the act itself can be stressful for dogs. Some males will refuse to eat if they are around a female in heat, and hormonal swings can make females tense and anxious. Sterilization also can prevent some unwanted behaviors in males, such as "marking" of territory (including your furniture), mounting behavior, or aggression toward other males. If you own a female, spaying will prevent messy heat cycles and the constant unwanted attention of male dogs in the neighborhood during these times.

Unless you are willing to become a genetics expert and consider breeding a not-for-profit hobby, you should spay or neuter your Boxer. The procedures are relatively simple and have fairly quick recovery periods. The vet anesthetizes the dog, and then removes either his testicles (neutering in the male) or her uterus and ovaries (spaying in the female). Most dogs go home the same

Spaying/Neutering Myths— Common Misconceptions About Altering Your Dog

○ It is unnatural to sterilize a dog.

○ Males are no longer "macho" and become wimps.

○ Females will never calm down.

○ Males no longer protect their homes and owners.

○ Females will not be as friendly.

○ Both males and females will become fat and lazy.

○ Both males and females will lose their playfulness.

day or the day after surgery, although their activity should be restricted for a few days.

There is no truth to the belief that females should be allowed to go into one heat before they are spayed. In fact, dogs should be spayed or neutered before they reach sexual maturity. Maturity traditionally has been defined as six months of age, although a female may go into heat as early as four months. Some humane societies spay and neuter at a very young age to prevent unwanted pregnancies later. Speak with your vet to decide the best time to spay or neuter your Boxer.

Sick Calls and Emergencies

You know that you need to visit your vet once a year for your dog's wellness exam, but what about if your Boxer is sick or hurt? What types of injuries or illnesses require immediate veterinary care, and what types can you treat yourself at home? The brief overview below identifies some signs that will help you make that decision. (First aid is discussed further in Chapter 5, Common Health Concerns.)

When to Call the Vet

Certain situations and/or symptoms demand emergency veterinary care. If your dog has been hit by a car, even if he seems all right, see a vet immediately. He should see a vet if he has been involved in any other type of traumatic event as well, such as a fall from a substantial height, a fight, or even been a passenger in a car that was involved in an accident. If he loses consciousness or has trouble breathing or walking, also seek care right away. Other symptoms that need immediate professional attention include uncontrollable bleeding, trauma to the eyes, bloody diarrhea, difficulty urinating, and seizures. Heat stroke, which is evidenced by excessive panting, difficulty breathing, and an increased heart rate, is an emergency condition. Bloat, as well, demands immediate treatment. If your dog appears restless, drools, attempts to vomit but cannot, and has a swollen, painful abdomen, rush him to the vet—his life may depend on it.

Other symptoms, while still needing veterinary attention, are not emergencies. If your dog experiences these symptoms you don't need to rush him to an emergency clinic, but you should see your vet within 24 hours if the symptoms don't get better or respond to at-home treatment. These symptoms include: straining to defecate; diarrhea (without blood); irritated eyes that are not traumatized; signs of minor discomfort, such as increased scratching; and minor behavioral changes, such as depression or a decreased appetite.

Many symptoms can be caused by a number of problems, ranging from the mild to the severe. One example is limping. If your dog suddenly begins to limp, you'll first want to figure out where the problem lies. Check your Boxer's pads. A stone or sliver of glass could be embedded there, causing your dog pain. If so, gently remove the foreign object and wash out the wound. If you don't see anything in the pads, check the legs for any signs of swelling or tenderness. In many breeds, including Boxers, lameness in the rear can be an early sign of hip dysplasia. In general, if your dog's limping continues for more than a day or two or seems to be getting worse, see your vet.

A lack of appetite is one of the first signs of many illnesses. While your dog may not be particularly hungry on a given day or may just feel a little out of sorts, if your Boxer skips two or three meals, make an appointment with your vet.

Vomiting should be approached cautiously. If your Boxer has eaten a lot of grass or had one too many treats, he may just need to clean out his system. If your dog vomits several times during one hour or also has diarrhea and/or a fever (above 103°F), or the vomiting continues, see your vet. Also, as mentioned above, unproductive vomiting may be a sign of bloat. This is an emergency that requires immediate veterinary care.

Diarrhea, too, can result from many causes. First, see if you can clear your dog's system by withholding food for 24 hours. Make sure to provide him with plenty of fresh water to prevent dehydration. After the 24-hour fast, feed meals of cooked rice and boiled, drained hamburger for several days, gradually adding your pet's regular food. If the diarrhea

Did You Know?

A dog's heart beats between 70 and 120 times per minute, compared with 70 to 80 times per minute for humans.

continues, occurs several times during an hour, contains blood or mucus, or has a particularly foul odor, it may indicate a more serious cause. Your vet should always investigate blood in the stool, urine, vomit, or nasal discharge.

How to Administer Medication and Pills

Chances are that sometime during your Boxer's life you will need to medicate him. This is much less traumatic for you and your dog if you proceed calmly and confidently.

If you need to give your dog a pill, you'll want to ensure that your Boxer swallows the entire tablet, so the medicine can do its work. If your dog usually doesn't investigate his food before eating it, you can try wrapping the pill in a piece of cheese or cooked meat. You'll need to watch your dog carefully to be sure that he doesn't eat the treat and spit out the pill. If your dog seems to be on to your tricks, open his mouth and gently place the pill on the back of his tongue near the center. Never haphazardly drop the pill in your dog's mouth or it could lodge in his windpipe. Tilt your dog's head back, shut his mouth, and stroke his throat until he swallows. Carefully open his mouth again to make sure he really has swallowed the pill.

If you need to administer a liquid, your vet should give you a special syringe that measures out the proper amount of medication. Hold back your dog's head at a slight angle, place the syringe between the cheek and back teeth, and shoot the medicine onto your dog's tongue. Hold his mouth shut until he swallows every last drop. Be prepared: Some medicines taste extremely bitter, and your dog may react by trying to spit out as much as possible. Be persistent and hang on for dear life! If your dog doesn't get enough medicine down per

Emergency Instructions for the Boarding Kennel/Pet-Sitter

What if your dog becomes sick or hurts himself while you are away? If you leave your dog at a boarding kennel, first ask if they have a vet on staff or if they use a veterinarian in the area for emergencies. Even so, it's also a good idea to give them the name and number of your dog's veterinarian, especially if your Boxer has a specific medical condition. If you have hired a dog-sitter, leave an emergency list with your veterinarian's phone number, the phone number of the local emergency clinic, and the phone number for the National Animal Poison Control Center, (800) 548-2423. (There is a fee for a consultation with the NAPCC, but follow-up calls are free.) Also leave information on any medications your dog needs or any special medical conditions to watch out for. Prepare for the unexpected to ensure that your dog gets the care he needs should an emergency occur in your absence.

dose, you may end up having to give even more doses, which won't be fun for you or your Boxer.

If your dog injures his eye, you may need to apply ointment or drops. Pull down the lower lid and squeeze the ointment in a strip across the length of the eye, then blink the lids once or twice to make sure the medicine distributes evenly. To administer drops, hold the eye open and apply the drops directly in the center.

Costs

Some first-time dog owners are shocked at the high cost of veterinary care. Between spaying or neutering, vaccinations, heartworm preventive, flea and tick products, annual checkups, and

How to Make an Insurance Claim

It's your responsibility as a policyholder to make the best use of your insurance plan. Take these steps to get the most for your money:

1. Designate a file for pet insurance forms.

2. Always take a claim form with you to the veterinarian's office. Many companies require a veterinarian's signature.

3. Make copies of receipts. A receipt must accompany every claim form. Some companies require only copies; others require originals. Keep a copy for your records.

4. Make copies of completed claim forms. If a question or payment issue arises, a copy to review on your end of the phone line will be reassuring.

5. Note an acceptable payment period on your calendar. Reimbursement may slip your mind, and it may be delayed in cases where a problem is encountered and you forget to inquire about the payment's status.

6. Mark claims paid and date received. Leave a paper trail that's easy to understand. Looking back a year later, you'll be glad for the notations.

©1999 Solveig Fredrickson

the occasional visit with a sick or hurt dog, you may be thinking of putting a second mortgage on your house!

Why does it cost so much? First, you must realize veterinarians go through rigorous schooling similar to that of human doctors. You are paying for the expertise of a highly skilled and knowledgeable professional (although most vets make a fraction of a human doctor's annual salary). The vet must also cover the overhead costs of running a clinic, including rent or a mortgage for the building itself, employee's wages, equipment, supplies, insurance, and utilities. These costs add up and are reflected in the price you pay for your veterinarian's services.

What if an emergency happens and you don't think you can afford the vet bills? By all means, be up-front about your situation. Some clinics accept credit cards, while others may set up payment plans in dire situations. Do not take advantage of your vet's kindness, however. You should be prepared to pay for life-long medical expenses *before* you buy a Boxer. Distress over the expense of veterinary services does not provide a legitimate excuse for not paying your bill. Your vet may not offer payment options because of this potential for abuse.

Two options can help you pay your veterinary bills. The first is the pet insurance plan, which works similarly to the insurance plan you have for yourself and your family. Most pet insurance plans charge a yearly fee in exchange for accident and major illness coverage. A deductible may apply and preexisting conditions may not be covered. Most insurance plans exclude wellness exams and preventive care such as spaying/neutering and vaccinations. Still, if an emergency or major illness strikes your dog, insurance may allow you to seek advanced treatment that you otherwise could not afford.

The second option, which is offered by some clinics and veterinary hospitals, is the savings plan. With this option, you pay a monthly fee, but do not pay for specific routine veterinary visits. Your dog will receive general care, such as vaccinations, check-ups, yearly fecal exams, and even nail trimmings, all covered under the plan. Some plans even include office visits when your pet is sick and certain diagnostic tests. These plans allow you to budget payments monthly, instead of contending with a big expense at your dog's annual visit or when your dog is sick, and can result in significant

Ten Questions to Ask Every Provider

Before choosing a pet insurance or membership plan, be sure to get straight-forward answers to all your questions. If it makes you more comfortable, get the answers in writing.

1. Does your policy follow fee/benefits schedules? If so, please send me your detailed coverage limits. In the meantime, please give me examples of coverage limits for three common canine procedures so I can compare them to my current veterinary charges.

2. Does your policy cover basic wellness care, or does it cover only accidents and illnesses? Do you offer a wellness care endorsement that I can purchase on top of my basic plan for an additional fee? What other endorsements do you offer, and how much do they cost?

3. Under your policy's rules, can I continue taking my dog to his current veterinarian, or do I need to switch to another veterinarian?

4. Does your policy cover hereditary conditions, congenital conditions or pre-existing conditions? Please explain each coverage or exclusion as it pertains specifically to my dog. Is there a feature where pre-existing conditions will be covered if my dog's pre-existing condition requires no treatment after a specified period? What is that period?

5. What happens to my premium and to my dog's policy if your company goes out of business? What guarantees do I have that I won't be throwing my money away?

6. How quickly do you pay claims?

7. What is your policy's deductible? Does the deductible apply per incident or annually? How does the deductible differ per plan?

8. Does the policy have payment limits over a year's period or during my pet's lifetime? How do the payment limits differ per plan?

9. What is the A.M. Best Co. rating of your insurance underwriter, and what does that rating mean?

10. Is there a cancellation period after I receive my policy or membership? How long do I have to review all my materials once I receive them, and what is the cancellation procedure?

savings. Many plans also offer discounts on other products and services available at the clinic, such as prescriptions or grooming.

Veterinary costs can seem overwhelming at times. If you reach a point at which you are unable to afford the care your dog needs, discuss your concerns openly and honestly with your veterinarian. Also, investigate pet insurance and savings plans. One of these options may be right for you.

Common
Health Concerns

In This Chapter

o Parasites, Inside and Out
o Illnesses and Emergencies
o Obesity
o Health Concerns Specific to Boxers

N o matter how nutritious a diet you feed your Boxer, how much exercise he gets, and how diligent you are about preventive care, there will be times when your dog develops some kind of health concern. These concerns can run the gamut from the annoyance of parasites, such as fleas and ticks, to common illnesses, to emergencies and genetic diseases that affect the Boxer. When dealing with these problems, there is no greater advice than the Boy Scout motto: Be prepared. Know the signs and symptoms of potential health concerns and how to deal with them beforehand to prevent the problems you can, and help your pet recover more quickly from the problems you can't.

Parasites, Inside and Out

There's nothing more unsettling than thinking about these creepy, crawly (and in some cases, leaping) insects besieging your dog, and possibly your house and yard as well. Just keep in mind that the best defense is a solid offense. Arm yourself with knowledge about these insidious foes and their battle plans and you and your dog will be able to defeat them.

External Parasites

From your puppy's first day in his new home, begin what I like to call the "Puppy-Pampering Period." Set aside a few minutes of quiet time, get down on the floor with your dog, and go over his entire body with your hands. This will let you search for any signs of fleas, ticks, or other external parasites, as well as odd lumps or bumps that you may want to have checked by your veterinarian. Although going over your puppy each and every day might seem excessive, it pays off in the long run by making him comfortable with having his body examined. When he's an adult, you may only need to check him once a week or after he's been playing in a field or wooded area. By then, he'll probably look forward to his "doggie massage!"

Fleas Fleas have long been the bane of dogdom. Historically, they have been very difficult to get rid of once an infestation is underway. They can cause everything from mild itching to disease. Thankfully, new advances in the flea-fighting arsenal have given us effective weapons against this prevalent parasite. But before I address how to prevent and/or treat fleas, let's take a good look at the enemy.

Fleas are a highly prolific species. At any one time, adult fleas in an environment account for only 1 to 5 percent of the total flea population. At the right temperature and humidity (65 to 80°F with 70 to 80 percent humidity), fleas multiply rapidly.

Fleas jump on a dog and feed for 2 to 3 days before they start to lay eggs (up to 40 to 50 per day). These eggs then drop off your pet and land in bedding, furniture, floor cracks, and the lawn outside. Within a day or 2, the eggs hatch into larvae. Flea larvae burrow deep into carpet pile and are extremely difficult to destroy. After the larvae have fed on debris for 5 to 12 days, they each spin a cocoon. The cocoon is virtually indestructible—no insecticide can kill the flea during this stage. The cocoon can survive up to a year, just waiting for the ideal conditions to emerge. Vibration, heat, or pressure stimulates the adult to hatch. Depending on the environment, the entire life cycle of the flea, from egg to adult, can be as short as 21 days or as long as a year to complete.

How can you tell if your dog has fleas? Excessive scratching may provide your first clue. To look for evidence of these parasites on your Boxer, part the hair along his back and around his tail and hindquarters. Fleas also favor the groin area and armpits. Running a flea comb through your dog's fur in these areas will usually catch any adult fleas that are around. Be sure to kill the flea quickly or it will leap into the environment, only to jump back on your dog later. Even if you don't actually see these pests, you may spot their calling cards— white flea eggs or brownish red "flea dirt" (excrement).

Fleas feed on pets, but they live throughout the environment. If you end up with an infestation, you'll need to

Did You Know?

Dogs see color less vividly than humans but are not actually color-blind.

treat not only your dog, but also every part of his environment, from his bed to the carpet, furniture, and yard.

How can you prevent an infestation in the first place? People used to rely on flea collars with very limited success, partly because they provide the most protection around a dog's head while fleas tend to gather at the other end. If their dog did end up with fleas, they would treat him with a wide variety of products, from shampoos to sprays to dips. While these were helpful, they had to be used repeatedly over a period of time to be sure all the fleas were killed. Many of these products, because of their chemical content, were dangerous. If used too often or in an improper amount, or if mixed with other products, they could prove harmful to pets.

> If you end up with an infestation of fleas, you'll need to treat not only your dog, but also every part of his environment, from his bed to the carpet, furniture, and yard.

Fortunately for today's pet owner, new advances in flea-fighting technology offer safer and more effective solutions. You'll want to begin your search for the best product for your Boxer at your veterinarian's office. He or she can recommend flea preventive products, or flea treatment if you already have an infestation. In fact, many of the new flea products require a prescription. These tend to be safer than their over-the-counter cousins.

One type of the new breed of flea preventive comes in pill form. These pills contain an ingredient that actually prevents eggs from growing into adults and is harmless to people and dogs. Although this pill can help to control fleas overall, it does have drawbacks. For one, it doesn't kill adult fleas. For another, a flea must actually bite your Boxer in order for the drug to take effect, since it is absorbed into and transmitted to the flea through the dog's bloodstream. In other words, the product won't kill a flea that jumps on and off your dog without feasting first.

Topical, spot-on treatments take care of this problem. Squeeze a small amount of the product on one spot (for small dogs) or two spots (for larger dogs) of the dog's body each month. A Boxer, unless he is very young, will require two-spot treatments, one between the shoulder blades and the other along the back by the base of the tail. The product provides protection over your dog's entire body within a day. These treatments will kill—on contact—any flea that dares to jump on your dog, regardless of whether it stops for a snack. These spot treatments are sold under a number of product names. As mentioned above, prescription treatments usually are safer for your dog than those sold over the counter.

What if you haven't tried one of these preventives yet, and your dog is already crawling with these pesky critters? Again, first consult your vet. He or she will determine whether shampoos, dips, powders, sprays, or a combination are in order. Remember that some of these products can be very dangerous if haphazardly used together, so only combine products on the advice of your veterinarian.

If you already have an infestation, you'll need to treat your dog's environment as well as your dog himself. First, thoroughly vacuum your house, your furniture, and your dog's bedding and immediately throw out the vacuum bag, since any adult fleas the vacuum sucked up will jump back into the environment the first chance they get. Use a fogger or spray on your home that not only contains an insecticide to kill fleas, but also an insect growth regulator (IGR) to keep immature fleas from developing. While both foggers and sprays work effectively, sprays can be useful for getting into hard-to-reach spots, such as deep in carpet pile. Another option is to sprinkle borax or borate powder on your carpet. Read the labels of all products carefully for safety instructions, and keep all people and animals away from the entire treated area until it is completely dry.

In addition to treating your house, you'll need to treat your yard if you have an infestation. Rake up leaves and other debris in which fleas thrive. After that, you have several options. Some owners spray their yards with IGRs to interfere with the flea's life cycle. These compounds are effective and are safe for your pet, but they are dangerous to all insects. If you want to make sure you don't kill the "good" bugs with the "bad," there are more natural treatments available. Parasitic worms called nematodes, parasitic wasps, and diatomaceous earth (a fine dirt composed of the cell walls of one-celled sea creatures) all can help rid the environment of fleas without harming people, animals, or other insects. If you do still opt to use IGRs or a pyrethrin spray, distribute it sparingly and in limited areas.

Ticks Ticks, which are found in fields and wooded areas, love to attach themselves to warm-blooded mammals. They latch on for a blood meal and then drop off to lay eggs. As soon as you get home after a long walk in the woods with your Boxer or a romp through the tall grass by a lake, check him thoroughly for ticks. Some of the new flea preventives also kill ticks. If you find a live specimen on your pet, however, you need to remove it immediately. Use tweezers or a special tick remover, never your bare hands (if the tick is carrying a disease, touching it could expose you). Grasp the tick as close to your dog's skin as possible and pull it out quickly. Don't injure the tick while it is attached or it may spit diseased saliva into your dog. For your Boxer's sake, never try to remove a tick with a lit match—you'll only succeed in burning your dog! Afterwards, flush the tick down the toilet or drop it in alcohol or turpentine to kill it. Flush the bite area on your pet's skin with warm soapy water or hydrogen peroxide. If the area swells, try an ice pack and some antibacterial ointment. If the area doesn't clear up after a day or two, see your vet.

> As soon as you get home after a long walk in the woods with your Boxer or a romp through the tall grass by a lake, check him thoroughly for ticks.

Ticks are more than just a nuisance. They also carry a number of diseases, some of which can affect you as well as your dog. Rocky Mountain spotted fever, erhlichiosis, babesiosis, tick paralysis, and Lyme disease, to name a few, all are transmitted by tick saliva. That's why it is extremely important that you check your dog regularly; the longer a tick feasts on your pet, the more likely it will transmit a disease to him.

All of these diseases are dangerous, but Lyme disease, especially, has been in the news lately because of its effects on both dogs and humans who have encountered an infected tick. Lyme vaccines are available; if you live in or are planning a vacation to an area where ticks are prevalent, talk to your vet about vaccinating your dog.

Skin Mites (Mange) If your dog scratches intensely but you see no sign of fleas, he may suffer from mites. To diagnose mites, which are much smaller than either fleas or ticks, a vet must examine skin scrapings from your dog. Several types of mites affect dogs.

The scabies mite digs under the skin to lay its eggs. Although scabies can live anywhere on a dog, they tend to congregate around the elbow, hocks, ears, and face. These mites cause a condition called sarcoptic mange. When infected with this mite, your dog will scratch incessantly at his unbearably itchy skin, sometimes causing it to swell and form pus-filled scabs. Treatment usually consists of medicated dips, plus cortisone to relieve the itching. In addition, your vet may give an oral medication such as ivermectin for relief.

The demodex mite causes demodectic mange, or red mange. This mite actually lives on virtually all dogs and is passed on to puppies from their mothers during nursing. Only a small percentage of dogs are bothered by the demodex mite. Symptoms of the demodex mite often first appear on the skin around the dog's eyes, elbows, and feet, which becomes inflamed and hairless. Puppies with immature immune systems are the usual victims of red mange and often can beat the disease as they grow older. Some dogs whose immune systems never fully develop or are defective may be bothered for life. Your vet will treat your dog with medicated dips.

Cheyletiella mange, or walking dandruff, is caused by the cheyletiella mite and, again, is most often seen in puppies. These mites are very active, and tend to move under the flakes of skin they have created when your dog scratches, making it appear he has walking dandruff. See your vet for dipping treatments.

Ear mites live in the ear canal of dogs and cats and can cause intense itching as they feed on the dead skin and wax debris found in the ear. They can cause irritation of the canal that allows serious secondary bacterial or yeast infections to take hold. Left untreated, ear mites are the source not only of great misery, but can cause a head tilt, trouble walking, and occasionally, the secondary infection can cause an abscess in the brain. Your veterinarian can dispense medicine to clear up ear mites within a few weeks of treatment or may choose to give ivermectin by mouth.

Ringworm Although ringworm is external, it is not a parasite. Contrary to what its name implies, ringworm actually has nothing to do with worms, but rather is a fungus that can cause a rapidly spreading circle of hair loss surrounded by a red ring. Although it usually isn't itchy, scabs and crusts can form, leading to draining sores. Ringworm is contagious not only to dogs, but also to humans, especially children. If your Boxer has ringworm, don't let any children pet him until the condition is cleared up. Ringworm is diagnosed by flooding the skin with an ultraviolet light (ringworm may glow green), by examining skin scrapings under a microscope, or by running a fungus culture. Your vet may treat the disease by clipping away the infected hair follicles and may recommend bathing the skin with a special shampoo. If that doesn't seem to heal the infected area, your vet will administer antifungal medication by mouth.

Internal Parasites

Internal parasites can be even more elusive foes than fleas or ticks, since they are not creeping, crawling, or jumping on your pet. Many types of internal worms are quite common. In fact, most puppies have some type of worm, and adult dogs can also be affected. If you note any of the symptoms below, take a fresh fecal sample to your veterinarian for diagnosis. Your dog's stool also should be checked during his yearly exam to discover internal parasites that are not producing symptoms.

Roundworms If your puppy has an especially round potbelly and dull coat, he may be plagued by roundworms. Other symptoms of these spaghetti-like worms, which range in size from one to seven inches long, include vomiting, diarrhea, weight loss, and failure to thrive. If your Boxer is heavily infested, you will even see worms in his stool or vomit—they are white, stringy worms that can either be coiled or stretched out. Puppies can get roundworms from their mother while they are still in the uterus or later while nursing, or from an infected environment. It is best to treat all puppies for roundworms by giving deworming medication every two weeks from as early as two weeks of age. If left untreated, an infestation of roundworms can cause stunted growth or even death.

Roundworms also can affect adult dogs. Dogs acquire round-worms by eating infected soil and feces. In these older dogs, roundworms may not produce symptoms. But, if a stool sample shows roundworms, your dog will require treatment, for both his health and yours, since roundworms can be transmitted to people if they handle infected stool.

Hookworms Hookworms—small, thin worms about a quarter-inch to a half-inch long—are most prevalent in warm climates. Hookworms live in the small intestine, where they suck blood from the intestinal wall. As they move on to new feeding sites, the old wounds continue to bleed. Puppies usually get hookworms from their mothers while nursing, although the rare puppy will acquire them in utero. This condition can pose a serious danger, and many pups die soon after exposure. The signs of infestation are anemia (due to intestinal bleeding), pale gums, weakness, emaciation, and dark-colored, thick diarrhea. Puppies with serious conditions may need blood transfusions as well as medication to get rid of the worms.

Older dogs can also contract hookworms, although chronic hookworm infections in adults are rare. Adult dogs typically pick up hookworms through contact with contaminated feces or soil. Hookworms can still pose a danger even after it seems that they have been eradicated, since dogs that recover from hookworms can form cysts in their tissue, which carry the hookworm larvae. Stress or illness can trigger the release of the larvae, causing a new outbreak. Your vet can diagnose hookworms by examining a stool sample and prescribe medication as treatment.

Whipworms Whipworms are small, thin worms that live in the large bowel of dogs and puppies. Although they usually don't cause severe disease, their presence can cause irritation that leads to bloody diarrhea, weight loss, and unthriftyness. Your veterinarian can diagnose an infestation by finding eggs in your dog's stool—although it can be difficult because these worms lay eggs infrequently. Treatment is any one of several veterinary-prescribed wormers, and usually the dog must be re-treated in one to two months. The eggs can persist in infected soil or kennel for years.

Tapeworms These nasty worms can range in length from less than an inch to several feet. They are made up of a head and a multi-segmented body. Each segment contains eggs, and these segments pass out of your dog's body in his feces. When dried out, the segments resemble grains of rice. Sometimes, you can see moving segments attached to the fur around your Boxer's anus. Other symptoms include mild diarrhea, loss of appetite, and a change in the texture and condition of your dog's coat.

The flea is the main host that transmits tapeworms. If your Boxer swallows a flea that carries tapeworms, he becomes the tapeworm's host. If you

Did You Know?

The tallest dog on record was 42 inches tall at the shoulders and weighed 238 pounds.

weren't convinced your dog needed flea protection before, this should do the trick!

Your dog also can get certain kinds of tapeworms by eating raw meat, rabbits, or certain rodents. If your veterinarian diagnoses tapeworms through a stool sample from your dog, he or she will prescribe medication.

Heartworm The heartworm is one of the most dangerous parasites affecting dogs. Carried by the common mosquito, heartworm can kill your pet. When an infected mosquito bites a dog, it imbeds larvae into the dog's skin. Over a period of three to four months, these larvae go through several stages to develop into adult worms. At that point, they find a vein and travel to the right side of the heart and pulmonary artery, where they multiply. One dog plagued by heartworm had 250 worms in his heart. Symptoms include intolerance to exercise, coughing (especially after exertion), weight loss, and general fatigue. Treatment is expensive and complicated. If heartworm is left untreated, dogs can develop severe disabilities or even sudden death.

When dealing with heartworm, prevention is the answer. Dogs older than six months should be blood-tested for heartworm before starting any preventive (puppies less than six months old don't require testing). If they are worm free, they should be placed on a once-a-month preventive either during the mosquito season or year-round, depending on the climate.

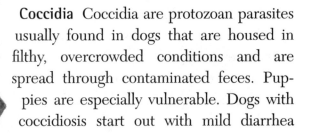

Coccidia Coccidia are protozoan parasites usually found in dogs that are housed in filthy, overcrowded conditions and are spread through contaminated feces. Puppies are especially vulnerable. Dogs with coccidiosis start out with mild diarrhea that worsens and eventually becomes mucuslike and bloody. If the disease isn't treated promptly, the dog may suffer loss of appetite, weakness, dehydration, and anemia.

Stool sample analysis diagnoses the problem. An infected dog should receive medication from the vet. You must also thoroughly sterilize the dog's housing which can be very difficult because the coccidia form hard-coated, microscopic cysts that survive most standard cleaners. Unfortunately, even though the dog recovers, he may carry the disease to other pets and could experience flare-ups in the future when stressed or sick.

Giardia Another protozoan, giardia is becoming more prevalent. Your dog can catch giardiasis by drinking from puddles or other stagnant, fecal-contaminated water. Mucuslike, blood-tinged diarrhea is the main symptom. Giardiasis responds well to medication; however, make sure to test and treat all animals that may share dirty water or contaminated yards in your household. Pets can also pass giardia to humans through infected water sources, which will result in unpleasant diarrhea and can make you and your family very sick.

Illnesses and Emergencies

The best way to prepare for potential illnesses or emergencies affecting your Boxer is to expect the unexpected. Prepare yourself ahead of time by knowing what signs to look for, what action to take, and by having a fully stocked first-aid kit handy at all times. Someday, your dog's life may depend on it.

The best way to prepare for potential illnesses or emergencies affecting your Boxer is to expect the unexpected.

Insect Bites/Stings

Dogs can be curious when it comes to bugs such as bees or spiders, and may get too close for their own good. If your Boxer gets stung, first check to see whether a stinger is still in your pet. If so, brush it out with a firm object, such as a credit card. Don't try to pick it out as you would an ordinary splinter, since squeezing or breaking it could release additional toxins into your dog. Next, apply a paste of baking soda and water directly to the sting, and use ice packs (always place a cloth or paper towel between the skin and the ice pack) if there is swelling. If your dog experiences a severe reaction to the sting—such as extreme swelling, hives that spread over her body, or extreme itchiness, trouble breathing or collapse—take her to the vet. Facial swelling demands emergency attention, since the swelling can spread to the upper airways and throat and prevent air from reaching the lungs.

Vomiting

Many things cause vomiting, from eating a foreign object to infectious illness, motion sickness, and certain diseases. If your dog is vomiting and she is under a year old, is older than eight or nine, or has a serious medical condition such as diabetes, she should see the veterinarian right away. Also see your vet the same day if your Boxer is running a fever (a temperature greater than 103°F). If your dog is a normal, healthy adult and starts vomiting yet seems to feel well otherwise, withhold food and water for eight to twelve hours. If she doesn't vomit during the fast, give her a few ice chips to lick every two or three hours. Vomiting or not eating can rapidly lead to dehydration, so it is essential to give your Boxer fluids. If she is able to keep this liquid down, after a few hours add about a half-cup of water and repeat this every two or three hours. If she

still hasn't vomited after 24 hours, give her a bland diet of two parts boiled rice mixed with one part boiled, drained hamburger, fed a little at a time. If she holds down this food and water, gradually mix her regular food back in over the next 48 to 72 hours. If your dog vomits again at any stage during the treatment, take her to the vet.

Unproductive vomiting (when your dog tries but is unable to vomit) calls for a different course of action. This may be a symptom of bloat, and demands emergency veterinary attention.

Diarrhea

Like vomiting, diarrhea can stem from many causes. One avoidable precipitator is changing your dogs diet too quickly. Although we enjoy and can tolerate variety in our meals, dogs can't. Don't change dog foods unless your dog isn't thriving on the brand she is eating. If you do decide to change foods, do so gradually or your dog may end up with digestive problems.

Other potential causes of diarrhea include eating something spoiled or toxic, parasites, stress, and disease. If your dog's diarrhea continues for more than 24 hours, contains blood, or is accompanied by vomiting, or if your Boxer is less than a year old or older than eight years, see your veterinarian. Regardless of her age, you should take your dog to the vet when a fever (103°F or greater) or dehydration accompanies the diarrhea or if she looks or acts sick. Check for dehydration by lifting the skin at the back of your dog's neck. If it doesn't spring back into position within a second or two of you letting go, your dog is dehydrated and needs emergency attention.

If your pet has none of the above complications, withhold food for 24 to 48 hours, but supply plenty of water (as long as your

Taking Your Boxer's Temperature

The key to taking your Boxer's temperature is to remain calm. If you're nervous, your dog, too, will become agitated. Use a rectal thermometer, available in traditional glass or digital versions, lubricated with petroleum jelly or a water-based lubricant. Have your dog stand or lie down (whichever seems more comfortable) and insert the thermometer about one inch into the dog's rectum. Leave a glass thermometer in for three minutes and a digital thermometer until it beeps. The normal temperature range for a dog is 100.2 to 102.8°F. Temperatures less than 100 or over 104°F signal an emergency.

Boxer isn't vomiting). Then, switch to a bland diet of one part boiled burger or boiled chicken (with the skin, fat, and bones removed) and two parts boiled rice. If the diarrhea seems to subside after two or three days on this treatment, gradually add your pet's normal food back into her diet.

You can give your dog anti-diarrheal medicine, but only at the onset of diarrhea and only after first calling your vet to ask his or her opinion. Your vet should be able to suggest a medication and dosage over the phone. If your dog doesn't improve, seems to be getting worse, or vomiting or fever accompanies the diarrhea, take your pet in for an examination.

Choking

Choking is a potentially life-threatening situation that must be treated at once. A choking dog might struggle or gasp for breath, act anxious, and her gums may turn blue or white. Choking can be due to a number of causes. Your dog may be choking on vomit, have an upper respiratory disease, her tongue may be swollen due to an allergic reaction, or she may have a foreign object caught in her throat.

Toys are one form of foreign object dogs frequently ingest. It is very easy for a Boxer to ingest bitten-off parts of toys or even the entire thing; it is not unheard of for a small ball to slip down a dog's throat. Select your Boxer's toys carefully, and inspect them frequently to make sure your dog isn't chewing them into dangerous pieces.

Although your dog loves you, she may become distraught when choking, so take care not to get bitten while helping her. If your dog is conscious, don't stick your hand in her mouth. If she is unconscious, open her mouth and gently sweep your hand from side to side to try to feel any foreign object, being careful not to push an object further down into her throat. Pull your Boxer's tongue forward and remove any obstruction or vomit. Dogs normally have a hard object, called the hyoid apparatus or "Adam's apple" in the back of their throat. Don't pull on this or you may cause serious harm. If you still can't dislodge the object or she is conscious, help your dog to stand on her hind legs or hold her in this position and place your arms around her waist from behind. Close your hands together to make a cupped fist, then place your fist just behind or on the last rib. Rapidly push up with your fist, repeating as necessary until the object is forced out.

Once the object comes out, check your pet's vital signs. If she isn't breathing or has no heartbeat, you will have to perform cardiopulmonary resuscitation (CPR).

If you are having difficulty getting the object out, don't waste a lot of time trying—get your dog to the vet. In all instances of choking, a veterinarian should check your dog anyway to ensure all obstructions have been removed. Your pet also requires immediate veterinary care if the choking did

How to Perform CPR on Your Boxer

If during an emergency, you discover that your dog is not breathing and/or has no heartbeat, you need to administer cardiopulmonary resuscitation (CPR). Please understand beforehand, however, that CPR isn't foolproof, even when performed by a professional. Also, you must be sure a dog is unconscious, or you could be bitten. Never take time out to perform CPR for a dog in this condition if you have transport to a veterinary clinic—rush him to the vet immediately and perform CPR on the way. Although CPR is very difficult to execute, it certainly is worth trying when your dog's life is in danger.

To perform CPR, you need to know your ABCs—airway, breathing, and circulation. First, look into your dog's throat and clear any foreign obstructions. Then, check for breathing. Watch his ribs for the slightest sign of movement, or hold a mirror by his muzzle to see if it fogs up. If the dog is breathing on his own, move on to circulation (heartbeat or pulse). If he is not, place him on his right side and hold his muzzle closed, then place your mouth over his nose and exhale deeply enough to slightly raise the dog's rib cage, which shows his lungs are inflated. Remove your mouth from the dog's nose and allow the lungs to deflate. Repeat this procedure every three to five seconds, and check for a heartbeat every third time by pressing down with your palm on the left side of the chest just behind the bent elbow. Continue treatment until the dog is breathing on his own.

If your pet has a heartbeat, skip the following step. If he has no heartbeat or pulse, lay your dog on his right side and stand or kneel with his back to you. Cup your hands over each other and compress the chest where the left elbow lies when pulled back to the chest. Compress inward about three inches each time, at a rate of 100 to 120 compressions per minute. If you are alone, give two quick breaths after every 15 cardiac compressions. If you have an assistant, have one person perform each task and synchronize your procedure so that you are providing one breath per every three to five compressions, followed by a breath, then check for a pulse. Stop CPR every three to five minutes or if you detect movement to see if there is now a heartbeat. Don't stop artificial respiration for more than 30 seconds if the dog is not breathing on his own or he could experience permanent brain damage.

not result from an object and instead indicates symptoms of disease or an allergic reaction.

Bleeding

If your dog is bleeding, hold a piece of gauze or other sterile material over the wound, applying direct pressure. If you don't have anything sterile, grab a clean cloth. If blood soaks the material, add more material on top. Removing the original cloth might prevent a blood clot from forming (blood clots help stop blood flow). Keep applying direct pressure until you can reach your veterinary clinic.

If the bleeding continues and spurts, keep applying direct pressure to the wound while also holding the area slightly closer to the body with your hand. If this technique fails, apply a pressure bandage by wrapping gauze around the wound and securing it with tape. Make sure the bandage is tight enough to stop the bleeding but not so tight that you cut off circulation. If the injury is on a limb, keep checking your Boxer's toes for swelling and temperature; if his toes start to swell or feel cold, loosen the bandage.

If you still cannot stop the bleeding, you need to apply pressure to pressure points in your dog's body that correspond to the injured area. If your dog is bleeding from a front leg, place three fingers up in the armpit on the side of the injury. If your dog is bleeding from a back leg, apply three-finger pressure to the area of the inner thigh where the leg connects to the body on the side of the injury. If your Boxer is bleeding from her head, place three fingers at the base of the lower jaw, on the same side and below where the bleeding is occurring. If she is bleeding from the neck, place three fingers in the soft groove next to the windpipe on the same side as the wound.

Never apply pressure to the windpipe itself, and never apply pressure to your dog's neck if you think she may have a head injury. Note: When using pressure points, you must release pressure for a few seconds at least every 10 minutes, or your dog could suffer permanent damage.

The final resort to staunch a bleeding limb is the tourniquet. Because of its potential to cause long-term, serious damage, a tourniquet should only be used on an animal that is unconscious and may die without it. If you must employ this technique, wrap a two-inch strip of gauze around the limb above the wound, but don't knot it. Wrap each end of the gauze around a stick, then turn the stick slowly and just enough to stop the bleeding. Loosen the tie for several seconds at least every 10 minutes. Although you may need to apply this technique to save your dog's life, realize that she may lose a limb because of the interrupted blood flow.

> If your dog is bleeding heavily, the most important thing is to get her to the vet immediately.

As you can see, bleeding is an extremely dangerous situation that must be handled properly. If your dog is bleeding heavily, the most important thing is to get her to the vet immediately. If possible, ask someone else to drive you and your dog to the clinic, so you can apply the above techniques in the car.

Fractures

If your pet breaks a bone, you need to keep her calm and quiet. Check her breathing and pulse and give CPR, if needed. If the bone protrudes through the skin, take your dog to the vet immediately. Loosely place a nonstick pad or gauze sponge on the wound and secure the dressing with tape, taking care not to move the bone or wrap too tightly.

You'll need to keep your dog completely still while you take her to the vet. If you have someone with you, place your dog on a large flat piece of wood as a makeshift stretcher. If you are alone, try to pick up your dog by placing one arm under and around her neck and the other behind her hind leg or, if her hind leg is injured, under her stomach. If you think she will not lie still in the car, which may injure her further, you may need to try to splint the fracture.

Applying a splint, like performing CPR, is very difficult to do correctly and can actually worsen a fracture if done improperly. You'll need to place something rigid, such as rolled-up newspaper or sticks, on each side of the fractured limb. Hold the splint in place with lots of tape all along the splint or cloth strips tied up and down the splint. Again, make sure not to move the bone or wrap too tightly. Test the tension by placing two fingers between the cloth and the limb, to guard against tying so tightly that you cut off circulation.

Car Accidents

Nothing is more upsetting than seeing an animal struck by a car. You can do your part to prevent this from ever happening to your Boxer by always keeping her on a leash or in a fenced yard.

But, as we all know, people may accidentally leave the gate open, a leash could break or pull out of your hands, and accidents happen. If you witness your dog getting hit by a car, try to pay attention to what part of the dog's body the vehicle struck—this is important information for your vet. Wave

Shock

Different causes bring about different symptoms of shock. Your dog may be weak and subdued. His body temperature can range from below normal to normal or above normal (in cases of shock caused by a bacterial infection). His pulse may be rapid and weak, and his gums may not exhibit a normal capillary refill time of one to two seconds. Test capillary refill time by pressing on your dog's gums and counting the time it takes the gums to change from white back to pink. If your dog's gums seem to be responding normally, but he is acting lethargic and confused, he may be in early stages of shock.

In all cases of shock, immediate veterinary care is imperative. Control any bleeding, wrap your dog in a blanket, towel, or piece of clothing to keep him warm, and rush him to the veterinary clinic.

down traffic and gently pull your dog off the road as quickly as possible, being careful not to cause more injury. Many dogs will jump up after an accident and try to run off. This is a survival mechanism and shouldn't be misinterpreted as meaning the dog is fine. If your pet can't move at all, she may have a broken back. Place her on a stiff board or on a blanket and get someone to help you carry her carefully to a car, so you can get her to the hospital. Again, have someone else drive, if possible. Check her breathing and pulse and perform CPR if necessary. Try to control any bleeding. Check for signs of shock and treat accordingly (see sidebar). In all cases, even if your dog seems fine, take her to the vet immediately.

Heat Stroke

Dogs can fall victim to heat stroke when left outside without proper shelter or when exercising excessively in hot, humid conditions. A common cause of heat stroke in dogs is being left in a parked car. Never leave your Boxer in the car on a warm day. Even if the windows are slightly open, the temperature in your car can quickly reach unbearable levels, which can prove fatal to your pet. Always monitor your Boxer on a hot (or even warm) day and use your air conditioning if your dog seems uncomfortable.

Signs of heat stroke include excessive panting or difficulty breathing, drooling, an increased heart and respiratory rate, and lethargy. If untreated, your dog could have a seizure or fall into a coma. Since the Boxer is a brachycephalic breed (one with a flat-nosed face) she is more susceptible to heat stroke than dogs with a longer snout.

If your dog is suffering from heat stroke, get her out of the heat source immediately. She must receive emergency veterinary care, since delayed treatment could mean death. In addition, complications from heat stroke, such as kidney failure and respiratory arrest, may not show up for hours or even days. Cool your Boxer down with towels soaked in cold water, place her in an air-conditioned car, and rush her to the clinic, where the vet will give her IV fluids and carefully reduce her body temperature.

Seizures

Seizures, like many other symptoms, can result from a variety of causes, from poisoning to diseases, organ failure, and epilepsy. Dogs seem to sense the onset of a seizure, and may act dazed or anxious, or try to stay by you or hide in a safe place. When the seizure hits, the dog usually loses her balance, falls over, and twitches. She may also drool, urinate, or defecate. Some appear to stare at nothing or to bite at imaginary things. A dog having a seizure often doesn't recognize her owner. After a seizure, your dog may act normally right away, or she may be disoriented and walk into walls or furniture.

If your dog experiences a seizure, make sure she is in a safe spot (away from sharp objects or the top of stairs, for example). Don't disturb her, and especially don't touch her near her mouth. She may not know who you are and may bite as a reflex. Take note of when the seizure started, how long it lasted, and whether anything seemed to trigger the episode. When the seizure stops, take your pet to the vet as soon as possible. The vet might place your dog on anti-seizure medication, which will not prevent all seizures but will help reduce their frequency and severity.

Poisoning

Many different substances in various forms can poison your dog. Some are eaten, while others are inhaled, and still others are absorbed through the skin. Treatment varies widely, so it is important not to haphazardly administer antidotes on your own.

Signs of poisoning include drooling, staggering or trembling, seizures, vomiting, diarrhea, and swollen, irritated skin or eyes. Check your pet's breathing and pulse and begin CPR, if necessary. If you suspect your pet has been poisoned, but you don't know by what, take her to the veterinarian immediately. If you know what poisoned your pet, call your vet and tell him or her the exact name of the poison (keep the container or label to take to the vet). You must also tell the vet how long ago your dog was exposed, how much she ate or was exposed to, her vital signs (including temperature and heart rate), and her weight. Your vet may prescribe an antidote over the phone that you can administer before bringing in your pet, or the vet might tell you to rush your dog to the clinic immediately. You also can call the National Animal Poison Control Center at (800) 548-2423 or (900) 680-0000. The center, which charges a fee, may be able to prescribe an antidote over the phone.

Fish Hooks

If your Boxer is your constant companion and accompanies you everywhere, you may take her on a fishing expedition so you both can enjoy the great outdoors and each other's company. If you do, you need to exercise caution and prevent your Boxer's access to the fishing equipment, which probably smells like a seafood feast to her. If your dog gets a fish hook embedded in any part of her body take her to the vet immediately to have the hook removed. If you can't get to a vet quickly and the hook is in your dog's paw, try to push the hook through the skin until you can see the barb. Cut the barb off with a wire cutter and then pull the hook out in the reverse direction from the way it went in. Wash out the wound with warm water or a salt/water solution of one teaspoon of salt mixed with a quart of warm water. If your dog embedded the hook in her mouth or swallowed it, however, never try to remove it yourself.

Even if you have successfully removed the hook, take your dog to the vet in case she needs antibiotics to prevent infection.

Burns/Electric Shock

Burns fall into one of three categories: thermal, chemical, or electrical. Examples of thermal burns include scalding from hot water and getting too close to an open flame. If your dog receives a

Did You Know?

Dogs have extremely sensitive hearing and a sense of smell up to 1,000 times better than humans to compensate for their relatively poor eyesight.

thermal burn, first check for signs of shock. If she is in shock, rush her to the veterinarian immediately. If she is not showing signs of shock, cover the wound with cold compresses, made by soaking rags in ice water then wringing them out. Place a sterile, nonstick gauze pad or a clean, moist cloth over the burn to keep it cool and clean. Then take your dog to the vet.

Chemical burns can come from either alkalis or acids. If your dog sustains a chemical burn, again check for signs of shock and seek emergency care if shock is present. Wear protective gloves and clean the wound immediately. If the offending substance was an alkali, such as oven or ammonia cleaner, wash the wound with equal parts vinegar and water. If it was an acid, such as toilet bowl or drain cleaners or automobile battery fluid, wash with one teaspoon of bicarbonate of soda mixed with one pint of lukewarm water. If you do not know what kind of chemical caused the injury, rinse with plain water. Follow the instructions for antidotes that are printed on the chemical's container, if accessible. Take your dog to his veterinarian immediately.

The third type of burn, electrical burn, often brings an added consequence—electric shock. Wires fascinate some dogs, especially puppies. If your dog chews through a wire, she may experience severe burns and shock. If you see your pet actually bite a wire, turn off the power source or remove the cord with a wooden or plastic broom, to prevent you, too, from being electrocuted. Never touch a dog who is still in contact with a live power source. If you didn't actually witness the incident, your only indication that your dog has been burned may be blisters around her mouth, excessive drooling, or a foul odor coming from her mouth. Check your dog's airway, breathing, and circulation and perform CPR, if needed. Check for shock, and take your dog to the vet immediately.

You can prevent electrocution by covering cords with plastic cord covers or by securing them to the floor with duct tape and covering them with carpet. Other options are to unplug all appliances not in use and/or rub the cord with Tabasco sauce or a bitter tonic such as Bitter Apple from a pet store. Finally, you should never leave puppies unsupervised near live wires. (You can now purchase a "Smart Cord"—an extension cord that automatically shuts off the instant it's damaged. It's available from One Step Ahead catalog, P.O. Box 517, Lake Bluff, IL 60044, 800-274-8440 or www.onestepahead.com.)

Allergic Reactions

Any number of things in your dog's environment—including food, grass, bugs (bites), household cleaning products, or even a new shampoo—can cause allergies. If your dog develops a sudden, severe allergic reaction, such as facial swelling or trouble breathing, get her emergency care. If the reaction is relatively mild, such as irritated, itchy skin, bathe her with a gentle, hypoallergenic shampoo. Apply cold compresses to any red, itchy areas, then follow with a baking soda and water paste. If your vet recommends it, an over-the-counter antihistamine might help your allergic dog. (Ask your vet for the proper dosage).

> Any number of things in your dog's environment–including food, grass, bugs (bites), household cleaning products, or even a new shampoo–can cause allergies.

If this doesn't clear up the problem, take your pet in for an appointment with the vet. Food allergies are common and may require a change in diet. Seasonal allergies also occur frequently, and your vet may be able to prescribe medication to relieve your dog's symptoms.

First-Aid Kit Essentials

○ Your veterinarian's phone number

○ An after-hours emergency clinic's phone number

○ The National Animal Poison Control Center's hotline number, (800) 548-2423 or (900) 680-0000

○ A book on emergency care (<u>First Aid for Dogs and Cats</u>, by Dr. Bobbie Mammalo, is available through the American Red Cross)

○ Rectal thermometer

○ Tweezers

○ Scissors

○ Penlight flashlight

○ Rubbing alcohol

○ Hydrogen peroxide (three percent)

○ Syrup of ipecac and activated charcoal liquid or tablets (antidotes for poisoning)

○ Anti-diarrheal medicine

○ Dosing syringe

○ Nonstick wound pads, gauze squares, and roll cotton to control bleeding

○ Adhesive tape

○ Elastic bandage

○ Styptic powder (in case nails are cut too short)

○ Emergency ice pack

○ Latex examination gloves

Eye Injuries

If your Boxer's eyes are red, swollen, or watery or if she keeps pawing at them, she may have something in her eye or a condition such as conjunctivitis (a swelling of the pink tissue lining the inside of the eyelids). If you see a foreign object in your dog's eye, flush it out with a sterile saline eyewash or with large amounts of tap water. Even if you remove the object, you'll want your vet to examine her eye, in case her cornea has been scratched. Whenever your pet's eyes are involved in a health concern, take her to the vet. Many eye conditions can be serious if not treated. Your dog's eyesight is too precious to risk.

Obesity

Maintaining the proper weight in your Boxer is more than a matter of vanity. An overweight dog not only looks less attractive than a thinner dog, he also is less healthy. Extra weight puts strain on every part of a dog's body, from his heart to his lungs and bones.

Maintaining a Healthy Weight

It is important that you monitor your Boxer's weight throughout his life. Adjust the type and amount of food your dog eats as he moves from puppyhood into adulthood and eventually old age. Make a habit of performing the rib-check test every month or so. Stand above your dog and look down. Does he have a waist? When viewed from the side, does his abdomen tuck up from his ribs to his pelvis or does his belly look like a sagging potato sack? Place your hands along his sides and run them lightly over his ribs. With slight pressure, you should be able to feel each rib. If you have to press hard to find his ribs or you can't find them at all, you have an overweight dog! (The rib-check test and Boxer nutrition are discussed further in Chapter 3, Food for Thought.)

If your dog is overweight, there's a good chance you are at the root of his problem. Although some dogs gain weight because of a medical condition, the number one cause of obesity is overfeeding, and we all know who controls the food bowl! Let's start by examining snacks. No matter how cute and pleading your Boxer may look, don't allow snacks to make up more than 5 to 10 percent of his diet at the most, and only feed snacks that are healthy. If your dog has a weight problem, check his daily intake of dog food. Remember that the cups per day listed on the dog-food bag are just recommendations, and each dog is different. Feed your dog the amount of food that keeps him trim and healthy.

If your dog is overweight, you first need to consult your veterinarian. He or she can work up a weight-reduction diet and an exercise plan that will shape up your dog slowly and safely and keep him that way. In general, when dealing with adult dogs, it is better to feed the same amount of a lower calorie food than to cut back the amount of your dog's normal food. If your dog notices he is eating less food, he will feel hungrier than if he eats the same amount of food, but with fewer calories. Most premium dog foods come in low-calorie versions, or your vet may put your dog on a prescription weight-reduction diet. Keep in mind, however, that your dog can't do this alone. If you are not diligent in sticking to the diet, and if you keep slipping your Boxer treats, he'll never lose the weight.

> If your dog is overweight, there's a good chance you are at the root of his problem.

Diet, however, is only half of the equation. Your dog also will need to step up his exercise. Ask your vet to recommend the proper amount and type of exercise to rid your dog of his excess weight. Overweight dogs shouldn't be pushed too hard too fast, or they can injure themselves. Agility, for instance, is an excellent exercise option for dogs who are already in decent shape, but can be harmful to an overweight dog who could injure himself jumping or navigating other obstacles. Instead, your vet may recommend road work. Always start out slowly, gradually walking (or jogging) greater distances with your dog.

Trimming Down a Chubby Puppy

Trimming down overweight puppies requires a slightly different approach. Feeding a low-calorie adult diet to a puppy may deprive him of the essential nutrients he needs to grow properly. Instead, feed your pup slightly less of his normal diet and keep monitoring his condition until he reaches an ideal weight. You also don't want to put a puppy on a strictly regimented exercise program. It could do some real damage to his growing bones.

Health Concerns Specific to Boxers

Sadly, every breed of dog is prone to specific diseases and illnesses. It is important that you educate yourself beforehand about the maladies that can affect the Boxer, and what kind of tests, prevention, and cures are available for each. If you are educated about the diseases and disorders that run in Boxers, you'll know what questions to ask a breeder to ensure that he or she is doing everything possible to breed healthy dogs. Not only should you ask a potential breeder if he or she tests for these disorders, you should ask to see proof. You are making a lifelong emotional investment in your Boxer; you want to be sure you are buying a healthy dog.

Genetic Diseases and Disorders

Hip Dysplasia Hip dysplasia (HD) is a disorder that affects many dog breeds, including the Boxer. This progressive, degenerative joint disease, in which the thigh bone does not fit correctly into the hip joint, ranges from mild, asymptomatic cases to severe cases that cause serious pain and/or debilitation. If your Boxer experiences difficulty getting up, appears lame, or is reluctant to run and play, your vet should check him out for dysplasia. A definite diagnosis requires x rays.

Since this genetic disease can be so devastating, the Orthopedic Foundation for Animals (OFA), the Institute for Genetic Disease Control in Animals (GDC), or the PennHip system should evaluate all breeding stock and determine if they are free of this condition. When considering purchasing a puppy, make sure that both parents have been certified clear of hip dysplasia by one of the above methods.

As HD is rarely detected before six months of age; accurate diagnosis typically cannot be made until two years. A poor diet is believed to worsen this genetic problem. That's why it is vital that your Boxer pup grows slowly, eats the right foods, and doesn't become overweight. Overexercise and injury at a young age can also contribute to HD. Hip dysplasia is treated with medication and/or surgery, depending on the condition's severity.

Cancer Many different types of cancer—including those affecting the skin, brain, thyroid, sex organs, and pancreas—can befall the Boxer. Treatment of malignant cancers includes surgery, chemotherapy, and/or radiation. Benign skin tumors thankfully can usually either be left alone or removed under local anesthesia. But because cancers are so common in this breed, never take for granted that any lump or bump is benign. Always visit your vet when you notice a lump anywhere on your Boxer.

Gingival Hyperplasia Tumors of the mouth, called gingival hyperplasia, affect mainly middle-aged to older Boxers. Since Boxer's lips tend to collect pieces of food, owners must clean the areas regularly. Although affected dogs often have many gingival swellings, which may distort a dog's appearance, they usually are not a major health concern. If your dog develops tumors anywhere in its body, however, see your vet to make sure that the tumor is benign.

Heart Disease There are two main types of heart disease seen in the Boxer: aortic stenosis and cardiomyopathy. Aortic stenosis, detected as a heart murmur, is a narrowing of the outflow tract from the left ventricle of the heart to the aorta. If this defect appears below the aortic valve, it is called subaorticstenosis (SAS). Mild cases often are never even detected and don't shorten a dog's life span, while severe cases can cause heart failure that frequently is fatal. Surgery is not an option to treat aortic stenosis, but therapy can be used to correct any irregular heartbeats that may accompany the disease.

> Because cancers are so common in this breed, never take for granted that any lump or bump is benign. Always visit your vet when you notice a lump anywhere on your Boxer.

Cardiomyopathy is a disease of the heart muscle that strikes middle-aged Boxers for no apparent reason, although it can be traced to a number of causes in other breeds, including poisoning, viral infection, and diabetes. It causes rhythmic abnormalities that often lead to heart failure and death. Since it is so widespread, it is vital that you have your Boxer examined by a veterinarian if he exhibits early symptoms of the disease, which include fainting or sudden weakness. Cardiomyopathy can be treated with several types of drugs, which can add a number of symptom-free years to a dog's life.

Hypothyroidism Hypothyroidism is an increasing problem among Boxers. A deficient thyroid can affect a number of functions in the body, including the heart. Obesity, lethargy, and hair loss are some of the symptoms; a blood test can confirm if thyroid hormone levels are low. You may have to give your dog replacement hormones, which will rid him of most symptoms, for the rest of his life.

Temperature Intolerance Intolerance to temperature extremes is another health concern in the Boxer. Their single coat and lack of body fat leaves them vulnerable to the cold, while their flat faces make them susceptible to heat stroke. Always be aware of your Boxer's comfort in extreme conditions. Winter may call for booties and a doggie coat, while summer days are great for lounging in air-conditioned houses, soaking in a wading pool, and drinking lots of fresh water.

Epilepsy Primary or "idiopathic" epilepsy is a disorder of the brain that causes seizures. Although many things—from low blood sugar to infections and toxins—also cause seizures, in the primary form the cause is not known, but may be hereditary in the Boxer. The seizures come and go throughout the dog's life usually beginning between six months to five years old.

Epilepsy can be treated with medication, although some dogs cannot be well-controlled even with high doses of multiple medications. Working closely with your veterinarian will give you the best chance of diagnosing and controlling the problem. Because this disorder may be inherited, always ask about a history of seizures in the line when choosing a puppy. Unless your vet is certain that your Boxer has a non-hereditary seizure disorder, you should not breed a dog who has seizures.

Follicular Dysplasia Some Boxers develop a condition called canine follicular dysplasia (CFD) in which the hair thins, becomes brittle, and sometimes falls out completely. The problem isn't with the hair itself but with the follicle—the growth bud that lies within the skin. CFD is considered to be hereditary, so always choose puppies from parents who have luxurious, healthy coats.

Dogs with CFD do not become ill, but don't look very good, either. Treatment consists of flushing with medicated shampoos and possibly oral treatment with retinoid drugs. Work closely with your vet or veterinary dermatologist to improve this condition.

Bloat Bloat can affect Boxers as well. Bloat occurs when the stomach swells from excess gas, fluid, or both. The stomach may even flip over, causing a life-threatening emergency called torsion. Although the causes of bloat are still somewhat of a mystery, it is believed to be precipitated by overeating or heavy exercise immediately before or after eating a meal or drinking large quantities of water. Feed your Boxer two smaller meals per day, rather than one large daily meal throughout his lifetime to lessen his chances of developing bloat. Limiting his exercise before and after meals and regulating his water intake before and after exercising are also good ideas.

You may feel discouraged after reading the above list of health concerns, and may be wondering how you'll ever find a healthy Boxer. While Boxers can be affected by the disorders mentioned here, there also are many healthy representatives of the breed just waiting to find a home. You are better off knowing about potential health problems up front so you can do your best to buy a healthy puppy, rather than learning about a disease only when your beloved dog is suffering from it.

Did You Know?

Dogs and humans are the only animals with prostates.

Basic Training for Boxers

By Liz Palika

In This Chapter

○ When to Begin Training
○ The Teaching Process
○ What Every Good Boxer Needs to Know

Why train your Boxer? Does your dog try to jump up on every person she meets? Does she constantly want to play? Does she grab your belongings (instead of her toys) because she knows you will chase her? Does she sometimes get a little too protective? Does she drag you down the street when you go for a walk? These are all normal behaviors for a healthy, active young Boxer, but they are also unnecessary, annoying, and potentially dangerous behaviors that can be changed (or at least controlled) with training.

Just because these are natural behaviors doesn't mean they should continue. Jumping on people is a bad habit that can result in dirty or ripped clothing, scratched skin at the least, and more injuries should your Boxer knock someone down. Grabbing your things and playing keep-away can cause harm to your belongings and even your dog. Dragging you down the street is hard on your dog's neck and your shoulders and arms, and can even result in injury to you should you fall.

With training, your Boxer can learn to control herself so that she's not reacting to every impulse. She can learn social rules such as to sit when greeting people (rather than jumping on everyone) and to walk nicely on the leash. When your Boxer behaves herself at home, you will be more likely to allow her to spend more time in the house with you instead of shutting her outside, exiling her to the backyard. When your Boxer learns to behave herself in public, she is a joy to take for a walk instead of an embarrassing annoyance; you will be more likely to take her places because you'll be proud of her.

Jake is a two-year-old dark red Boxer owned by Thelma Jacobson of Oceanside, California. When he was younger, Thelma brought Jake to training because he was a handful. He would try to jump on everyone, try to pull her in any direction he wanted to go, and felt he needed to visit with every dog he saw. Thelma had owned Boxers before and knew what Jake was capable of doing. "I had trained my previous Boxers," she said. "I knew Jake was smart and could learn manners, and he did." Now, with some training behind him, Jake is well behaved. He sits when he greets people, even when you can tell by his wiggling

A well-trained dog will accept your guidance even when he would rather be doing something else.

Basic Commands
Every Dog Should Know

Sit: Your dog's hips should move to the ground while his shoulders stay upright.

Down: Your dog should lie down on the ground or floor and be still.

Stay: Your dog should remain in position (sit or down) when you walk away from him. He should hold the stay until you give him permission to move.

Come: Your dog should come to you on the first call, no matter what the distractions.

Walk Nicely on the Leash: Your dog can walk ahead of you on the leash but should not pull the leash tight.

Heel: Your dog should walk by your left side with his shoulder by your left leg.

stub of a tail that he really would rather jump up! He no longer tries to drag Thelma down the street, and he restrains the urge to visit with friends, neighbors, and other dogs. He's not perfect yet; Thelma is still working on his Come command, but he is getting better at it. "It's all a matter of training, practice, and consistency," says Thelma.

As Thelma knows, training is an ongoing process and is more than just teaching your dog to Sit or Stay. Training teaches her to behave herself at home and respect your household rules. Training teaches her to comport herself properly in public, too—greeting people respectfully instead of jumping on them. Training applies to every aspect of the dog's life.

When to Begin Training

Boxers are working dogs with a strong desire to please. This can make training much easier, especially when training starts early.

Characteristics of a Trained Dog

A trained dog knows:

- The appropriate behaviors allowed with people (no biting, no mouthing, no rough play, and no mounting);
- Where to relieve himself and how to ask to go outside;
- How to greet people properly without jumping on them;
- To wait for your permission to greet people, other dogs, and other pets;
- How to walk on a leash nicely so that walks are enjoyable;
- To leave the trash cans alone;
- To leave food alone (on the counters or coffee table) that isn't his;
- Not to beg;
- To chew on his toys and not your personal things;
- To play with his toys and not the kids' toys;
- That destructive behavior is not acceptable; and
- To wait for permission before going through doorways.

A trained dog is a happy dog, secure in his place in the family.

Boxer puppies are ready to start training as soon as they join their new household. At eight or nine weeks old, a puppy can begin learning the basic rules. He can learn that biting isn't allowed, that he should sit for every meal, and where he should go to relieve himself. By 10 weeks of age, you can start attaching a leash to his collar and let him drag it around for a few minutes at a time so that he gets used to the feel of it. Puppies have a very short attention span, but are willing and eager students—especially when you make training fun.

Keep in mind as you start teaching your Boxer, that this adorable puppy is going to grow up to be a big, strong dog. Don't let the puppy do anything now that you will regret later. For exam-

Puppy Kindergarten

The ideal time to start group class training is as soon as your Boxer puppy has had at least two sets of vaccinations. Some veterinarians recommend that you wait longer; consult your vet about the best time for your puppy to begin his training. Most puppy classes recommend that puppies start between 10 and 12 weeks of age. Puppy kindergarten teaches you how to teach your puppy and includes the basic commands of Sit, Down, Stay, and Come—all geared for the puppy's short attention span. In puppy classes, your Boxer will also spend time socializing with other people and other puppies.

ple, if you teach the puppy to cuddle with you on your lap now, will you still want him on your lap when he weighs 65 pounds?

If you adopt a little older puppy or an adult, you can still start training right away. While your Boxer will need time to get used to your household, especially if he was a stray, from a breeder's kennel, or in a shelter, training helps him learn what you expect and, as a result, makes that adjustment easier.

Jenny is a one-year-old Boxer who was turned in to a Southern California Boxer Rescue group. A family with three children adopted her. Although she was very patient with the kids and showed no aggression, she obviously didn't know how to behave around them so her new family enrolled themselves and her in a training class just two weeks after they adopted her. She learned to sit for

Start training early so that your puppy learns good behavior instead of bad habits.

Basic Obedience-Training Class

Most dog obedience instructors invite puppies to begin the basic class after they have graduated from a puppy class or after the puppy reaches four months of age. If your Boxer is older than four months and has never attended a puppy class, he still goes to the basic class. This class teaches the traditional beginner's commands: Sit, Down, Stay, Come, and Heel. In addition, most instructors spend time discussing problem behaviors such as jumping on people, barking, digging, and chewing. A group class such as this helps your Boxer learn to control himself around other dogs and people—serious distractions!

petting and, by doing this, stopped knocking over the younger children. She learned that mouthing wasn't allowed and she learned to play with her toys instead of the kids' toys. By the time she finished class, the kids had learned how to work with her, too, and she had adjusted well to her new family.

Start teaching your new Boxer the rules you expect of him right away. For example, if you don't want him to get up on the furniture, never allow him to get up there. Don't make excuses, as in, "Oh, this is a new house to him and he's upset. We can teach him later to stay off the furniture." If you don't want him up on the furniture, teach him right away what your rules are. Breaking bad habits later is much more difficult!

Is It Ever Too Late?

Do you have a three-year-old Boxer who is not as well behaved as you would like? It's not too late—you can still train him. The downside to starting training later is that you then have to break bad habits as well as teach the new behaviors. With a young puppy,

Private Training

Private training is usually recommended for Boxers with one or more serious behavior problems. In private sessions, which are one on one either at your home or at the trainer's facility, the trainer can tailor the training to your dog's specific needs.

you're starting with a clean slate and can teach the proper behavior before he learns any bad habits. If you've ever tried to stop a bad habit (smoking, for example), you know it can be very difficult. With most Boxers up to about seven years of age, however, you can control most bad habits, with consistent training and lots of patience.

If your dog is older than eight or nine years of age, your success at changing bad habits will be much more limited. You can teach new commands—Heel, Sit, Down, Stay, or Come—and your dog will be able to learn those without too much trouble. However, changing bad habits in an older dog—especially if the habits are of many years' duration—will have limited success, depending on the problem. In some cases, his age may work with you. For example, if your Boxer has been jumping on people for eight years, you can probably change that by teaching him to sit instead. As an older, heavier, and possibly arthritic dog, he's going to be less apt to jump anyway, and the praise he gets for sitting will make it more worthwhile.

Basic Dog Psychology

People and dogs have a long, shared history. Archeologists have found evidence of this history in archeological sites dating back thousands of years. Why did this relationship develop? Researchers don't know for sure, but guess that the wolf, as an efficient predator, had hunting skills early man could use, or perhaps people learned to watch the wolves as early warning systems against other predators or trespassers. But why did the wolf decide to cooperate with man? Again, we don't know. Maybe some wolves learned to follow people, scavenging the scraps of hunts or the garbage people always leave behind them. All of this is speculation, as we have no written history telling us exactly what happened. We do have the end result: domesticated dogs who have been protectors, helpers, and companions for thousands of years.

Families and Packs

In the wild, wolves live in packs. The pack is made up of a dominant male, a dominant female, several subordinate adults, a juvenile or two, and the latest pups. Only the two dominant adults breed; the others help hunt for and protect the resulting puppies. This pack has some important social rules (besides limiting the breeding to the two dominant adults) and these rules are rarely broken. The leaders usually initiate the hunt, and then direct where and when the hunt will take place. They eat first and best, with the subordinate animals grabbing what they can until the leaders back off. The leaders decide where the pack's den will be and the rest of the pack follows. These and other rules help keep the order among the pack members. There is usually little disruption in the pack unless one of the wolves decides to try to move up in the pack order. If an older wolf is disabled, dies, or leaves the pack or if a younger wolf gets ambitious, then there may be some posturing or fighting until the new pack order is established.

Dogs today fit into our family life because they have this pack history. Our family is a social organization similar to a pack, although our families have significant differences from a traditional wolf pack. We do often have an adult male and adult female, although today there may be just one adult. There are rarely any other adults in the pack, as a wolf pack might have, and there may or may not be juveniles (teenagers) and children. In addition, the rules of our family are rarely adhered to as strongly as the social rules in a wolf pack are. For example, in a wolf pack, as mentioned above, the leaders eat first. In our families, people eat any time and the order of eating has no specific rhyme or reason. These family rules, or lack of rules, can be very confusing to our dogs.

What Does It Mean to Be Top Dog?

"Top dog" is a slang term for the pack leader. In the wolf pack, the top dog is the dominant male or dominant female, often called the alpha male or alpha female. In your family pack, the top dog should be you, as the dog's owner, and any other member of the family.

> In your family pack, the top dog should be you, as the dog's owner, and any other member of the family.

Often during adolescence, a Boxer with a particularly bold personality may make a try for leadership of his (or her) family pack. Adolescence usually strikes at sexual maturity, between eight and twelve months of age, and lasts for several months.

Unfortunately, Boxers can be quite dominant and do often try to dominate their owners. Benjamin Hart, D.V.M., and Lynette Hart, authors of *The Perfect Puppy* (Freeman & Co., 1988), queried veterinarians, dog trainers, and other pet professionals about several behavior traits of many of the most common breeds.

Don't let your dog use his body language to show dominance. Your dog should recognize you (and your children) as above him in the family pack.

Boxers scored very high in the category of dominance over owners with "high" meaning this is a common trait in the breed.

If the dog's owner is less dominant than the dog, or if the owner is unaware of the signals that the dog relates to dominance, the dog may actually think he is in charge. For example, as mentioned, eating first is one signal dominant dogs use. When do you feed your Boxer? Many dog owners feed the dog first to get him out from underfoot while cooking. If your Boxer eats first and you eat later, he could interpret this as weakness on your part—even though it means nothing to you! Going first is important, too. Who goes through first when you open the door? Have your dog wait for you to go first.

A dog who takes over can make life miserable around the house. This is when we see mounting (sexual) behavior toward the owner. The dog may growl whenever you try to do something—such as make him move off the furniture—and the growl may escalate to a snap or bite. Your dog cannot be the top dog in your household; after all, it is your house!

Although it is very important that your dog regard you as the leader or top dog, don't look at every action your dog makes as a dominance challenge. After all, he knows you're important—you supply the food! For dogs who do have a dominant personality, though, this training during adolescence is very important.

You Are the Top Dog!

- You always eat first, even if it's just an apple or carrot.

- You go through doors and doorways first; block your dog from charging through ahead of you.

- Go up stairs ahead of your dog; don't let him charge ahead and then look down at you.

- Give him permission to do things. If he picks up his ball, tell him, "Get your ball! Good boy!" even though he was going to do it anyway.

- Practice your training regularly.

- Have your dog roll over for a tummy rub daily.

- Do not play rough games with your Boxer– no wrestling on the floor or tug-of-war.

- Never let your dog stand above you or put his paws on your shoulders; these are dominant postures.

The Teaching Process

Training your dog is not a mysterious process although sometimes it may seem so. Teaching your dog is primarily communication and then rewarding the behaviors you want—or interrupting the behaviors you do not want—to continue happening. For example, if you want to teach your Boxer to stay off the living-room furniture, watch him when he's in the room with you. When he goes over to the sofa, sniffs it, and starts to climb up, stop him, using a deep, growling tone of voice: "Rover, no! Get off the furniture!" When he moves away from the sofa and lays down on the floor, praise him in a higher-pitched, happy tone of voice: "Good boy!"

Did you notice I specified different tones of voice? Dogs are verbal animals, just as we are, and tone of voice is very important to their communication. When your dog wants to play, his barks or yelps are much higher in tone than when he is warning you of someone coming up the walk to the front door. You can aid the training process by copying some of these tones. When you give your dog a command, such as Sit, use your normal speaking voice at a normal speaking strength. When you praise your dog to let him know that he has done something right, use a higher-pitched tone, such as when you say, "Ice cream!" When your dog makes a mistake, use a deeper tone of voice, a "Grrr!" type of voice.

> Volume isn't important; instead, when you give your dog a command, or praise or correct him, sound as though you mean what you're saying.

When using these different tones of voice, don't raise your volume. Your dog hears very well; in fact, much better than we do. Volume isn't important; instead, when you give your dog a command, or praise or correct him, sound as though you mean what you're saying. If you tell your dog something and then giggle, he's not going to take you seriously. For example, if he tears something up and you catch him in the act and tell him "No!", you cannot laugh at him no matter how cute he looks with sofa cushion stuffing hanging out of his mouth.

You must also keep in mind that your dog wasn't born understanding English, French, German, or any other human language. You need to teach your dog that some of your spoken words (or to your dog, sounds) have meanings. The tone of your voice can teach him a lot. He learns that "Good dog" is a positive thing because you say it in a high-pitched tone of voice and you usually pet him when you say it. He learns that "No!" means something bad because you say it in a deeper, growling tone of voice and you look unhappy when you say it.

But how does your Boxer learn what the word "sit" means? Or "down"? Or any other spoken command? You need to teach him. When teaching him, say the word as you help him follow

A treat can be a wonderful training tool to help teach your dog to pay attention to you. When he looks at you, praise him, give him the treat, and then follow through with other training.

through with what you ask him to do. Tell him "Rover, sit!" as you take a treat and hold it above his nose, moving it slowly back over his head toward the stub of his tail. As his head goes up, his hips will go down. When his hips touch the ground, praise him "Good to sit!" and give him the treat. The treat is what is called a lure. It helps your dog to do something by causing him to move or assume a position. In addition, when he does what you ask, the lure becomes part of your positive reinforcement, letting the dog know he has done something right.

Your timing is very important when teaching your dog. Praise him as he does something right and let him know he's making a mistake as he makes it. Let's continue with the living-room furniture example. Interrupt him *as he starts to get up* on the furniture. Praise him when he makes the decision to stay off the furniture, even if you helped him make that decision. Let him know *as he does something right* that it is right or *as he does something wrong* that it is wrong.

During the training process, don't hesitate to set your dog up for success. We all—dogs and people—learn more from our successes than our failures. Your Boxer will be more willing to try again (whatever it is that you are teaching him) if he succeeds and is rewarded. When setting your dog up for success, think about what it is you are teaching him. If you want to keep your Boxer off the furniture, ask him to lie down at your feet *before* he jumps up on the sofa. If you want him to stop jumping on people, ask him to

Training Vocabulary

Training involves certain terms you will need to understand in order to work with your Boxer. The following is a basic canine training vocabulary:

Positive Reinforcement: Anything that your dog likes that you can use to reward good behavior. This can be verbal praise, food treats, toys, tennis balls, or petting.

Praise: Words spoken in a higher than normal tone of voice to reward your dog for something he did right; part of positive reinforcement.

Lure: This can be food treats or a toy. You use a lure to help position the dog as you want him, or to gain his cooperation as you teach him something.

Interruption: The moment when you catch your dog in the act of doing something and you stop him. This can be a deeper-toned verbal sound, "Leave it alone!" or a sharp sound like dropping a book to the floor.

Correction: Usually a deep, growling tone or words used to let your dog know that he has made a mistake, delivered as he is doing it, to interrupt the behavior. A correction can also be a snap and release of the leash. It should be enough to get your dog's attention and stop the behavior at that moment and that's all.

sit *before* he jumps on your neighbor. When you learn to think ahead, you can prevent a lot of problem behavior from happening and, at the same time, teach your dog the right way to do things.

Do not rely too heavily on corrections to teach your dog. You can let your dog know that he's made a mistake when you catch him in the act—his nose in the trash can—but do not correct him after the fact. He may associate the correction with many things—the trash on the floor, you catching him in the kitchen or with the trash—but he may not actually associate the after-the-fact correction with the act of dumping over the trash can. A correction or interruption is effective only when you catch him making the mistake.

A properly timed correction lets your dog know when he's making a mistake, but it doesn't tell him what to do instead. For example, if you want to teach your Boxer not to jump on people, you can correct him with "No jump!" and he may learn what that means, but it doesn't teach him how to greet people. After all, his jumping on people is a greeting. Training needs to give him an alternative. A better approach is to first teach him to sit to greet people. Then, after he knows how to do that, you can let him know when he makes a mistake and jumps up.

Corrections should be given as the dog is making the mistake, not after the fact.

A training program that relies too heavily on correction will not be successful with most Boxers. Most Boxers, as working dogs, are more than willing to cooperate with a training program when they understand what is being asked of them. They need some motivation to want to do this, however, and that motivation can be your approval, verbal praise, food treats, or toys. If the Boxer feels that there are too many corrections or the corrections are too harsh, he will stop cooperating. He may refuse to move, lie down, or play dead, or he may even become depressed, showing the classic signs of depression—lack of appetite, lack of interest in surroundings, and no desire to play. Training a Boxer must have a balance. Let him know when he's making a mistake as he is doing so, but use a lot of positive reinforcements to keep him upbeat, positive, and motivated.

Teaching Your Dog to Be Handled

Your Boxer cannot care for herself. That's your job. You need to be able to comb her, check for fleas and ticks, and look for cuts,

The Training Process at a Glance

To teach a new command:

○ Show the dog what to do, with a lure, your hands, or your voice.

○ Praise him for doing it and reward him with the lure.

○ Correct him for mistakes only when he knows and understands the command and chooses not to do it.

To correct problem behavior:

○ Prevent the problem from happening when possible.

○ Set the dog up for success by teaching him to do something else and then rewarding it.

○ Interrupt the behavior when you catch the dog in the act. Let him know he made a mistake.

○ Show him what to do instead.

scrapes, bumps, and bruises. When she has a problem, you need to be able to take care of it, whether it's cleaning and medicating her ears when she has an ear infection, caring for her stitches after spaying, or washing out her eyes if dirt gets in them.

It's important to teach your dog before you need to do anything that she can trust you when you touch her body. When you bring your Boxer home, either as a puppy or an adopted adult, one thing you can do every evening is to teach your Boxer to accept social handling. Sit on the floor and invite your Boxer to lay down in front of you. Start giving her a tummy rub to help her relax. When she's relaxed, start giving her a massage. Begin massaging at her muzzle, rubbing your fingers gently over the skin, and at the same time, check her teeth. Then move up her head, touching the skin around her eyes, looking for a discharge or problem in her eyes. Move up to her ears, stroke the earflaps, massage around the base of each ear, and, while you're there, look

Make a Negative into a Positive

Many dogs dislike having their toenails cut and Red, a red brindle Boxer, was one of those dogs. When his owners tried to trim his nails, he would struggle, cry, growl, and sometimes even try to bite. His owners didn't want to continue this way and wanted to teach him at least to tolerate toenail trimming.

I suggested using peanut butter as a distraction and had Red's owner give him a spoonful of peanut butter as her husband trimmed his nails. Red was still uneasy about the nail trimming, and would pull his paws away, but he was so busy licking the peanut butter off the roof of his mouth that he allowed the toenail trimming to take place without any additional bad behavior.

inside the ears for potential problems. Continue in the same manner all over your dog's body, from her nose to the tip of the stub of her tail. If at any time your Boxer protests, go back to a tummy rub for a moment, or offer her some peanut butter to distract her.

Do this exercise daily and incorporate grooming. Comb one side, then roll her over, and do the other side. Trim her nails after you've massaged her feet and checked them for cuts and scratches.

If your dog needs medication or first-aid treatments, you can do that while massaging, too, so that the treatment doesn't turn into a big fight. It simply becomes matter-of-fact and a part of the daily massage.

A tummy rub can help relax your dog if he's over-stimulated. You can also follow through with any needed grooming. In addition, this is a wonderful time for bonding with your dog.

A Side Benefit of Boxer Massage

There is a welcome side benefit to the daily massage you give your Boxer. When you are finished massaging him, he is totally relaxed—like a limp noodle! Massage him when you would like your dog to be quiet and calm. If he's over-active in the evening when you want to sit back and watch television, turn the TV on while you're massaging your dog. Then, when you're finished massaging him, he'll fall asleep and you can watch the rest of your show!

The Importance of Good Socialization

Socialization is a vital part of raising a mentally healthy, well-adjusted Boxer. A young Boxer who has been introduced to a variety of people of different ages and ethnic backgrounds will be a social dog, one who is happy to meet people on a walk and is not afraid of certain people. Dogs who are not properly socialized may grow up afraid of children, senior citizens, or people of a different ethnic background than their owners. These dogs often become fear biters and may eventually be destroyed as dangerous dogs.

Socialization also refers to meeting other dogs and pets. A well-socialized dog gets the opportunity to meet dogs of a variety of sizes, shapes, colors, and breeds and learns how to behave around these other dogs. Your dog should also meet dog-friendly cats, ferrets, rabbits, and other pets. The important lesson is the more strangers your Boxer is introduced to—whether a senior citizen, child, cat, or Poodle—the better.

Socialization also includes introducing your Boxer to the world around him, the sights and sounds he will experience during his life with you. He should see and hear a motorcycle going down the street, kids on skateboards and inline skates, the garbage truck on trash day, and birthday party balloons. Walk him past the construction crew working on the house down the street and let him stop and watch the road crew working on the intersection. The more he sees and hears, the better his coping skills as an adult. Don't introduce your Boxer to everything all at once, however. You may overload him!

> Dogs who are not properly socialized may grow up afraid of children, senior citizens, or people of a different ethnic background than their owners.

You can start socialization when your puppy is nine to ten weeks old. Begin by introducing him to friendly neighbors. Let them play with him, pet, and cuddle him. Don't allow rough play or handling, however. Keep this contact positive. As your puppy grows up, continue introducing him to different people, sights, and sounds. Take him to the local pet store and let people pet him. While there, he can see a shopping cart and follow it with you as you go shopping. Socialization is an ongoing, gradual process.

Should your puppy be frightened by something, do not hug him, pet him, or otherwise try to reassure him. Your puppy will assume those soft words are praise for being afraid. Instead, use a happy tone of voice, "What was that?" and walk up to whatever scared him. Don't force him to walk up to it—just let him see you walk up to it. For example, if your puppy sees a trash can rolling in the street after the wind has blown it over, hold on to

Introduce your dog to other friendly, well-behaved, healthy dogs. Avoid rowdy, poorly behaved, aggressive dogs; they could scare your dog and ruin the socialization you've done so far.

your puppy's leash (to keep him from running away) and walk up to the trash can. Ask your puppy in an upbeat tone of voice, "What's this? Rover, look!" Touch the trash can. Pat it several times so that your puppy can see you touch it. If he will walk up to it, praise him for his bravery.

Luckily, Boxers are by nature highly social dogs. That doesn't change the need for good socialization, however. Kindergarten puppy class is a wonderful way for Boxer puppies to meet other people and other puppies. In addition, most instructors have playground equipment and toys that the puppies can play on and with to increase their socialization skills and confidence. Adult Boxers can still be socialized, although the best time to do this is during puppyhood.

How a Crate Can Help

Originally built as travel cages, crates have become popular training tools for a variety of reasons. A crate can help you house-train your Boxer puppy by confining him to a small place during the night and for short periods of time during the day. Since your puppy doesn't want to soil his bed, he will develop better bowel and bladder control.

The crate is also a good training tool to prevent other problems from occurring. If your Boxer sleeps in his crate during the night, he can't sneak away to chew up something or raid the trash can. When he's confined, he won't be shredding the sofa cushions while you go to the store. When your dog is prevented from getting into trouble, he is also prevented from learning bad habits. As he grows up, he can gradually be given more freedom; but not until he is mature mentally and emotionally—two and a half to three years old for most Boxers!

A crate helps your puppy develop bowel and bladder control, prevents accidents from happening, and becomes your puppy's special place.

As you use the crate, it becomes your dog's special place. He can retreat to his crate for a nap when the household is quiet or he can go to his crate when he's overwhelmed or doesn't feel good. He can hide his favorite toys in his crate or chew on a special rawhide there. It is his place, his refuge.

Many first-time dog owners initially have a problem with the idea of confining their dog to a crate, likening it to a jail cell. But dogs are den animals. In the wild, wolves and coyotes give birth in a den or cave and the puppies are restricted to that den until the mother feels they are old enough to venture out. Most mother dogs are the same way and prefer to give birth in a quiet, secure spot. This is why most breeders give their pregnant bitches a whelping box designed to provide the mother and puppies with such a place.

Introduce your Boxer to the crate by propping the door open and tossing a treat or toy inside. Let him reach in to grab the treat and then back out. Praise him for his bravery! Repeat this several times. Then offer him a meal in the crate. Keep the door propped open, but set his dinner bowl inside the crate so he needs to step inside to get it.

As you are introducing him to the crate, start teaching him a command. As you toss the treat in, wait for him to move toward the crate. When he steps inside, tell him, "Rover, crate!" or "Rover, go to bed!" Use a command that is comfortable to you. In

Choosing the Right Crate

Crates come in two basic styles. There are solid-sided plastic crates that are used for airline travel and wire crates that look like cages. Each style has pros and cons. The wire crates provide more air ventilation and are good if you live in a very warm climate. As they are more open, however, some dogs feel vulnerable in these crates; they don't provide as much security for the dog. Wire crates are usually collapsible but, even when collapsed, are very heavy. The plastic crates do not collapse and take up more room when you store them, but are lighter in weight. They do not allow as much air circulation as the wire crates, but do provide more security for the dog. To choose the right style of crate for your dog, consider your needs and your dog's personality.

The crate should be big enough for your dog as an adult to stand up and turn around. You will use the crate for many years, so get one that will be big enough for your dog when he has grown to his full size. If you aren't sure what size to get, ask for help at the pet store.

the early training steps, give him a treat incentive each time he goes inside the crate. Not only will this make him go inside faster and with more enthusiasm, it also will make him think of the crate as something positive instead of something confining.

The best place for the crate is in your bedroom. I moved my nightstand into the garage, put the dog crate right next to the bed, and use that as the nightstand. This way I can hear the dog and know when she needs to go outside. In addition, she gets to spend 8 uninterrupted hours with me. In our busy society, that's important time! She can hear me and smell me. Even though we really aren't doing anything together, it's still time for her to be with me, a member of her family pack.

If you don't want the dog crate in your bedroom, maybe you could put it in one of the kids' rooms. Or perhaps you could put it in the hallway outside your room. Whatever you decide to do, do not isolate your Boxer. Do not put him out in the backyard alone, or out in the garage or laundry room alone. Remember, dogs are social animals; isolation causes many behavior problems, including self-mutilation and destructiveness.

Your Boxer can spend the night in his crate and a few hours in it here and there during the day, preferably no more than three or four hours at a time. He needs time out of the crate to play, exercise, follow you around, and learn the rules of the house.

What Every Good Boxer Needs to Know

If your Boxer lacks good social skills, your life with him can be horrible, frustrating, and downright embarrassing. Fortunately, social skills are fairly easy to train.

No Jumping on Visitors!

Boxers like to jump up on people. That's how they are and how they got their name, according to one theory (Boxers jump up and box with their front paws). Your Boxer is much too big and strong to jump on people, however. Teach your Boxer to sit each and every time he greets people—you, your spouse, your kids, guests, and people on the street. We'll talk about how to teach the Sit command later in this chapter. Once he knows how to sit, you can enforce it every time he greets someone.

There are several ways to teach your dog to greet by sitting. First of all, if he doesn't have his leash on—say when you come home from work—make sure you at least greet him with empty hands. As your dog dashes up to you and begins to jump, grab his buckle collar (which he should be wearing with his ID tags), tell him "Rover, no jump! Sit!" and with your hand on his collar, help him sit. Keep your hands on him as he sits, so that you can help him maintain that position. Praise him for sitting, "Good boy to sit! Yes, you are!"

The leash is also a good training tool to help the dog sit. When guests come to your house, ask them to wait outside for a moment as you leash your dog. (They'll be more than happy to wait!) Once your dog is leashed, let your guests in. Have your dog sit before the guests pet him. If he bounces up, have your guests back off, and don't let them pet him again until you have him sit. This, of course, requires training your guests, too, to make sure they cooperate. If your dog learns that he can jump on some people, he will never be reliable about not jumping.

You can do the same thing while out on walks. Have your dog sit prior to allowing people to pet him. If he gets too wiggly and bounces up, have the people step back for a minute until he's sitting again.

When training a young dog of my own, I have found that some people protest when I'm doing this training. "Oh, I don't mind," they say, usually as they are brushing paw prints off their clothes. But I consider this important training. I don't want my dogs ruining people's clothes, scratching people, or knocking them down. So if people take offense, I just try to explain why it's important to me and I find that most will then cooperate with my training efforts.

To Bark or Not to Bark

All dogs bark; it is their way of communicating. And while some barking is acceptable—say when someone comes to the front door or a trespasser is climbing over the back fence—too much barking is annoying. In addition, neighbors are quick to complain when a loud barker disturbs the peace of the neighborhood. Luckily, Boxers are not normally problem barkers, although when they do bark, their bark can be very loud!

The easiest way to stop problem barking is to first control it when you're at home. Invite a neighbor over and ask her to ring your doorbell. When she does and your dog charges the door, barking loudly, step up to your dog, grab his collar, and tell him "Rover, quiet!" If he stops barking, good; praise him! If he doesn't stop, close his mouth with your hand, just wrapping your fingers around his muzzle as you tell him again to be quiet. When he stops, praise him.

Many dogs will learn the word "quiet" with repeated training like this. Some dogs are a little more persistent, more protective, or just like to bark. With these dogs, the correction needs to be a little stronger. Take a squirt bottle and put about a half-inch of white vinegar in the bottom. Fill the remainder of the squirt bottle with water.

> Luckily, Boxers are not normally problem barkers, although when they do bark, their bark can be very loud!

Squirt the mixture on the palm of your hand and smell it. There should be just a whiff of vinegar smell—not strong—just enough so you know some vinegar is there. If it's stronger, dilute it with more water.

This time, when the dog charges the door after the doorbell, follow him, and very quietly say, "Rover, quiet!" If he stops barking, fine; praise him. If he doesn't, squirt a mist of the vinegar water toward his nose, but be sure to keep it out of his eyes. He will smell the vinegar and, because he has such a finely tuned nose, will not like it. He will stop barking, back off, and lick the water off his nose. Praise him for being quiet! The squirt bottle

Bark Collars

There are several different types of bark control collars on the market. There are some that give the dog an electric shock or jolt when he barks, some that make a high-pitched sound, and one that gives a squirt of citronella when the dog barks. The citronella collar works on the same concept as the vinegar/water squirt bottle; the smell is annoying enough to the dog to make him stop what he's doing. This is the collar I generally recommend; it is effective for most dogs and a humane training tool.

works as an interruption because it can stop the behavior (the barking) without giving him a harsh correction.

Use the same training techniques (verbal correction, collar, closing the muzzle, or squirt bottle) to teach your dog to listen to your Quiet command around the house. When he's reliable there, then move the training outside. If he barks at the gate when kids are playing out front, go out front (out of your dog's sight) and be prepared to correct him as soon as he barks. Always, of course, praise him when he's quiet.

No Begging

There is no reason for any dog to beg while you're eating; some dogs are very aware of food, however, and begging for scraps or a dropped tidbit is normal behavior for the dog. Begging is a bad habit because it usually escalates. The dog may start by hiding under the table waiting for a tidbit to fall, but quickly moves to laying his head in your lap hoping to catch the tidbit before it hits the floor. It can lead to stealing food from the children's hands or sneaking food off the table or counters.

Begging is relatively easy to solve. Later in this chapter, you'll learn how to teach the Down-Stay command. Once your Boxer has mastered the Down-Stay, use this to make him hold his position while people are eating. I don't like to exile the dog to the backyard—that just creates more frustration—but by having the dog lay down in a corner of the room, out from underfoot and away from the table, the dog can learn to be

Teach your dog to hold a Down–Stay while you're eating. He will learn that he gets to eat when you are finished so he must be patient.

still, control himself, and wait. When everyone has finished eating, the dog can then be given a treat *in his bowl* away from the table.

When you first begin this training, make sure you use the leash and collar on the dog because if the dog has been doing some begging, he is not going to want to give it up. Before you sit at the table, have him do a Down-Stay and drop his leash next to him. When the dog gets up from the Down (which he will probably do!), tell him "No!" and put him back in the Down-Stay at the same place where you originally left him. (Don't let him crawl across the dining-room floor!) Your first meal under this new regime will probably require several corrections, but be persistent. After all, you're teaching a new behavior and breaking a highly rewarding bad habit.

No Biting!

Dogs have received a lot of bad press lately, especially regarding dog-bite situations. Every time a dog bite ends up on the evening news, legislators introduce another anti-dog bill. It is now illegal to own certain breeds of dogs in some parts of the United States. England has outlawed some breeds of dogs, as have other countries and Boxers have often been included in these bans. Dog owners should be very frightened by this—our ability to own a specific breed of dog is being curtailed.

All dog owners should take training very seriously. All it takes is one bite and your dog could be taken from you and euthanized—plain and simple.

A dog bite is legally defined as an incident in which the dog's teeth touch skin. Breaking the skin is not necessary nor are puncture wounds. If the dog touches skin with an open mouth, that is a dog bite. Vicious intent is not required, either. If your dog is in the backyard with the kids and grabs the neighbor's son with his teeth, it's a dog bite, even if the dog just wanted to be a part of the play.

> It's important to teach all dogs that teeth are not allowed to touch skin—ever!

It's important to teach all dogs that teeth are not allowed to touch skin—ever! That means the dog is not to grab at your hand when he wants you to do something; nor is he to protest (with his teeth) when you take something away from him. He should not use his mouth when you play with him; no grabbing your arm or pant leg. To keep your dog safe, simply do not ever allow him to touch teeth to skin no matter what the circumstances.

It's easy for young puppies to learn not to use their mouth. Each and every time the puppy grabs skin or clothes, tell him "No bite!" in a deep tone of voice, and take your hand away. If he does it during games, simply stand up and end the game. If he does bite hard, say "Ouch!" in a high-pitched, hurt tone of voice, being very dramatic. Then tell the puppy "No bite!"

No Wrestling or Tug-of-War!

For many boys and men, in particular, one of the favorite games to play with the family dog is wrestling. The owner and dog get down on the floor and roll around, pinning each other and having a great time. Most dogs and their male owners enjoy the game.

Another game that most dogs love is tug-of-war. Your dog has one end of a toy (or something of yours, such as a shoe) and you have the other end. Your dog may think it's a game, but you may not, especially if you're trying to get your shoe back!

Unfortunately, although these are often your dog's favorite games, they are not always good games for dogs. If you have a dog with a tendency to use his mouth (and Boxers, as a breed, have this tendency)—to grab and hold on—wrestling and tug-of-war both reinforce that tendency. In other words, these games teach the dog that he can use his mouth on people. This is a bad lesson for the dog to learn.

If the puppy is persistent and keeps trying to use his mouth, take hold of him by his buckle collar with one hand and close his mouth with the other hand as you give him a verbal correction. Do not let go until he accepts the correction. If he struggles and fights you, simply sit down on the floor and hold him on your lap or between your legs until he relaxes. If you let go too soon, he will simply turn and try to get you again.

Older puppies or adult Boxers who have been allowed to use their mouth will have a little harder time changing this bad habit. Again, you must let the dog know each and every time he does it that it is no longer acceptable. Tell him "No bite!" and take your hand away. End the games if he does it during play. Don't let him mouth you while you're grooming him, petting him, or trimming his toenails. Be consistent and make sure other family members are, too.

Time-Out!

If your puppy throws a temper tantrum when you correct him—that is, he throws himself around and acts like a wild animal—simply take him back to his crate, put him in, and close the door behind him. Don't yell at him or scold. Just put him away and give him a 15- or 20-minute time-out. This gives him a chance to relax and you a chance to take a deep breath. Most puppies will throw a temper tantrum at some point during puppyhood, but you don't want to give in to that kind of behavior. Set the kitchen timer and let him out in 15 or 20 minutes.

If your dog seems intent on mouthing you, or if you have a bad feeling that your Boxer may actually bite you one day, call a professional trainer or behaviorist for help. Don't wait until a bite has already happened. Get help if you feel that you simply cannot control the situations in which your dog may want to use his mouth (or teeth).

Where to Dig (And Where Not to!)

Dogs dig for a number of reasons, all of which are natural and normal to the dog. Your Boxer may think the dirt smells good after a rain or after the sprinklers have been on. Perhaps you have a gopher or mole and he wants to investigate this intruder. If the weather is hot, he may want to dig down to some cool earth to lay in. Your dog has no idea why you are so upset about digging; the concept of a smooth, green lawn with no holes in it is beyond your dog's comprehension!

Since digging is so natural, it's a good idea to give your dog a place where he can dig. If there is a particular spot he really likes, perhaps in a corner behind the garage or next to the back porch, let him have that spot. Frame it off with wood if you want, or with bricks. Dig it up even more, so it's nice and soft, then bury and partially bury some dog toys and treats. Invite him to dig there.

In the rest of your yard, fill his holes and sprinkle some grass seed over them. If there are a couple of holes that he has dug up repeatedly, fill the holes, spread some hardware cloth (wire mesh) over them, and anchor it down. Let the grass grow up through this mesh; you can leave it permanently if it's anchored well enough. If your dog tries to dig his hole again, he will hit the wire mesh. He won't be able to dig and the wire mesh won't feel good on his pads.

If you catch the dog in the act of digging, you can correct him as you would for any other misbehavior—but don't count on catching him. Most dogs seem to dig when they are alone, usually in the morning just after their owner leaves for work. A strenuous morning run or a good game of catch might alleviate the digging problem; it's worth a try!

Destructive Chewing

As with many other undesirable activities, chewing on things is a natural behavior for puppies. Your Boxer puppy started chewing to relieve the discomfort of teething, but probably quickly discovered that chewing was fun. It gave him something to do when he was bored; after all, if he chewed the corner off a cushion and shook it, stuffing would go flying everywhere. What fun!

Unfortunately for your dog, chewing can be destructive and costly so it is a behavior that needs to be controlled. Notice I didn't say "stopped"—I said "controlled." Your puppy needs to be able to chew, so you need to teach him what to chew on and prevent him from destructive chewing.

Too Many Toys?

If your dog is a chewer, don't try to change his behavior by giving him lots of toys. Too many toys may give him the idea that everything is his and that he can chew on everything! Instead, just give him two or three toys at a time. If you like getting him toys, that's fine; rotate them. On Monday, give him a rawhide, a squeaky toy, and a Kong toy. On Tuesday, you can give him a new rawhide, a rope tug toy, and a tennis ball. By rotating the toys, you can keep him interested in them, but at the same time, you aren't overwhelming him with too many toys.

As with the other problems we've discussed, prevention is important. Close closet doors, make sure shoes and dirty clothes are put away, and have the kids put away their toys. Don't let your Boxer have free run of the house until he is grown up and totally reliable. Keep him close to you and prevent him from wandering away. When he picks up something he shouldn't have, take it away from him as you let him know that was wrong, "No! That's mine!" Then hand him one of his toys, "Here, this is yours!"

When your dog chooses to pick up one of his toys on his own, praise him! Tell him what a smart dog he is and how proud you are of him! Really go overboard. When he learns that this is a good choice, he will be more likely to repeat that later.

On the other hand, if you discover that he has chewed something up when you weren't around, don't do anything. After the fact, corrections don't work.

Other Undesirable Behaviors

Boxers are usually pretty good dogs. Unlike some other breeds, their owners don't have to deal with too many problem behaviors.

The common problems faced by most Boxer owners (especially the owners of young Boxers) are rowdy behavior, lack of self-control, and jumping on people. Training can help all three of these problems, and maturity (combined with training) will help the first two.

If your Boxer has any other behavior problems not covered above, you can approach them using the same methods. What is your dog doing? When does he do it? Why does he do it? Does he need more training? More exercise? Can you catch him in the act so that you can teach him? Can you set him up so that you can catch him in the act? If you can't catch him in the act, can you prevent it from happening?

If you are unable to solve behavior problems, don't hesitate to call a reputable trainer or behaviorist for some help. Ask your veterinarian to recommend someone.

House-Training

Earlier, I said that a crate is a wonderful training tool to help you house-train your puppy. Puppies are born with an instinct to keep their bed clean and toddle away from their bed as soon as they are able. A crate builds on that instinct. When the puppy is confined to the crate during the night, the puppy can develop greater bowel and bladder control. Of course, that means you must let the puppy out of the crate and get him outside when he cries to be let out.

Puppies who have been purchased from a pet store are often harder to house-train than other puppies, often because the puppy has had to learn to relieve himself in his cage at the pet store. His instinct to get away from his bed was lost because he had no alternative.

Older puppies and adult Boxers can still be introduced to a crate even if they were never in one as a puppy. The process is the same. (Review the earlier section on how to teach the dog to use the crate.)

House-Training Guidelines

Using a crate is not all that needs to be done to house-train a baby puppy, older puppy, or adult Boxer. House-training is primarily a matter of taking the dog outside when he needs to go, making sure he does relieve himself, teaching him a word, and then restricting his freedom in the house until he is reliably house-trained.

Just sending the dog outside when he needs to go won't work. If you just open the door and shove the dog outside, how do you know that he has relieved himself when you let him in a half an hour later? He may have spent that half-hour hunting for a gopher! You need to go outside with your dog. When you take him out and he sniffs the ground, tell him "Go potty!" (or whatever command you wish to use). When he does what he needs to do, praise him, "Good boy to go potty!"

Once he's done what needs to be done, take him back inside but don't let him have free run of the house. Put up baby gates or close doors so that you can restrict his activities. Do not consider him house-trained for at least six to eight months. If he has no accidents, it just means you're doing everything right!

One of the most common mistakes dog owners make in regard to house-training is giving the puppy (or dog) too much freedom too soon. Many dogs don't want to take the time to go outside to relieve themselves, especially if their family is inside. The puppy will, instead, go hide behind a sofa, or wander off to a

House-Training Timetable

Your dog will need to relieve herself after:

○ Each meal

○ Drinking water

○ Playtime

○ Waking up from a nap

○ Every two to three hours in between

Alert: When you see the puppy sniffing the floor and circling, grab her quick and get her outside!

back bedroom and relieve himself there. You may not find the "accident" for hours and then it's much too late to do anything about it. By restricting the puppy's freedom to the room where you are, you can keep an eye on him and the puppy will be less likely to have an accident.

When Accidents Happen

If you catch the puppy in the act of relieving himself—it's still happening—you can let him know he made a mistake. Tell him "Oh no! Bad boy!" and take him outside. If you find a puddle, however, don't scold him. It's too late.

Keep in mind when you're teaching the puppy that he has to relieve himself, having a bowel movement or emptying his bladder is not wrong. If he does it in the house, the place is wrong, not the actual act of relieving himself. If the puppy misunderstands you or if you convey the wrong message and the puppy believes that urination and defecation are wrong, he will no longer relieve himself in front of you and will become sneaky about it. He will

Ask to Go Outside

Barking dogs cause many neighborhood complaints so teaching a dog to bark when he needs to go outside can be counterproductive. Your dog needs some way to tell you he wants to go outside, however, so teach him to ring some bells instead.

Go to a craft store and get two or three bells (each about two inches across). Hang them from the doorknob or handle where you want the dog to ask to go outside. Make sure they hang at your dog's nose level. Cut some hot dogs in tiny pieces. Rub one bell with the hot dog and then invite your dog to lick it. When he licks the bell and it rings, open the door quickly, invite your dog outside, and then give him a piece of hot dog as you praise him, "Good boy to ask to go outside!"

Repeat this training three or four times per session for a few days. Then start using it (still with hot dogs) whenever your dog needs to go outside. When he starts ringing the bell on his own, make sure you hear the bells and praise him enthusiastically!

sneak to a back bedroom, or will go behind the sofa. He may hold it for hours when you're nearby and then when his bladder is ready to burst, he will go somewhere that is inappropriate.

You can make sure you convey the correct message by going outside with him and praising him when he relieves himself outside, restricting his freedom inside, and correcting only those accidents that you catch happening.

Five Basic Obedience Commands

Sit

When your Boxer learns to sit, he also learns to control himself and his actions. Once he knows how to sit on command, you can

Hold a treat in your hand and let your dog sniff it. Then take the treat up and back over his head. As his head comes up, his hips will go down.

prevent him from jumping on people, you can feed him without him knocking the food bowl out of your hands, and you can get his attention to have him do other things. This is an important lesson for most bouncy young Boxers.

There are several ways to teach any dog to sit and any method is right if it works. The easiest way is to shape the dog into the position you want as you tell him the word. Have your Boxer on-leash, and hold the leash in your right hand. Place your right hand on the front of your Boxer's neck, under his chin. Slide your left hand down his back and tuck his hips under as your right hand pushes up and back. (Think of a teeter-totter—up

When your dog sits and his hips are on the ground, praise him.

and back at the front and down in the rear.) At the same time, tell your dog "Rover, sit!" When he sits, praise him.

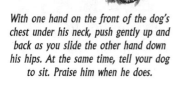

With one hand on the front of the dog's chest under his neck, push gently up and back as you slide the other hand down his hips. At the same time, tell your dog to sit. Praise him when he does.

Down

When combined with the Stay command, the Down command teaches your Boxer to be still for gradually increased lengths of time.

You can have him do a Down-Stay at your feet in the evening when you would like some peace and quiet. You can have him Down-Stay when guests come over so he isn't pestering them. He can also do a Down-Stay in a corner of the dining room so he isn't begging under the table. If you drop a glass on the kitchen floor and it shatters, you can tell your dog to Down-Stay right where he is so he doesn't walk in and cut his feet. The Down-Stay is a highly useful command.

Have your dog sit and then show him a treat. Tell him to lie down as you take the treat from his nose down to the ground in front of his paws.

Start by having your dog sit. Once he's sitting, show him a treat in your right hand. As you tell him "Rover, down!" move the treat from his nose to the ground right in front of his toes. As he moves down, rest your left hand on his shoulder. If he tries to pop back up, the left

As your dog lies down, praise him.

hand can help him stay down. Once he's down, praise him and give him the treat.

Stay

You want your dog to understand that Stay means hold still. Use the Stay command when your dog is sitting or lying down. In either case, it tells your dog to remain in that position until you tell him he can move.

If your dog doesn't lie down for the treat, just scoop his front legs out from under him and gently lay him down. Praise him even though you're helping him do it.

Start by having your dog sit by your left side. Use one hand to make the Stay signal, an open palm in front of your dog's nose, as you tell him "Rover, stay!" At the same time, exert a little pressure backward (toward his tail) on the leash so the leash helps him remain in place rather than move forward. When you're comfortable your dog isn't going to move, release the pressure on the leash and step away. After a few seconds, go back to your dog, pet him and praise him.

As he learns the command, you can *gradually* increase the time and distance between you for the Stay. For example, for the first few days, take one step away and have him Stay for 10 seconds. Later that week, take two to three steps away and have him Stay for 20 seconds. Increase the time and the distance very gradually. If your dog makes quite a few mistakes, that's a sign you are progressing too quickly. Make your increments smaller.

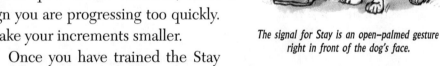

The signal for Stay is an open–palmed gesture right in front of the dog's face.

Once you have trained the Stay with the Sit, introduce the Stay with the Down. Since your dog is more comfortable lying down and you've already taught the Stay, he should be able to hold the Down-Stay for longer periods of time. Again, though, if your dog is making a lot of mistakes, don't increase the time and distance quite so rapidly—slow down.

Walk Nicely on the Leash

Taking your Boxer for a walk should be a pleasurable experience. I enjoy walking my dogs; we visit with neighbors, watch the herons down in the riverbed, and stop to sniff the spring flowers. Our walks are enjoyable because my dogs are well behaved in public. They have learned their social manners and do not jump on people or bark at other dogs—nor do they pull on the leash! A walk is no fun for you or your dog when he's got the leash so tight your arm hurts and he's choking himself. Your dog needs to learn to pay attention to you and to treat the leash as something fragile.

Start by hooking the leash to your dog. Have some really good dog treats in one hand and hold the end of the leash in the other hand. Show your dog the treats and back away from him, encouraging him to follow you.

Use a treat and your happy verbal praise to encourage the dog to follow you on the leash as you back away from him. Praise him when he follows you.

When he does, praise him. If he doesn't follow you or doesn't pay attention, show him the treat again and back away. If he is very distracted and doesn't seem motivated by the treats, try using a squeaky toy or different treats.

If your dog still wants to fight the leash or wants to ignore you, continue with the treats and backing away, but this time when he ignores you, use the leash to give a snap and release correction with the collar. A snap and release is like the bounce of a tennis ball, snap to pull the leash tight very quickly and release to let off the leash tension. The

When your dog is following you nicely, turn so that the both of you are walking forward together. Keep a treat handy to pop in front of his nose should he get distracted. Praise him.

force of the snap should be only as much to get the dog's attention and *no more*. When he reacts to the snap by looking at you, praise him, show him the treat, and encourage him to follow you.

When you can, back up and your Boxer will follow you; then, as you're walking, turn so that you're walking forward with your dog walking close to your left side. If he pulls ahead, let him go as you hold on to the leash and back away. When he hits the end of the leash, act surprised, "Wow! How did that happen?" and continue walking. Show him that when he walks with you and pays attention to you, good things (praise and treats) happen, but when he pulls ahead, he may get a leash correction as well as a verbal reprimand.

Come

Life is much easier when your dog comes when you call him. Daily life is much calmer when you don't have to chase your dog all over the house to put him outside and when you don't have to worry about the dog dashing through the open door to play keep-away with the neighborhood kids.

To teach the Come, put your dog on-leash and have his box of dog treats in one hand. Shake the box of dog treats, tell your dog "Rover, come!" and back away from him. When he follows you, praise him and give him a treat. You are using a sound stimulus (the box of dog treats) to make him pay more attention to your verbal command. Continue using the box of treats for as long as you need

Make sure your dog will come to you reliably all the time before you try it off–leash.

Training Collars

A variety of training collars is available to dog owners. Which one is right for your Boxer?

Buckle collar: This collar is used to keep identification on the dog and is often the first collar worn by puppies. This collar does not give the dog any correction at all and is useful simply for ID or for holding the dog.

Chain collar: Often called a choke chain, this collar works by constriction. When used properly in correction, it is snapped tight and then released. This gives the dog a quick snap and release (tight and then loose) correction and he understands you are trying to get his attention. When used incorrectly, the collar can tighten and constrict the dog's neck, possibly causing neck damage. As the collar works by constriction, it can choke the dog and should never be left on an unsupervised dog.

Prong or pinch collar: This collar looks like a medieval torture device, with its inward pointing prongs. The prongs are flat, however, and do not threaten the dog's skin. This collar does not choke the dog and works by making corrections feel uncomfortable. If you put it around your leg and give a snap and release correction, you can feel that it's uncomfortable but not painful. This collar works for strong, powerful dogs who are trying to overpower their owners.

Head halters: This collar is good for many breeds because it gives the owner more control without giving a hard correction. It should not be used on Boxers, however, because of the breed's short muzzle.

Each of these training tools has pros and cons. You may want to try a couple of different tools and see what works best for you and your dog.

them to create a good response to the Come command. With some dogs, that might even be months. Use the treats as long as you need to use them.

When your dog is responding well to the Come on-leash (usually very quickly), make up a long leash—20 to 30 feet of clothesline rope works well—and practice the same thing. Hook the long leash on your dog and take him out to play, letting the leash drag.

Call him to come, using the treats. If he comes, praise him and give him a treat. If he doesn't come, use the long line to make him come and praise him anyway—since you made him do it— but don't give him a treat.

Train the dog to come on-leash and on-long-leash for quite a while before trying it without a leash. Dogs learn very quickly that the rules are different off-leash! Make sure your dog will come to you reliably all the time before you try it off leash.

Training Is an Ongoing Process

Training your Boxer can be a lot of work. It requires that you pay attention to your dog and think about what your dog is doing. You may also need to make some changes around the house and in your daily routine. Other family members will have to cooperate and you may even need to ask some neighbors to help.

The payoff, however, is well worth all the effort. A well-trained dog who reliably behaves himself both at home and in public is a joy! When your dog behaves himself, he won't be exiled to the backyard and will, instead, be a part of the family. When your dog behaves himself, you will want to spend more time with him. A well-trained dog can be your friend, companion, and confidant.

A well–behaved dog is a joy to own and a pleasure to spend time with.

7

Grooming

If you consider yourself "grooming-ability challenged," you'll be happy to know that the Boxer is a wash-and-wear breed. Still, don't make the mistake of thinking you can neglect your Boxer's grooming. He needs to be brushed and bathed regularly to keep his coat gleaming with good health, and his teeth, ears, and nails need regular upkeep.

Whether you choose to do all of your dog's grooming yourself or opt to take your dog to a professional, you still need to learn the basics of grooming. Unless you plan on paying a professional to brush your dog every week, or every day during the shedding season, you'll want to acquire that skill. You'll also need to become comfortable with cleaning your dog's teeth, ears, and eyes, and clipping his nails to keep him looking and feeling his best.

Home Grooming Versus Professional Grooming

It's important that you help your puppy or adult dog get used to being handled from the first day you bring her home. This will make her comfortable with the entire grooming process and will make grooming go smoothly in the future for you and/or a professional groomer. Take five minutes every day to sit on the floor with your Boxer and examine her entire body, keeping up a running monologue of praise all the while. Look in her eyes, and check her ears. Open your dog's mouth and examine her teeth, lightly massaging your finger along her gum line. Next, run your hands along her body, paying extra attention to her feet. Pick up each paw, massage it, gently part the toes, and touch the nails. Many dogs become anxious when their nails are trimmed. For some dogs, anxious doesn't even begin to describe how they feel about the process. Ease your dog's fears, and make your job easier, by helping your pet get comfortable with the procedure from the start. This daily "puppy-pampering period" also will help you catch any coat or skin problems, such as fleas or suspicious lumps, early on.

If your puppy or adult dog was not handled often from birth (if she was a rescue dog, for example), you may need to work harder at getting her used to being touched. Gently manipulate any part of your Boxer's body about which she seems sensitive. The minute your dog calms down and stops resisting, praise her.

If you feel at ease grooming her on the floor, then stick with it. If you prefer to use a grooming table or plan on taking your dog to a professional (who will definitely use a table), you'll want to accustom her to being up off the ground. If you don't want to invest in a grooming table, you can put a rubber mat on top of a table that is a comfortable height or even on top of the clothes dryer, while your dog is still a puppy.

First, simply hold out the brush or currycomb and allow your pup to sniff it. If the puppy seems calm, you can try running the brush lightly through her fur. Although young puppies require little grooming, brushing for a few minutes each day acquaints them with the process. Your puppy may initially react to this strange sensation by biting at the brush. If you realize you are pulling or tugging her fur, you should, of course, stop what you're doing and proceed in a gentler manner. If you know you're not hurting the puppy and she's merely trying to assert herself, don't give in. Otherwise, she'll quickly learn that biting is a means of getting her own way. Instead, ignore the behavior and continue brushing.

> Although your puppy may be too young to know any commands, it is never too early to begin training.

If your Boxer continues to mouth the brush, calmly but firmly command "Off" or "Leave it." Don't shout; you don't want to scare the puppy into compliance. Although your puppy may be too young to know any commands, it is never too early to begin training. Your voice usually will distract your Boxer from what she's doing. As soon as she lets go of the brush, praise her. You also can offer her a treat for behaving, but don't over-reward, since that creates its own problems (she'll expect a treat every time she does what she's supposed to do).

What to Look for in a Groomer

The groomer you select for your Boxer should:

○ Possess certifiable knowledge and hands-on experience.

○ Treat clients with courtesy and listen to their concerns.

○ Handle each dog firmly but gently.

○ Show a genuine love of dogs.

○ Never allow puppies that are not fully vaccinated to be around older dogs.

The grooming facility should:

○ Be sterile and clean.

○ Have an adequate number of crates in all sizes to house its clients' dogs.

○ Have a special outside area for potty breaks.

Sometimes owners inadvertently make grooming difficult by trying too hard to make the experience fun for the dog. While grooming should be enjoyable, don't turn it into a play session. Don't let your Boxer play with the grooming equipment, or she'll never hold still for future grooming sessions.

Even if you usually take care of your dog's coat yourself, there may come a day when you want a professional to groom your Boxer. How do you go about finding a groomer?

First, ask other dog owners or canine professionals for their recommendations. Your breeder, veterinarian, or pet-sitter may know of good groomers in the area. Once you have a few names, visit the shops personally. Ask what kind of training the groomers have received. Have they graduated from a grooming course and/or apprenticed with an experienced groomer? Pay attention to how the staff treats the dogs. Are they confident, yet gentle, when they are working with difficult dogs? Are they patient with puppies or dogs who have never been groomed? If the groomers enjoy their job, chances are their upbeat attitude will rub off on their clients' dogs.

Check out the facility carefully. While the reception area will most likely be neat and tidy, you'll also want to be sure that the grooming area is clean and sterile. The staff should wash out and sanitize tubs after each dog's bath as well as sterilize crates between dogs.

If you must leave your dog for several hours beyond the time it takes to groom her (for example, if you leave her for the day, while you're at work), ask how often the groomer will take your Boxer out to relieve herself. A dog that is left in this new environment for hours on end may have an accident in her crate, causing her more stress and anxiety.

Once you decide on a shop, take your pet for an introductory appointment. Inform the groomer that this is your Boxer's first visit, and ask if he or she will spend a little extra time making sure your dog has a pleasant experience. If you have done your homework and spent time preparing your dog at home, this first grooming session and those that follow should be pleasurable for everyone. After all, what dog wouldn't like an occasional day at the spa?

Routine Care Every Boxer Needs

Let's get down to the basics. How often will your Boxer need to be groomed? What equipment do you need? And just how do you go about convincing a Boxer he needs a bath when he has other ideas in mind?

Brushing

The Boxer has a dense, short coat that is fairly simple to care for. While the breed does shed substantially throughout the year, it sheds most heavily during the spring and fall. You should brush your Boxer for 15 to 30 minutes at least once a week year-round, but increase to daily brushing during the shedding seasons. Boxer hair tends to stick to everything it comes in contact with, from your furniture and carpet to your clothing. It's much easier to brush your dog regularly and throw out the accumulated hair than to vacuum every surface in your house daily. Keep in mind, however, that no matter how often you brush your Boxer, you'll never be able to keep your home free of hair. As with most breeds, sharing your life with a Boxer means not getting upset over a stray hair floating across your kitchen table, and learning to coordinate your clothing—and your furniture—with the color of your dog!

When brushing your Boxer, first use a currycomb or natural bristle brush to loosen and remove dead hairs. The currycomb, which is made of hard rubber, should be used in a circular motion while the bristle brush should be used against the hair's natural lie. Once you have thoroughly brushed your dog, taking care around the sensitive areas including the ears and stomach, you can go over your dog's body with a hound glove. A hound glove is a mitt you wear on your hand that is covered with short fiber bristles or rubber nubs. "Pet" your dog with the glove all over his body—smoothing down his coat in the natural direction of his hair—this conditions your dog's coat by evenly distributing

> You should brush your Boxer for 15 to 30 minutes at least once a week year-round, but increase to daily brushing during the shedding seasons.

its natural oils. To make your Boxer's coat really shine, you can apply a lanolin coat conditioner after brushing and then buff with a chamois cloth. And don't forget to use your flea comb if you see evidence of those pesky critters.

Bathing

I mentioned brushing before bathing for two reasons. First, you'll brush your dog more often than you'll bathe him, so you need to feel comfortable with the different brushing tools and techniques your Boxer requires. In addition, you should always thoroughly brush your dog before you bathe him. Although a Boxer's fur won't mat during a bath like the coat of longer-haired dogs can, brushing your dog before a bath removes any excess hair that will just serve to clog your drain.

Where are you going to bathe your dog? Since the Boxer is a substantial-sized breed, some people like to bathe their Boxer outside during the summer. If you opt for outdoor bathing on a warm day and use a garden hose, run the hose through a window and attach it to an inside faucet so you can control the water temperature. Even on a hot day, icy cold water is too shocking for a bath. Never bathe your Boxer outdoors on a cold or cool day, and, no matter what the temperature, always allow him to dry in a draft-free area inside the house.

Another option is the do-it-yourself grooming tub, a service that an increasing number of grooming salons offer. You pay a nominal fee to bathe your dog yourself in a large, waist-high tub at their facilities. Not only does this save you from an aching back, but also the arrangement

Did You Know?

Nose prints can be used to identify dogs just as finger-prints are used to identify humans.

typically includes use of a quality shampoo, conditioner, towels, and a professional dryer at no extra cost.

If you don't live near a do-it-yourself grooming salon, your best option is your own bathtub. Before corralling your dog, gather all your supplies, including shampoo, conditioner, cotton balls, and lots of towels. Cover the bottom of your tub with a rubber mat and then place or entice your dog into the tub. He may resist at first, so it is important that you remain calm but assertive. If you are upbeat but show you won't stand for any nonsense, he'll realize you mean business and that baths are nothing to fear. If you're bathing your dog in the tub, ignore ringing doorbells, jangling phones, family squabbles, and other distractions. You must never leave your dog unattended, or he could hurt himself trying to jump out.

Clean out your Boxer's ears (see the section on ear cleaning to follow) and then put a cotton ball in each ear to keep out water. Rinse his coat with lukewarm water, starting at the rump and working backward to your dog's head. Cups of water just don't do the trick; invest in a spray attachment for your shower. Hold the nozzle close to his body to penetrate the fur and to keep the water from spraying and frightening him. Soak him thoroughly before applying shampoo.

Once your dog is wet, lather him well, and work the shampoo deep into his coat. Use only a high-quality canine shampoo. People shampoos contain a different pH factor than dog shampoos and are bad for your Boxer's coat. Make sure you lather every inch of your dog. Some owners forget that their dog is three-dimensional and only shampoo his back and the outside of his legs. Take extra care to clean the easy-to-miss groin, armpit, and anal areas. When washing your dog's head, be careful around his eyes. If you do get shampoo in them, flush them out immediately with clean water.

After giving your dog a sound lathering, rinse him well. Residual shampoo in your dog's coat can make his skin itchy and irritated. After he is fully rinsed, lather him up again. Two full shampoos will get him squeaky clean. Follow the final shampoo with a canine conditioner. Read the instructions to determine how long to leave in the conditioner. Many conditioners are applied like shampoos, while some can be sprayed in and left.

Once you are convinced you have removed all traces of shampoo and conditioner, turn off the water and grab a large towel. Towel-dry your Boxer by squeezing out excess water. Keep toweling until your dog is just damp (you may go through several towels). You can let your Boxer air-dry as long as you keep him inside in a warm, draft-free area. A dog can become chilled even on a hot day if a breeze is blowing. If you decide to blow-dry your dog with your own hair dryer, be sure to use the cool setting, since human dryers can easily burn a dog's skin. For a final touch, apply a finishing spray and polish with a chamois rub.

> **B**oxers, in general, require a bath every three to four months, or more often if they get dirty or develop doggie odor.

How often should you bathe your dog? Don't believe the old wives' tale that dogs should only be bathed once or twice a year. As long as you use a high-quality shampoo, dogs can be bathed regularly without losing essential oils. Boxers, in general, require a bath every three to four months, or more often if they get dirty or develop doggie odor.

Nail Clipping

While it is true that exercising on hard surfaces, as in long walks on pavement, wears down a dog's nails, all dogs still need their nails cut occasionally. You will need to clip your adult Boxer's nails every few weeks or whenever you hear them clicking on a hard surface such as your kitchen floor. Puppies' nails grow even more quickly and need to be trimmed every week. Long nails are not only unsightly, but also can interfere with your dog's movement. Nails that are allowed to grow unchecked can cause the toes to splay and can even begin to curl under and cut into a dog's pads. You should keep your dog's nails short, so that they rest just above the ground when he stands.

There are two basic types of nail clippers: the scissors and the guillotine. You also can use a nail grinder, but it may take some time to get your dog used to the noise. Grinding also is more time-consuming, and the friction of the grinder can burn your dog's foot if you work on one nail too long. The advantages of a nail grinder are that it leaves the nails smoother and prevents you from cutting into the quick—the blood vessel that runs through your dog's nails.

If you use scissors or guillotine clippers, keep them sharp and clean. Dull clippers won't make a clean cut, and rusty, dirty ones can infect your dog if you cut the quick and your pet bleeds. The objective when clipping nails is to trim as close to the quick as possible without accidentally nicking it. Dark nails are more difficult to cut than light-colored ones, since it is impossible to see the pink vein. Remove the dry-looking hook at the tip of the nail, cutting off small bits of nail at a time. As you cut the nail shorter, you'll notice it becomes softer and you'll see a small grayish-white dot under the nail, which is the end of the quick. When you reach this point, this nail is short enough; you can now move on to the next one. Keep in mind that the more often you trim, the shorter you can get the nail, since the quick actually recedes with frequent trimming. Cut each nail as quickly and cleanly as possible. Cutting slowly tends to pinch the nail and cause your dog discomfort.

If you accidentally cut the quick, don't panic. Apply a styptic powder to staunch the bleeding, and continue clipping the other nails. Don't stop and make a big fuss over your mistake, as it may make your dog even more apprehensive the next time you attempt to clip his nails.

When clipping your dog's nails, also check the pads of his feet and remove any pebbles or other small debris that may be lodged there. Check your dog's feet frequently during winter to make sure they're not irritated from road salt or ice. Petroleum jelly applied to the pads or canine booties can protect your Boxer's feet during cold months. If you notice your dog excessively biting at his paws, wash them thoroughly to keep him from ingesting road salt.

Ear Cleaning

During each grooming session, you (or your groomer) should check your Boxer's ears for irritation, such as mites or ear infections. The ear should be a pale pink and relatively odorless; a red, smelly ear or one with yellow, brown, or black debris usually indicates a problem. If you notice any of these conditions, see your veterinarian.

Did You Know?

The pom-pom cut used on Poodles was originally developed to increase the breed's swimming abilities as a retriever. The short haircut allowed for faster swimming but the pom-poms were left to keep the joints warm.

Boxer Grooming Essentials

○ Bristle brush

○ Currycomb

○ Hound glove

○ Chamois cloth

○ Flea comb

○ Quality dog shampoo and conditioner

○ Nail clippers or grinder

○ Styptic powder

○ Cotton balls

○ Ear cleaner

○ Dog toothbrush or thimble brush

○ Dog toothpaste

To maintain a healthy ear, wipe the flap out regularly with a cotton ball soaked with 3 percent hydrogen peroxide, light mineral oil, or a canine ear wash to remove any wax buildup (don't pour peroxide or mineral oil down the ear canal unless directed by a vet). Cropped ears tend to have fewer problems than natural ears because of the increased airflow, but all ears need regular attention regardless. Clean only the outer part of the ear; never reach into the ear canal or you could damage it. Also carefully pluck any stray hairs you find growing inside your Boxer's ears, as they can tickle and cause your dog to scratch and possibly injure his ear.

Tooth Care

One area of grooming that dog owners tend to overlook is dental care. Unhealthy teeth in dogs can lead to inflamed gums and tooth loss which, in turn, can make it painful or even impossible for a dog to eat. Long-neglected teeth can cause serious conditions such as heart or digestive problems. Your dog requires both at-home teeth brushing and veterinary dental care. Although you'll need to periodically take your dog to the vet for dental scalings and cleanings, brushing his teeth regularly will reduce the plaque buildup and help keep your pet healthy. Ideally, you should brush your dog's teeth every day or two, but even brushing only once a week or once a month will provide some benefits.

Your dog should already be used to you massaging his gums from your daily puppy-pampering sessions. To prepare him for his first teeth brushing, put some canine toothpaste on your finger and again push back your dog's lips and massage the teeth and gums. Once your dog accepts this, you can graduate to using a finger brush (which looks like a rubber thimble) or a dog toothbrush. Never use human toothpaste; it often contains foaming detergents that, if swallowed, can irritate a dog's stomach.

In addition to your Boxer's teeth, you'll need to regularly clean his muzzle. Food particles can get stuck in the muzzle's folds and cause infection if they aren't removed. Get in the habit of cleaning your dog's lips with a moistened towel after every meal. The wrinkles and folds of his face should also be wiped clean. If you take it upon yourself to wipe your dog's mouth, he'll also be less likely to use your jeans or your couch as a napkin!

Anal Gland Care

Every dog has two anal glands or sacs in the anal area. These sacs are sometimes called scent glands and may be a way dogs identify each other. This explains dogs' propensity for nose-to-rear sniffing. The anal sacs normally empty when the dog defecates, and the secretion that comes out is liquid and brownish. Anal

Conquering Grooming Disasters

No matter how well groomed your dog, there may be times when you run into an unforeseen grooming challenge. Here are some of the more common grooming problems you may encounter and the best ways to handle them.

Burrs Although romps through fields or wooded areas offer wonderful exercise for your dog, you may pay the price of burrs, seeds, twigs, or other things sticking to your dog. Fortunately, Boxers have short hair, but burrs are pretty stubborn and may still attach themselves to your dog. Try to remove them immediately with a fine-toothed comb. Mink oil conditioners, available at grooming shops or supply stores, can make the coat sleek, which makes it easier to remove burrs.

Skunk Spray You may have heard that tomato juice takes out the smell of skunk. Before you douse your dog, I have to tell you that this is not true. Tomato juice does not take the smell out, and it leaves you with a pinkish, sticky dog! Instead, use a high-quality skunk shampoo; your pet supply store or groomer should be able to recommend one. Brush your dog thoroughly before bathing him (plugging your nose if need be) since any dead, loose fur will only retain the smell and prevent the shampoo from penetrating all the way down to the skin. No matter what you use, your dog still may continue to smell slightly skunky every time he gets wet for several weeks or even months afterward.

Paint If your dog brushes against or rolls in latex paint, wash it out immediately, before it hardens. This paint, which is toxic, thankfully is water-soluble. If your dog gets into oil paint, you'll have to cut away the fur with paint on it. Never use paint thinner or turpentine on your dog, and never let your dog lick or chew at the paint.

Gum When your back is turned, your child decides to decorate your dog, and you discover a bright-pink wad of bubble gum stuck to your Boxer's fur! Don't rush to get out the scissors yet. First, try rubbing the gum with ice cubes to make it brittle. If the gum is stuck only to the ends of the hairs, you should be able to break or lift it off. If it's down in the coat, however, try using peanut butter as a solvent. If your dog steps in gum, try rubbing it with ice and then peeling it off the pads. If the gum is attached to the hair on the paw, cut it away.

Tar Hot tar can scald your dog. If your pet has come in contact with hot tar, apply cold water immediately and take him to your veterinarian. If your Boxer has a too-close encounter with cooled, sticky tar, apply ice cubes to harden the tar and then cut it away with scissors.

sacs can also be emptied after a sudden contraction of the anal sphincter, which might happen if the dog is frightened or upset.

In some dogs, the anal sacs fail to empty normally. Although this condition is most common in small breeds, it can happen to any dog. Soft stools, a small opening, or overactivity is usually the cause. When the sacs don't empty normally, they can become impacted, which may lead to infection. A dog with anal gland irritation or impaction may scoot on his rear, bite as if in pain, or whine.

Impaction is treated by expressing the glands, which is a messy and smelly job. Since large, healthy dogs generally don't suffer from impacted glands, you probably won't need to express your Boxer's anal glands unless directed by the vet.

8

Family Life

In This Chapter

○ Playtime
○ Playing Nicely with Children
○ Making Your Boxer a Good Neighbor
○ Traveling with and Boarding Your Dog

Above all else, the Boxer is a family dog. While proper nutrition, training, and veterinary care are vital to your dog's health and well-being, happily integrating your Boxer into your household is also important.

You know by now that the Boxer is an energetic dog, to say the least. What are the best ways to expend some of that energy, while at the same time strengthening the bond between you? Is the Boxer really as good with children as you've heard? What about other pets? Can the Boxer get along in close quarters with dogs, cats, and other animals? Since ill-behaved dogs are a leading cause of tension between neighbors, how can you ensure that your neighborhood will welcome your Boxer, instead of viewing him as a nuisance?

What about when you leave home to go on vacation? Should you bring your dog along? Should you find someone to watch your pet and, if so, how do you locate a suitable kennel or pet-sitter? By now your head may be spinning from all these vital questions. Don't worry—you'll find the answers here! By the end of this chapter, you'll know the best ways to make your Boxer a full-fledged member of the family.

> Playing with her owner keeps a Boxer both physically and mentally fit, and bonds her more closely to her special person.

Playtime

Every dog needs to play, for a number of reasons. Playing with her owner keeps a Boxer both physically and mentally fit, and bonds her more closely to her special person. You can "play" with your Boxer in many different ways, from taking long walks in the park to making up creative games or joining a competitive canine sport. Whatever you choose to do, you'll reap the rewards of a happy, healthy dog.

Exercise

Boxers are full of boundless energy. While they can adapt to any living accommodations, from a home in the country to a city apartment, they need adequate exercise to keep them fit and content. A bored, restless Boxer can quickly turn into a mischievous scoundrel, finding ways to occupy her time that may not meet with your approval—such as feathering the living room with throw-pillow stuffing or excavating doggie archaeological digs in the backyard.

A fenced yard provides a Boxer lots of opportunity to stretch her limbs. Many Boxers will tear around the yard on their own, providing great self-exercise. Judy Schrimpf of Port Jefferson Station, New York, says her Boxer, Brandy, makes the most of her backyard jaunts. "She'll be outside and I'll hear the thundering of her feet. I'll look outside and she's running herself like a racehorse. It's a really beautiful sight."

As much as your Boxer enjoys time on her own, however, she'll really love her outdoor time if you and your family join in the fun. While Boxers aren't retrievers, they still enjoy a good round of fetch. (Always use a ball that is too big for your dog to swallow.) Hide-and-seek is another fun game that can be played indoors or out, and uses your pet's mind as well as exercises her body. For a real energy depleter, invite over a friend or two with their dogs, and hold an impromptu doggie party. There's nothing like canine companionship to wear out your energetic pal.

While backyards are wonderful for exercise, your dog will also need opportunities to exercise off your property (on-leash, of course). If you live in the city and don't have access to a backyard, you'll need to be especially diligent about getting out and about with your pet.

While your Boxer is young, exercise her lightly to prevent strain on her growing bones. This means taking frequent walks of moderate length and avoiding the jarring motions of jogging or running until your pup reaches developmental maturity at about a year old. Also, until your Boxer is full grown, do not ask her to jump great heights, such as those required in agility (to follow) or higher levels of obedience.

As your dog matures, she will need more intense exercise. Long, brisk walks and hikes are great forms of exercise. Boxers also make good jogging or biking companions. Take care to train your Boxer how to run next to a bike, however, or she may make a sudden turn one day, setting the two of you on a collision course! Also, keep in mind the Boxer's susceptibility to heat stroke when exercising in warm weather. Due to her shortened muzzle, you need to watch your Boxer carefully for signs of overheating and avoid exercising her vigorously in the heat of a summer day.

Swimming is a great alternative for hot days when you don't want to risk a brisk jog. Swimming is an excellent form of exercise for Boxers of any age, because it does not stress the joints. To ensure that your Boxer enjoys her first dip, introduce her to water slowly. If she's forced to dive right in, she may get frightened and in the future avoid water all together. Instead, try to entice her with a flotation toy, throw a stick into the water, or wade into the water yourself and call her to you. Beware: Once you get your Boxer into the wet stuff, you might have a hard time getting her out! After your dog spends time in the water, always hose her off thoroughly to wash away chlorine from a pool or bacteria from a lake. Also, wipe her ears dry to ward off an ear infection.

Juli Bechard of Jacksonville, Florida, regards Boxers' ceaseless energy as one of their amazing attributes. Of her Boxer, Corey, she says: "One of the biggest positive points about my Boxer is his unending stamina. I feel this is important for the amount of work I do with him [obedience, agility, and search-and-rescue]. He never gets tired. I've seen him brain dead, hot and bored, but never tired. I take him  horseback riding with me, and he often comes in ahead of my horse and asking for more after 10- or 15-mile rides! I wish I had that kind of energy."

Advanced Obedience

Obedience work is a more structured means of "play." All dogs should receive some training to teach them proper manners and to enforce the pack structure of your household. Perhaps, however, after attending a class or two with your Boxer, you've found yourself practicing a little more than you thought you would. Perhaps you've started to show up early for class and hang around afterwards, asking the instructor for extra pointers. Maybe you even felt a little depressed on graduation night, wondering what you were going to do without your weekly obedience fix. Face it, you've been bitten by the obedience bug!

If you decide you'd like to try competitive obedience, you can pursue this sport at as low or as high a level as you wish. A good way to introduce both yourself and your dog to a low-key judging situation is to sign up your Boxer for a Canine Good Citizen (CGC) Test. Sponsored by the AKC and hosted by dog clubs around the country, this test measures your dog's reactions to 10 real-life situations and results in a pass/fail grade. Don't be upset if your dog doesn't pass the first time—this only indicates your Boxer needs more training in the areas marked. There are books devoted to the CGC test, and many dog-training clubs offer classes designed to prepare your dog for taking it.

The 10 parts of the test are:

○ **Accepting a friendly stranger.** Demonstrates that the dog allows a friendly stranger to approach and to speak to the dog's handler in a natural, everyday situation.

> All dogs should receive some training to teach them proper manners and to enforce the pack structure of your household.

- ○ **Sitting politely for petting.** Demonstrates that the dog allows a friendly stranger to touch her while she is out with her handler.
- ○ **Appearance and grooming.** Demonstrates that the dog welcomes being groomed and examined and permits a stranger, such as a veterinarian, groomer, or a friend of the owner, to do so.
- ○ **Out for a walk (walking on a loose leash).** Demonstrates that the handler is in control of the dog.
- ○ **Walking through a crowd.** Demonstrates that the dog can move about politely in pedestrian traffic and is under control in public places.
- ○ **Sit and Down on command/staying in place.** Demonstrates that the dog has received training, responds to the handler's Sit and Down commands, and remains in the place ordered by the handler.
- ○ **Come when called.** Demonstrates that the dog comes when summoned by the handler.
- ○ **Reaction to another dog.** Demonstrates that the dog can behave politely around other dogs.
- ○ **Reactions to distractions.** Demonstrates that the dog remains confident when faced with common distracting situations, such as the sudden closing of a door or the clatter of a dropped pan.
- ○ **Supervised separation.** Demonstrates that the dog maintains her training and good manners when left in the presence of a trusted person other than her handler.

If your dog passes the CGC test, she will receive a certificate stating that she is a Canine Good Citizen. This certificate makes a wonderful addition to your pet's scrapbook and/or can be framed and added to your Boxer brag wall (along with her puppy pictures and pedigree). It also can be used as a selling point when trying to rent an apartment or stay in a hotel room with your dog.

If you enjoyed the CGC test, just wait until your first real obedience trial! Dogs can earn a number of obedience titles through the AKC, with each title progressively more difficult to obtain. The first level of obedience is called Novice. This program requires your dog to demonstrate her prowess in heeling both on- and off-leash at different speeds through a particular pattern, coming when called (Recall), and holding a Sit for 1 minute and a Down for 3 minutes. In addition, during the Stand For Examination exercise, your Boxer needs to stand still and remain calm while the judge approaches and runs a hand over her. Each dog starts with a perfect score of 200 and loses points for flaws in her performance. To earn the title of Companion Dog (CD), your Boxer must earn a qualifying score of 170 points or more during three different trials under three different judges. Top-placing dogs receive award ribbons; dogs who fail to earn a top score but score over 170 still earn a leg toward their CDs and take home a qualifying-score ribbon. Although obedience trials are competitive, the greatest competition your dog faces is against herself.

The exercises for the second level of obedience, called Open, are slightly harder than those in novice training. Open trials require the dog to perform off-lead Heeling and long Sits and Downs with the handler out of sight. It also includes new exercises such as navigating a broad jump and two retrieves, including one over a jump. Dogs who obtain three qualifying scores under three different judges earn a Companion Dog Excellent (CDX) title.

The next obedience level, the Utility level, is even more difficult. The dog performs drills of increased complexity, such

Did You Know?

According to the American Animal Hospital Association, more than 40 percent of pet owners talk to their pets on the phone or through the answering machine.

as the signal exercise, in which she responds to Sit, Stand, Down, and Come commands at a distance from her handler, who can use only hand signals. In another Utility exercise, scent discrimination, the dog must pick an article with her handler's scent out of 10 similar articles. Other tests in this category include a directed retrieve, in which the dog must pick up one of three cotton gloves under her handler's direction, and a directed jump, in which she must leap both a solid jump and a bar jump at a distance, under her handler's command. At this level, dogs earn a Utility Dog (UD) title.

Once a dog obtains the Utility level of obedience prowess, she can go on to compete for Utility Dog Excellent (UDX) and Obedience Trial Championship (OTCH) titles. A dog who qualifies in both an Open and Utility class on the same day and repeats this feat 10 times is awarded a UDX. To earn an OTCH, a dog must place first in both Open and Utility, and then place first again in either Open or Utility. In addition, the dog must accumulate 100 points (with points based on the number of dogs competing), either by winning or placing second in Open or Utility.

Although Boxers have the reputation of being difficult to train, even stubborn, this isn't quite true. Boxers are extremely intelligent dogs who bore easily with the repetition used by many to teach obedience. To bring out the obedience star in your Boxer, you need to be creative and keep training fun.

Juli Bechard learned this the hard way with Corey. "I started working Corey with the basics the first day he came home at seven weeks. Walk on a leash, sit, shake, don't chew the couch, don't chew the kitty, etc. For the first six months of life, he was fantastic. (I don't think he knew he was a Boxer yet). Training was easy and fun. He Heeled beautifully, Sit and Stay was down to almost a science, Down was pretty, and he was obeying hand signals.

"Then, Boxerdom kicked in, and he obtained what I call 'Boxer Transient Deafness,' or BTD for short. In other words, occasionally he just goes deaf. Doesn't matter what I do, he can't hear me. Of course, he *can* hear the food bowl, the squeaky, or Molly, my other dog. Corey is my first Boxer, so I didn't realize this was a breed-specific genetic trait! I was extremely relieved to find out that it wasn't just Corey. Anyway, about this time, Corey 'quit' doing obedience for me. He would lag along and not pay attention.

"I started doing some reading, and decided to change the way I worked him, going to a strictly positive reinforcement training plan. I disposed of his choke chain and started working him with praise and food rewards. This worked a lot better. He was more consistent and easier to work with. The BTD wasn't quite as severe.

"Once we discovered agility training, I started using operant conditioning and clicker-type training. I don't use a clicker, but I do use a marker word, 'Good.'"

Corey has gone on to qualify for two legs of his CD (although, Juli admits, "by the skin of our teeth"). With Juli's latest training modification, teaching Corey to focus on watching her during heeling, she is hoping to clinch his title at his next trial.

"None of this is easy," Juli says wryly. "After all, Corey *is* a Boxer. But it is fun and interesting."

Sometimes, if you can find that right balance of obedience and Boxer creativity and penchant for performance, you can wind up with a true performer. If you find that your Boxer actually begins to crave the limelight of going in the ring, there is one final area of obedience that can use this showmanship to its best advantage. If you'd like to try obedience with a little flair, you might find that

Did You Know?

The Beatles song "Martha My Dear" was written by Paul McCartney about his sheepdog, Martha.

freestyle is for you and your canine performer. This relatively new addition to the world of competitive obedience requires dog/handler teams to perform intricately choreographed maneuvers set to music. Freestyle obedience resembles a canine-human dance—complete with costumed partners!

In addition to the AKC, other organizations, such as the United Kennel Club and the Canadian Kennel Club, offer obedience trials. (The appendix contains contact information for these organizations.)

Canine Sports

What if advanced obedience isn't for you, and you're looking for a different outlet for your dog's inquisitive mind and high energy? What if you enjoy obedience work, but would like to add another dimension to your dog's play? You can always try any of the many canine sports in which Boxers can compete and excel.

One such sport, agility, is a fast-paced and exciting activity that tests your Boxer's ability to navigate various obstacles, including tunnels, jumps, weave poles, A-frames, and teeter-totters. Agility is a progressive sport, in which each level requires the dog to conquer additional obstacles at a higher speed within an increasingly narrow time frame. If intense competition isn't for you, you can simply take an agility class for some great canine (and human!) exercise without ever competing in a trial. Several different organizations offer competitive agility events, each with their own rules and titles. The AKC, UKC, North American Dog Agility Council (NADAC), and the United States Dog Agility Association (USDAA) all offer agility competitions.

Juli and Corey have found their niche in agility, although as with any Boxer endeavor, it isn't always easy.

"In agility, he's gone through several phases. His first couple of months, Corey was the star pupil. He picked everything up very fast and was doing short sequences. After about two months, he developed what we agility people call 'zoomies.' He would leave me and race around doing whatever came to mind, with no regard for me or anyone else. I think it's a stress response that came on as I asked him to do more difficult work. Anyway, I treated the zoomies by catching him and crating him for a couple of minutes to let him cool down. I also worked on his attention ability and teaching him that I was more fun than anything else going on. His attention span has always been pretty short, so it hasn't been easy to convince him to stay focused on me, but he's getting much better.

"Once we actually entered a trial, I discovered many things, such as my dog can launch off the top of a six-foot A-frame without hurting himself, that he really likes tunnels, and if I get upset, he quits. Right now, that's our biggest hurdle. Corey knows what to do, but he's very sensitive to my attitude. He senses when I get upset, nervous, or frustrated and he reacts accordingly. He either completely shuts down and refuses to work by wandering off, or he gets frantic, running madly. I am learning how to handle this by keeping a positive attitude no matter what he does."

Many Boxers also excel at flyball, another fun, fast-paced canine sport in which two teams of dogs compete side by side against one another in a type of relay race. The first dog from each team races over four hurdles to a box at the end of her team's row. Each dog hits her respective box with her paw, which releases a tennis ball into the air. The dog must catch the ball, turn, and race back over the hurdles to the rest of her team. When she crosses the starting line, the next dog from her team is immediately released, and the race continues until all dogs from one team successfully complete the drill. Two teams usually compete in best three-out-of-five heats. Tournament competition can consist of double elimination or round robin. With double elimination, each team that loses two races is eliminated until only one team remains. In round robin, all teams play all rounds, and the team with the best record at the end of the day wins. Individual dogs accumulate points based on the accumulated times of their respective teams, earning them titles ranging from Flyball Dog (20 points) to Flyball Grand Champion (30,000 points). A game of speed and accuracy, flyball calls for dogs with single-minded determination.

If your Boxer loves to play ball and gets along well with other dogs (team cooperation is a must), she may find that flyball is the sport for her! Contact the North American Flyball Association for more information (see the appendix).

If, on the other hand, your Boxer is more motivated by sniffing out gophers in the yard than chasing a tennis ball, she may prefer tracking. Tracking measures a dog's ability to follow a scent and to find one or more scented articles along the trail. Progressive levels of tracking competition steadily increase the challenge by aging the scented trail from one to several hours and by laying the track over increasingly difficult terrain, such as concrete or gravel. The AKC and UKC both offer tracking titles.

> Tracking measures a dog's ability to follow a scent and to find one or more scented articles along the trail.

If your dog truly excels at tracking, and if you would like to work side by side with her in a volunteer position, you may want to check out search-and-rescue work. Although search-and-rescue is not a sport, but a charitable pursuit, similar to volunteer fire fighting, it builds skills and provides great exercise for your pet, not to mention the thrill of providing such an important service to people in need. Search-and-rescue teams endure intense training and must be ready at any moment to help search for missing children or victims of disasters, such as earthquakes and tornadoes. You and your dog should not enter into this pursuit lightly. If you can dedicate yourself to the effort and want to help others, however, you and your Boxer may be perfect for the job. For more information, contact the National Association for Search and Rescue (see the appendix).

Another sport in which Boxers excel is Schutzhund. Originating in the Boxer's home country of Germany, this sport initially tested the quality of potential German Shepherd Dog breeding stock. Schutzhund offers three levels of competition: novice (SchH I), intermediate (SchH II), and advanced (SchH III). Each level tests three areas of skill: tracking, obedience, and protection. While the tracking and obedience phases resemble those found in AKC trials, the protection aspect truly sets Schutzhund apart. During the protection phase, the dog searches six blinds for a planted "bad guy." The dog must not attack until the staged person attacks the dog or handler first. At that point, the dog must execute a directed but full-force attack on the helper's protective sleeve. When the handler issues the command "Out" (this command is sometimes given in German), the dog must immediately release the sleeve.

Although many people who do not understand the sport fear it, Schutzhund actually conditions dogs to have tremendous control and to attack only with provocation. Schutzhund not only teaches owners how to train, handle, and control their dogs, it also teaches dogs to understand human behavior as well as what does and does not constitute a threat. A Schutzhund-trained dog poses much less of a threat to a person who means no harm than an untrained dog of any breed does. However, Schutzhund training cannot "correct" a poor temperament. Dogs who are aggressive or excessively shy will be unable to do the work required of this sport. The United States Boxer Association, a club dedicated to promoting the Boxer as a working breed, can provide information on Schutzhund, as well as obedience and tracking (see the appendix). Many Boxers who show an aptitude for tracking and protection work go on to become police K9s.

Conformation showing is another sport that was developed to test breeding stock. It is still used to find the best specimens of a breed according to the breed standard. Breeders use conformation shows to help determine which of their dogs should be bred to pass on desirable characteristics. Although a newcomer to the world of purebred dogs might view conformation shows as merely doggie beauty contests, they really are much more than that. Of course, looks do matter in conformation events. However, since the actual competition consists of measuring the dog's characteristics against the breed standard, it takes into account movement and temperament as well as physical attributes. Obviously, no dog is perfect. Conformation shows reward the best representatives of the breed—those dogs who physically and mentally define the ideal Boxer. It is hoped these dogs will pass down their desirable characteristics to future generations.

Conformation showing takes a lot of hard work and dedication. If you would like to pursue this sport, it is vital for you to understand the breed inside and out. Talk to your Boxer's breeder to determine his or her interest in serving as your mentor.

Although not a sport, therapy work provides another pastime option for your Boxer. Therapy dogs visit nursing homes, hospitals, and other facilities to provide companionship to elderly, ill, and disabled individuals. Many Boxers who are rambunctious clowns at home take this job seriously, exhibiting a careful, calm demeanor when brought into nursing homes or children's hospitals. Nothing is more heartwarming than seeing your pet elicit giggles of delight in an ill child, or a great big bear hug from a frail elderly person.

Pet therapy is becoming increasingly prevalent as doctors and health administrators realize the positive impact animals have on people of all ages. Not only do animals help patients mentally, they also can help patients in physical therapy regain coordination via brushing a dog or holding a leash. Boxers, with their gentle yet playful manner, are perfect candidates for this type of work. If participating in therapy with your Boxer interests you, you can contact Therapy Dogs International, Therapy Dogs Incorporated, Delta Society, or other organizations that run pet-therapy programs (see the appendix). You also can contact nearby hospitals and nursing homes for information on local therapy groups.

Playing Nicely with Children

There's no doubt about it—Boxers love kids! They seem to revel in them, playing hard with older children, yet approaching infants and toddlers with an uncanny gentleness. A Boxer playing with children is a Boxer in heaven.

> A Boxer playing with children is a Boxer in heaven.

Boxers also are naturally protective of children. It's difficult to reprimand a child with a Boxer in the room; the minute you raise your voice, chances are the Boxer will step between you and the child. There are also numerous stories of Boxers protecting children from danger, such as pulling children back when they have wandered too close to a road or an open fire.

Although even adult Boxers who have never been around children seem to immediately warm up to children they are introduced to later in life, it's still a good idea to socialize your Boxer with kids while he's a puppy. Use nieces, nephews, or neighborhood children if you don't have any of your own—you can be sure your Boxer and the children will delight in the experience. This early socialization will help ensure that your Boxer will understand how to behave around children should you add any to your family down the road.

No matter how well your dog may behave with and know children, however, it is still important that you supervise all interaction between your Boxer and kids. A small child may—intentionally or unintentionally—mistreat your dog. In some instances, dogs have launched seemingly unprovoked attacks on small children that actually resulted from the child shoving a pencil deep into the dog's ear or some other atrocity. While Boxers may be willing to put up with almost anything, they should not be asked to endure such mistreatment.

Although most Boxers are gentle with children, keep in mind that this is a large, rambunctious breed that may need to be taught how to curtail its exuberant energy around small children. You can combat this by teaching your dog not to jump on people, and not to brush too closely to young children, which could easily knock them down. If you already have a Boxer in your life and find you are expecting a new human addition to the family, it is important to get your Boxer used to the sights, sounds, and smells of an infant before the baby even comes home. Buy a realistic-looking baby doll and carry it around for several weeks before the real baby arrives. Let your dog sniff the doll, but tell him "Easy" or "Gentle" and reward him only when he is calm. Once the baby is born but before he or she comes home from the hospital, a member of the family should bring home a piece of clothing with the baby's scent for the dog to examine.

After you've settled the new baby at home, make sure you take some time out of your hectic schedule to give your dog attention as well. Chances are your Boxer will want to be by your side while you bathe, feed, and change your baby and will happily stand guard if you need to leave the room for a moment. Again, never leave your Boxer and child alone for long periods of time.

Your Boxer will likely have a strong instinct to protect your child. At the same time, he must also respect your child's authority. Although it may seem impossible to convince a muscular Boxer that this teeny person is his alpha, it is not only possible, it is imperative. If you have an infant, practice obedience commands while holding your baby in your arms and facing the dog. In your Boxer's eyes, you will share your alpha status with the baby. Later, you can instruct your toddler to give commands while you stand behind him or her.

As your child grows, start assigning age-appropriate dog-care duties to him or her. For example, toddlers can help fill the water dish, and school-age children can tell the dog to Sit, then give him his dinner when he has complied. Older children and teenagers can groom their Boxer and walk him. (Remember your dog's considerable strength, though, and never let a child walk a dog he or she

Did You Know?

Chinese royalty considered their Pekingese dogs to be sacred and provided them with human wet nurses, servants, and guards to protect them from other dogs.

Ten Great Games
Kids Can Play with a Boxer

Children should avoid playing certain games with your Boxer, such as tug-of-war or wrestling, which can put your Boxer in a position of power, or chase games, which can lead to your child getting knocked down. To help you find more positive activities, here are 10 safe games that your child and your Boxer can enjoy together. Remember, though, that an adult must supervise all play.

Hide-and-Seek. Start teaching this game with your child "hiding" in plain view across the room, then gradually make the game more difficult by having him or her hide behind furniture or in another room. It helps for your dog to know your family members by name. For example, you can hold onto your dog while your child hides and then release him with an encouraging, "Go find Johnny!" Johnny can reward the dog's find with praise and/or treats.

Marco Polo. This game is similar to hide-and-seek, but adds audio clues. While your dog searches the house for your child, Johnny can "bark" or make another noise to help your Boxer find him. Many dogs will respond with a bark of their own, with the barking continuing back and forth until the dog finds the child. It's best to "bark" when the dog is in another part of the house, otherwise the game becomes too easy!

Freeze Tag. This game requires several children and one dog as players. The children call the dog using whatever verbal and body language they want, but then they must freeze before the dog gets close enough to touch them. The dog moves from child to child. Whereas younger children may not understand that they should stand still when the dog chases them, they understand how to freeze in a game setting.

Fetch or Frisbee. These games give a dog a great workout and also teach him that he must give up the ball or Frisbee in order for the game to continue. Make sure your children play this game properly, with the dog actually retrieving the object, rather than turning it into a game of keep-away, which undermines your child's authority.

Tricks. Teaching tricks—from shake to play dead and roll over—provides an excellent way for your child to bond with your dog as well as enforce his or her alpha position.

Chase the Flashlight. With this game, your child can wear out your dog while barely moving a muscle (which may or may not be a good thing!). The child simply shines a flashlight on the ground and quickly runs it back and forth, in circles or in figure eights while the dog chases the light. Just make sure your child lets your dog see that he or she is taking out and putting away this toy. Since flashlight beams have no smell, appear out of nowhere, and can never be caught, they have contributed to the neurosis of a Boxer or two! The hot new variation of this game uses laser toys to the same effect. As with flashlight beams, let your dog know when the laser game is starting and stopping, and take care never to shine the laser beam in his eyes.

Find the Toy. Help your child teach your dog to know his toys by name and to retrieve them on command. You can do this by associating a name with each toy as your dog picks it up. For example, if your dog picks up his tennis ball, say "Ball" and then praise him. When he picks up his stuffed mailman say "Mail-man," again followed with praise. If you tell him to get his mailman and he instead picks up his ball, say "Wrong. Get the mailman!" Reward a correct find.

Doggie Soccer. If your Boxer loves balls of all sizes, this may be the game for him. Your child will love whiling away a summer evening passing a soccer ball back and forth with a canine friend. As a forewarning, though, you may want to wipe off the ball before you pick it up!

Backyard Agility. With a few homemade jumps, a fabric tunnel from a toy store, and garden stakes pushed into the ground to form weave poles, you can make your own mini agility course. Of course, always keep your dog's safety in mind and make sure obstacles are sturdy and safe.

Red Light, Green Light. If your dog has learned to follow the obedience command Down while he is moving, you might want to try an adaptation of this old childhood favorite. The game is played with several children and your dog. One child turns his or her back and says "Come," and then "Red light, green light, one, two, three." On the count of three, the child turns to face the rest of the players who have been moving forward, and commands "Down," at which point the children must all freeze and the dog must drop in place. The game continues until one of the children or the dog reaches the child who is "it."

cannot control.) Your older child might even bond so closely with the dog that he or she may decide to take up a sport with your Boxer, such as obedience or agility. Junior Showmanship also offers a wonderful way for children and dogs to bond. This sport judges kids on their handling skills in a conformation show setting.

Now, it's time to cover training your children to treat your Boxer with respect. In general, Boxers are extremely tolerant of the pushing and pulling they endure at the hands of children. However, they should not be asked to endure abuse, even at the hands of an innocent child. Children must be taught from an early age to be gentle. Your children's friends must also be taught how to behave around your dog.

Shanna Neal of Kenna, West Virginia, has first-hand experience of the Boxer's love for children. "My Boxer, Bones, was about two when my grandson, Kevin, made his entrance into the world. Kevin immediately took to Bones and vice versa. Bones was very protective over this child and even growled once at my daughter because she played too rough with Kevin and he squealed.

"The most amazing thing about their relationship was that Bones actually taught my grandson how to walk. Kevin would hold onto Bones' docked tail and Bones would pull him to his feet. I had never seen a dog that would allow a child to hang on to his tail, let alone seek to have it abused. At any rate, Bones would slowly walk across the floor and Kevin would follow, hanging on to this little stub. If Kevin lost his balance and sat down, that dog would go and lick his face and then sit down with his back to Kevin and wait for him to grab that stub again before standing up and walking some more. I don't know how many times poor Bones had to allow me to wash 'stickies' off his tail, but I do know that when Kevin was able to walk on his own, Bones and he were inseparable."

Judy Schrimpf says that although she had been told Boxers were good with children, she was a little nervous when her daughter was born four years after Brandy came into their lives. But Brandy proved a natural, sleeping halfway between the stairway to Amanda's room and the front door when Judy would sneak out to do yard work while Amanda napped.

"When I would come in, she would give me this worried look, as if to say, 'How could you leave the baby like that?' She didn't understand that I had the baby monitor with me and could hear everything—she just knew that I had left."

Even though Brandy is now nine years old, she shows incredible patience, simply getting up and leaving the room if things get too rowdy. "Even when new baby Tyler accidentally falls on her and she yelps, she never snaps," says Judy.

Your Boxer likely will be game for anything your child wants to do, from romping in the yard to lying side by side on the sun-soaked grass watching the clouds go by. Dogs listen to your deepest secrets and never judge. If you properly train both your child and your dog, you can help them truly become best friends.

Boxers and Other Animals

While many Boxers get along with all manner of other animals, some have a difficult time adjusting to sharing the limelight, and the family affections, with other pets. Boxers love attention, and can get competitive over who gets to lie on the couch next to Dad, or who is going to try to crawl onto a visitor's lap. If there are dominance problems in your

> Boxers love attention, and can get competitive over who gets to lie on the couch next to Dad, or who is going to try to crawl onto a visitor's lap.

multi-dog household, it is especially important that you are clearly the leader.

Donna Murphy of Baldwinsville, New York, says she has owned several Boxer bitches who hated all other dogs, and a male who loved cats, dogs, and all manner of pets.

"From my experience, the bitches appear to be more dominant than the males in this breed, and while you may be able to have two males coexist in a household, two alpha bitches will literally try to kill one another." Less-dominant females get along much more easily.

Kim Monroe from Scottsdale, Arizona, says her two male Boxers had a number of Boxer friends and they all got along without incident. "I go to a park on the weekends here in Phoenix sometimes just to get my Boxer fix. There are about five Boxers and they all play and run and jump, and all the while their owners sit back and enjoy their enthusiasm. I have never seen a group of dogs not from the same family play so hard and get so excited to see their friends. It is quite a sight to see."

While some dogs are naturally more accepting of other pets, you can certainly help the process by introducing your Boxer to all types of animals while she is a puppy. Take her to a puppy class, introduce her to the neighbor's dog-friendly cat, and volunteer to keep the hamster from your child's class over a weekend. If your Boxer has frequent, positive experiences with all types of pets from an early age, she will be much more likely to live peaceably with a menagerie of animals as she gets older.

Making Your Boxer a Good Neighbor

You've taught your dog how to behave with your family pets and your children. Now, let's make friends with the rest of the neighborhood!

Holiday Hazards:
Keeping Your Boxer Safe and Healthy

Your Boxer is an important part of your family, and you no doubt will want him to join in holiday festivities. You must keep in mind, however, that some of the very touches that make the holidays special for us, such as rich food and tinsel decorations, can spell disaster for your pet.

If you are diligent about watching what your dog eats on a day-to-day basis, don't let this diligence slip during the holidays. Many foods we indulge in at these special times are hazardous for your dog. Chocolate can kill him, as can turkey bones if he ingests them. Other holiday foods, such as rich sauces, gravies, and spicy meats, may not pose as much danger to your pet, but they can give him a pretty bad stomachache (not to mention messy stool). Warn children and guests about the dangers of these foods to ensure that no one sneaks your pet a hazardous treat when you aren't looking. If you want to treat your dog to special snacks around the holidays, pick up holiday treats at a pet supply store or bake your own fun-shaped dog biscuits. Your Boxer will appreciate one of these treats just as much as he would your table food, and they won't compromise his health.

Another danger, especially around Christmas, is holiday decorations. The sparkle and shine of tinsel, garland, and Christmas tree ornaments might entice a curious Boxer. Tinsel and garland are not digestible and may cause serious intestinal blockage. Fragile glass ornaments can break and pierce your dog's mouth or paw. Many dogs are attracted to the tree and like to chew on it or to drink the water from the tree stand, both of which can make them sick. Your best bet is to block your dog's access to these hazards by putting up dog gates or by placing electrically charged mats (available through pet supply stores and catalogs) around the tree and other decorations.

The holidays are a fun, but hectic time for most people. Take some time out to go for a walk with your Boxer or just to snuggle with him in front of the fire. You'll both appreciate the break!

First, think about what could potentially turn your dog into a bad neighbor. Excessive noise is one thing that can upset neighbors. A dog who whines or barks for hours at a time is certainly a nuisance. To avoid this problem, do not leave your dog outside for hours on end. Although Boxers tend to be quiet dogs, noise problems can arise when a dog grows bored after being isolated in the backyard for long periods of time.

If your dog barks in the house when you leave, he is probably exhibiting separation anxiety. You can avoid this by following several steps. First, analyze your behavior both when you leave the dog and when you come home. Do you hug and kiss your Boxer and apologize for leaving, and then shower him with more guilty love when you return? If so, naturally your dog gets upset when you leave. It is like sandwiching a barren desert of loneliness between two oases of attention! Try instead to make your departures and reunions matter-of-fact. Give your Boxer a special toy such as a Kong stuffed with treats when you are about to go out the door and don't even say good-bye—slip out while he is busy investigating his goodie. When you come home, ignore your dog for the first few minutes. Take off your coat, change into comfortable clothes, or busy yourself in some other way, then calmly greet your dog. This will help to "take the edge off" and to make your absences easier for your dog to handle. Of course, if your dog still seems unduly anxious or you come home one day to a shredded couch, consult an animal behaviorist to deal with your Boxer's anxiety.

Another habit that may cause tense relations with your neighbors is a dog's penchant for roaming the neighborhood. Any dog who is off-leash can seem like a threat. Your dog may be the gentlest canine on Earth, but a neighbor is wise to assume the worst of a stray. Not only will your dog potentially scare your neighbors, he also may damage neighboring flowerbeds, gardens, and other property. Keep your dog on-leash during walks and confined behind a sturdy fence when in your backyard. Never chain your Boxer in your yard. It will provoke aggression in your dog (a by-product of being constantly jerked back when he attempts to protect his property), which will surely contribute to your Boxer's "bad neighbor" status.

Unruliness on walks gives your neighbors another reason to cross your dog off the block party invitation list. A dog who barks or lunges at every passerby is unpleasant to be around. Teach your Boxer to greet strangers calmly and to sit at corners to allow cars to pass by. Practicing obedience heeling, Sits, and Downs while on walks around the neighborhood can show people how well trained your dog really is.

Traveling with and Boarding Your Dog

A point will surely come when you will need to get away from it all and take a vacation. Now, here's the dilemma—do you take your four-legged best friend with you and make it an all-inclusive family affair, or do you let your Boxer take a vacation of his own, either at a boarding facility or at home with a sitter? Each of these options has its pros and cons, and each requires some investigating and forethought on your part.

First, let's look at the plus side of bringing your pet with you. If you're like some dog owners, a vacation just wouldn't be a vacation without your Boxer at your side. Even if you breathe a sigh of relief at the thought of a week

Did You Know?

Forty percent of dog and cat owners carry pictures of their pets in their wallets.

free of 6:00 A.M. dog walks, you may surprise yourself during vacation by waking at sunrise and taking a lonely early-morning stroll along the beach, all the while thinking how much your Boxer would enjoy this! If your Boxer is your constant companion, you may actually feel lost without him sleeping on the floor next to you or waking you up with a rough-tongued face wash. Dogs also are marvelous tools for meeting new people, which can provide lots of fun when you're visiting a place foreign to you. Another advantage to bringing your dog with you is that you won't have to deal with the problem of finding a suitable person to watch your Boxer.

Now, let's look at the negatives of traveling with canines. You may genuinely want a week free of dog walking, dog feeding, dog-poop scooping, and all the other responsibilities that go with dog ownership. That is not to say you love your dog any less, you just need a break. Another factor to consider is whether you plan to visit places that do not allow dogs, such as historic sites or museums. You may decide your Boxer would feel more relaxed and happier staying at home or in a boarding facility than being cooped up in a hotel room day after day (if the hotel will even allow it). Finally, travel itself can pose dangers to the health and safety of your pet, from overheating in a car stuck in holiday traffic to the myriad stresses and potential risks of air travel.

A good boarding facility can be an excellent place to leave your pet while you're out of town. A well-run facility will provide your dog with his own living space, which may include both indoor and outdoor runs. Some facilities will walk your dog a number of times each day and will make sure that your pet receives plenty of individual attention. Some of the more posh places that are cropping up around the country will even give your dog his own room, complete with a cozy bed, fun toys, soft music, or even dog videos to watch on TV!

The cons of boarding include the fact that you are entrusting your dog's care to complete strangers. If the boarding staff mistreats your dog in any way, he won't be able to tell you about it. If a facility isn't kept clean and sanitized, your dog could pick up parasites, kennel cough, or other health problems. In addition, some dogs just don't take well to kenneling and may become depressed and refuse to eat.

Dogs that don't thrive in a kennel situation are perfect candidates for the services of a pet sitter. This extends to puppies who are not yet fully vaccinated and to older dogs who don't adjust well to a change in routine. Of course, you might rely on neighbors, friends, and relatives to watch your dog. On the other hand, if you want a professional to take care of your Boxer in your absence, you may find that a pet sitter is right for you. Pet sitters will come to your house a few times a day (some may even stay overnight if you request it and they are available) to feed, water, and exercise your dog, sticking to his normal routine. Pet sitters also may perform small household tasks such as taking in mail and turning lights on and off. These personal touches not only make things more pleasant for your dog, but they also give your house a lived-in look, which may discourage break-ins (as does the fact that your large Boxer is at home).

What are the cons of pet sitters? They tend to cost more than boarding facilities, and their costs typically increase with the number of services you ask them to perform. In the case of a pet sitter, you're not only trusting a stranger to care for your dog, you're also giving a

Did You Know?

Millie, President Bush's English Springer Spaniel, earned over four times as much as her owner in 1991.

stranger access to your home. You should thoroughly check out a pet sitter before giving him or her a key. Finally, unless you've made plans for the sitter to stay at your house, your dog may spend many more hours alone than he is used to.

Traveling with Your Dog

If you have made the choice to bring your dog along on your trip, you should plan and prepare carefully for your dog's travel needs ahead of time.

Before You Leave Teaching your dog to behave well on a trip shouldn't start on the day you are leaving. In fact, if you want your Boxer to be a pleasurable travel companion, you must introduce him to travel when he is a puppy. First, you'll need to ensure that he is crate-trained. Crates provide the safest haven for your dog during car travel and are a necessity for air travel (unless a dog is a certified assistance dog for the blind or disabled).

Next, you'll want to gradually get him used to riding in a car. First, place him in the car in his crate or strapped in by a doggie seat belt. This will keep him safe in case of an accident, prevent him from climbing on you while you are trying to drive, and deter him from hanging his head out the window. Although a grinning Boxer with tongue flapping in the breeze may look like the picture of contentment, your dog could get hurt, or worse, from flying debris or a jutting tree branch. Once you've put your dog in the vehicle, turn on the car and speak to him calmly and encouragingly. If he remains relaxed, reward him with praise and possibly a treat. Then, turn off the car and let your Boxer out. Repeat this process for a few days. Once you're sure he is not frightened, take him for a short trip to a friend's house.

Keep everything upbeat and fun. Continue taking him on lots of short trips around the neighborhood or while you run errands.

Remember never to leave your dog alone in the car on a warm day. Even if the temperature is not threatening, don't leave a young or newly acquired dog alone in the car for more than a few minutes, because he may become frightened. If he does, you will take a few steps backward in your training and will need to gradually reacquaint him with the car. The more often you expose your dog to the car and the more fun you make car travel, the more willingly he'll accept longer trips later in life. The last thing you want is for every ride to be made for "business purposes;" that is, going to the vet!

Next, you'll need to plan your vacation. Although you may pride yourself on being spontaneous, when taking a trip with your dog, spontaneity is usually not the best course of action. There's nothing worse than driving around trying to find a hotel that accepts pets when you are tired and in a strange area. Be smart and call ahead to find a hotel at your destination that allows pets.

When traveling out of the country, find out from the U.S. Department of Agriculture Animal Plant Health Inspection Service (USDA APHIS Veterinary Services, www.aphis.usda.gov) whether the areas you're visiting impose any restrictions on importing animals. England and even Hawaii, for example, have a quarantine period that will probably convince you to leave your Boxer home for the trip. Begin this search 60 to 90 days before you travel to make sure you hve time to meet any restrictions imposed by the foreign country.

Traveling by Car Having a well-trained dog is important when traveling by car, but it is only one part of the equation. Before loading your Boxer into the car for a trip, first pack all his necessities. Remember to bring the following items:

○ Your dog's crate

○ Your dog's leash

○ Travel bowls for food and water (dog canteens are useful for hikes as well as car rides)

○ A supply of your dog's food (in case it is not available where you are traveling)

○ A thermos of water from home (to mix with the water at the vacation destination to prevent stomach upset)

○ Proof of vaccination, especially rabies

○ Medication and health records (if your dog has a medical condition)

○ A health certificate (if you're driving across the border; for example, between Canada and the United States)

○ Lots of plastic baggies and towels (paper and cloth) for cleaning muddy paws and drying wet coats

○ A basic first-aid kit

Grooming supplies may also come in handy. Also, make sure your Boxer is wearing a flat buckle collar (rather than a choke or prong collar, which could catch on something and strangle him) with his ID and rabies tags attached. The last thing you want is for your dog to become separated from you without any identification in a strange town. It's also a good idea to prepare for the worst by making up some lost dog flyers with a blank space in which to insert the phone number where you are staying.

While driving, stop every couple of hours to let your dog stretch his legs and relieve himself. If you are traveling in warm weather, monitor your Boxer to ensure that he does not overheat and use air conditioning if possible. Again—and this deserves repeating over and over—never leave a dog in a parked car during warm weather; the results could be fatal. If you are traveling during cold weather and want to leave your dog in the car for a short time, while you get something to eat, for instance, provide your Boxer with a blanket to snuggle in. Boxers have thin coats and can easily become chilled in an unheated car.

Traveling by Air Air travel is more complicated than traveling by car. Unfortunately, a Boxer is too large to ride in the passenger compartment under the seat in front of you (which is an option for smaller dogs). Unless your dog is a certified assistance dog, he will have to travel as freight in the cargo hold. You should book your dog's flight as far ahead as possible, since the airline may limit the number of animals it will carry, and try to schedule a nonstop flight. As each airline has its own pet policies, you'll need to ask for detailed information, in writing if possible. When calling airlines, inquire whether their cargo holds are temperature controlled. Temperatures in cargo bays can fluctuate to extremes, from the heat of sitting in the sun on the runway to the cold of flying tens of thousands of feet above the earth. Even if the temperature is controlled, try to avoid temperature stresses on your pet by planning summer flights for early morning or evening and winter flights for the afternoon.

> Again—and this deserves repeating over and over—never leave a dog in a parked car during warm weather; the results could be fatal.

Within ten days before flying, take your Boxer to the vet for a full examination and ask for a health certificate stating that your dog is in good health and cleared to fly. If you are worried that your dog will experience exceptional stress during the flight, ask your vet whether he or she recommends tranquilizers. Your vet may advise against them, because individual dogs react differently to tranquilizers, making the results difficult to predict. Also, ask the vet whether your dog needs any special vaccinations to prevent diseases specific to your vacation destination, such as against Lyme disease if you're traveling to an area with a heavy tick population.

Most vets recommend that you withhold food for four hours before a flight and withhold water for two (although you can substitute ice cubes).

Make sure your dog fully relieves himself before you put him in his crate. All airlines require that you use a sturdy, federally approved crate. The crate must latch securely but without locks (in case airline personnel need to remove your dog from his kennel); allow enough room for your Boxer to stand up, turn around, and lie down in; and provide air flow on three sides (four for international travel). You must also label the crate "live animal" as well as with your name, permanent address and phone number, and contact information for your destination. You will need to attach empty food and water bowls to the inside of the crate (airline personnel will fill them, if necessary). You must also fasten a plastic baggie filled with your dog's food to the top of the crate (so your dog can't reach it).

As with car travel, your dog should wear a flat buckle collar with ID and rabies tags. For your own peace of mind, in case of an emergency, you may want to remind flight attendants that your dog is on board.

Hotels and Campgrounds When traveling to a hotel or campground, call ahead to confirm that the facility allows pets. Many travel books list pet-friendly hotels, motels, bed and breakfasts, and campgrounds. The Automobile Association of America (AAA) is another good resource. If the hotel doesn't have a definite policy on pets, news that your dog is obedience-trained or has a Canine Good Citizen certificate may help sway policy in your direction. Never try to sneak your pet into a hotel or other establishment that doesn't permit dogs. Not only will you spend a stressful vacation trying not to get caught, if you are found out, your actions will probably guarantee that the no-pets policy will never change in pet owners' favor. If you and your dog are good ambassadors, showing that animals can be calm and well behaved in a hotel setting, you and others like you will help convince more hotels to allow dogs. If, on the other hand, your Boxer barks incessantly, relieves himself on the carpet, or chews up the nightstand, you may convince a hotel never again to allow pets.

When staying in a hotel that allows pets, always follow the rules. If they state no animals on the furniture, make sure your Boxer stays on the floor, whether or not that is your personal policy. Some hotels require you to crate your pet if you leave the room, while others stipulate that you must never leave pets alone in the room. This rule doesn't necessarily prevent you from participating in activities without your canine, however. Ask the hotel about local boarding kennels or doggie day care. Some attractions, such as Six Flags and certain Disney locations, also provide onsite kennels.

Some people prefer the personal attention of bed and breakfasts or the privacy of rented condominiums or vacation homes. Again, call ahead to make sure the owner or manager allows pets. Some bed and breakfasts forbid pets altogether, whereas others offer free dog-walking services and additional pet-friendly amenities. Condos and vacation houses, on the other hand, often require a pet deposit and a written contract spelling out the pet owner's liability for potential damage to the unit, if they allow pets at all.

Campgrounds usually allow dogs, but it is still best to call ahead to avoid disappointment. When they do allow dogs, campgrounds typically require that owners leash their dogs, pick up after them, and keep them from barking excessively. Some campgrounds also demand that owners never leave their dogs alone at the site. When camping, remember to bring along water from home to mix with local water, at least for the first few days. Also, check your Boxer regularly for signs of fleas and/or ticks.

Boarding Your Dog

Don't feel guilty if you decide not to take your Boxer on vacation with you. If you make the right arrangements, your dog may have so much fun, he won't even notice you're gone!

You can board your dog at either a veterinary facility or a private kennel. Veterinary boarding facilities are ideal for dogs with medical conditions or for senior dogs whose health is a concern. If your dog is familiar with the staff at your veterinary clinic, he may feel more comfortable staying there than at an unfamiliar kennel. Veterinary boarding facilities are usually smaller than most private kennels, which is a plus if your dog is uncomfortable surrounded by a lot of dogs he doesn't know. Services at vet facilities run the gamut, from offering simple runs that dogs are expected to use for exercise and elimination to scheduling individual walks, playtime, or even grooming.

Private kennels, too, offer a wide range of services, depending on the individual facility. Some expect dogs to remain confined to their runs, while others offer dog walks and supervised playtime with other dogs, while still others feature private doggie rooms and jam-packed days filled with training classes, agility obstacle courses, grooming sessions, and dog-biscuit snack breaks! Whatever amenities you are looking for, your chances are good of finding a kennel out there that offers them.

To find a private kennel, ask your veterinarian or dog-owning friends and relatives for recommendations. You also can call the American Boarding Kennel Association (ABKA) for member kennels in your area. The ABKA requires members to adhere to a code of ethics. (For contact information, see the appendix.)

Once you've found several kennels in the area that sound promising, make an appointment to visit them personally. You'll want to make sure the facility is clean and the staff seems friendly and attentive to the animals. The kennel staff should allow you to see the area where your dog will actually stay and not just a front waiting room. If the kennel staff refuses to let you fully inspect the premises, don't leave your dog there.

Whether dealing with a veterinary or private boarding facility, you should ask several questions before entrusting your dog to them. How often are the runs and other boarding areas sanitized? Can you provide your dog's own food to lessen the likelihood of stomach upset? Where will your dog spend his time? Will he remain confined to a run, or will he be taken for walks or given supervised playtime? Is the facility staffed 24 hours a day? What plans are in effect in case of an emergency? Does the facility work in conjunction with a local vet in the event of medical emergencies? (Regardless of the type of medical and emergency provisions the kennel provides, always leave your own vet's number with a kennel.) What are the facility's rates? Of course, you'll also need to ask whether an

Did You Know?

The saying "three dog night" is attributed to Australian Aborigines, who would sleep with three dogs (dingos, actually) to keep from freezing on cold nights.

opening exists for the dates you are planning to be away. Kennels tend to book up quickly during holidays and peak summer vacation times, so make your reservations as far in advance as possible.

If you are impressed with the facility, it wouldn't hurt to leave your dog there overnight for a trial run. This will allow you to judge his reaction to kenneling and will ease your mind when you take him in for a longer stay. It's also a good idea to leave an article of clothing that has your scent, such as a recently worn T-shirt or sweatshirt, to help your dog feel more comfortable.

Hiring a Pet Sitter

If you decide your dog doesn't take well to kenneling, or if you just want the personal touch and extra services a pet sitter provides, this is an excellent option. But don't choose just anyone. This person will have access to your house, so you need to exercise extra caution.

Again, ask your veterinarian or dog-owning friends for recommendations. The National Association of Professional Pet Sitters and Pet Sitters International also can help you in your search (see the appendix). Check to make sure any professional pet sitter you consider is licensed, bonded, and insured. During your initial phone call, explain what you are looking for and ask if the pet-sitter offers these services. Virtually all pet sitters will feed, water, walk, and play with your dog, but some also will water your plants, feed your goldfish, and perform other small tasks. Ask the sitter about his/her background and experience. Also ask for several personal references and call these people to ask about their experiences with the pet sitter.

Once you pick out a candidate, invite him or her over to meet your dog. Watch how the sitter interacts with your pet. Let the sitter take your Boxer for a walk around the block and play with him in the yard. Boxers can be strong willed and take advantage of people who are not assertive, so you want to be sure that your sitter can handle your dog and earn his respect.

Your sitter should offer a contract that clearly states the services rendered. He or she should display a friendly demeanor and obvious love of animals. The sitter should have a working relationship with a local vet in case of emergencies (although you should also provide your vet's number). Also make sure the sitter has worked out a contingency plan in case he or she cannot attend to your pet because of illness or another personal matter.

Take the sitter through your house and show him or her where you keep the dog food, cleaning supplies, treats, toys, and other pet necessities. Explain any peculiarities in your dog's behavior (for example, he walks on your right side instead of heeling on the left, or he is afraid of thunder). On the day you leave on vacation, make sure your house is fully stocked with dog food, treats, any medication your pet needs, cleaning supplies, and other essentials. Also, leave your veterinarian's number and contact numbers for your destination in a prominent place. It's a good idea to arrange for the sitter to arrive just as you are leaving so you can make sure your dog doesn't consider him or her an intruder. Then, walk out the door and enjoy your vacation. Don't hesitate to call once or twice (or more) during your trip—your pet sitter won't mind and you'll feel better hearing how well your dog is doing without you!

Neighbors and Friends and Relatives, Oh My!

Although these people are not professionals, they can make good dog sitters—or not. If you are considering asking a neighbor, friend, or relative to watch your pet, confirm that he or she has experience with dogs (another dog owner is preferred), is responsible, and gets along well with your Boxer. You'll want to use someone who will treat watching your pet as seriously as a professional would. Payment can consist of whatever is mutually agreeable, from money to a dinner out or reciprocal dog-watching when the other person goes on vacation.

As with a professional pet sitter, leave phone numbers for your vet and your destination in a prominent place, as well as general care instructions and an ample supply of food and other necessities.

9

A Lifetime of Love and Good Health

In This Chapter

○ Your Aging Boxer—What to Expect
○ How to Keep Your Older Dog Comfortable
○ Saying Goodbye

There's no doubt about it—your Boxer truly is your best friend. From the moment he skidded into your life on gangly puppy legs, you knew he would be a pal for life. He has shared in your happiness, bouncing with joy as only a Boxer can, and comforted you with soulful eyes and an understanding kiss when you were down. You feel that your friendship will last forever.

But lately, you've noticed that your dog's bounce is not quite as buoyant as it used to be. His eyes, while still as caring, are slightly clouded. A few gray hairs even grace his grinning muzzle, and you feel a tug at your heart. Your dog is getting older.

Sadly, we usually outlive our dogs, and we may have several dogs come and go in our lifetime. The only thing you can do is make sure that your dog receives the best nutrition, exercise, and veterinary care throughout his life and, equally important, that he knows each and every day how much you love him. And when the time comes, your dog will need you to have the courage to say goodbye.

Your Aging Boxer—What to Expect

Boxers live an average of eight to twelve years. They seem to have a short period of old age, staying active for most of their lives. But no matter how young and puppyish your Boxer still looks and acts, changes are going on in his body that prove time is marching on. Learning what to expect as your dog ages better equips you for keeping him healthy and content in his sunset years.

> Learning what to expect as your dog ages better equips you for keeping him healthy and content in his sunset years.

Age-Related Disorders

A number of health problems can occur with advanced age. As with all health issues, it is important to educate yourself about these disorders ahead of time so you will know what signs to look for and what to do to keep your dog as comfortable as possible.

Arthritis

Virtually all elderly dogs develop stiffness in their joints. As a result, your aging Boxer may struggle to get up from a nap, stumble and fall occasionally, or just seem to experience difficulty moving. Arthritis is a catchall term for a number of degenerative joint diseases.

Some recent advances have made all the difference in dogs' lives, allowing some dogs to live out more comfortably many more years, whereas a short time ago, they may have been euthanized. Ask your veterinarian about these new pharmaceuticals and nutraceuticals (foods with health benefits), and whether any of them might be a good option for your dog. As with many medications, some of the new drugs present side effects that, unfortunately, may offset their benefits. For some dogs, however, these medications (or supplements) truly are miracles. Many owners choose alternative medicines, such as acupuncture and chiropractic medicine, to treat their pet's arthritis in conjunction with or in place of conventional medicine.

In addition to treating the arthritis medically, you'll want to make some adjustments to your Boxer's environment to offset the effects of aging, such as ensuring that he doesn't catch drafts and that he eats a high-quality, well-balanced diet suited for older dogs. While exercise is still vital, it should be toned down to reflect your older Boxer's slower pace.

Obesity

In general, older dogs require fewer calories. They tend to exercise less than younger dogs, and if they continue to eat the same type and quantity of food as they did in their prime, they usually gain weight. Obesity in a Boxer not only is unattractive, but also can predispose your dog to heart disease, cancer, musculoskeletal problems, and diabetes.

There are many excellent lower-calorie senior-formula dog foods on the market that will provide your dog with the proper nutrition, yet allow you to continue feeding the same amount of food so that your dog doesn't suspect he is on a diet. You also can try splitting your Boxer's food into several smaller meals during the day, just as you did when he was a puppy, to ease his digestion.

Again, exercise is important, but should not be overdone. Shorter, more frequent walks and swimming, which places less stress on limbs and joints, are good options. Ask your vet for more suggestions on how best to exercise your older Boxer.

Diabetes Mellitus

In this condition, the body's cells are unable to metabolize sugar in the blood due to a deficiency of insulin or the cells' lack of response to insulin. Diabetes is a serious disease that can result in death if left untreated.

Symptoms of diabetes include increased drinking and urination, dehydration, and weight loss. Blood and urine tests can confirm a diagnosis by measuring for elevated sugar levels and abnormally high or low insulin levels. The causes of diabetes range from genetic disorders to obesity and a poor diet.

If your Boxer is diagnosed with diabetes mellitus, he may require insulin injections for the rest of his life. Many owners find it easier to learn to give their pet insulin shots than to be constantly taking their pet to the vet for injections. In addition, the Boxer's diet must be carefully controlled and the obese dog must be slowly trimmed down, under a veterinarian's supervision.

Cancer

Cancer is as dreaded a disease in canines as it is in humans. Ask your breeder about any types of cancer that may run in your dog's family tree and then pass along this information to your vet, so he or she can look out for anything suspicious. Also continue to check your dog's entire body at least once a week for lumps or sores that don't seem to be healing. This body check becomes even more vital as your dog ages, since early detection can dramatically improve your Boxer's chances of survival.

In the past, dogs who were diagnosed with cancer frequently were euthanized as a matter of course. Today, cancer treatments, such as surgery, radiation, chemotherapy, and even gene therapy, are giving many dogs a new lease on life. Unfortunately, the high cost of some of these procedures still prohibits many owners from taking advantage of these life-prolonging options.

Some of the holistic methods of treating cancer include nutritional, herbal, and antioxidant therapies, organic diets, and stress reduction. Always consult with your veterinarian before embarking on any treatment plan.

Kidney and Liver Failure

Older dogs often suffer from kidney and/or liver dysfunction, which, like diabetes, may first be suspected due to increased thirst, urination, and dehydration. Luckily, there are special prescription diets aimed at helping these organs function properly. These diets alone may help prolong life, but combined with medical treatment may allow a dog to live normally—or nearly so—for years. Your vet will run tests on your dog's kidneys and/or liver and plot a course of action.

Cushing's Disease

A pituitary tumor or an adrenal lesion, leading to an abnormally high output of corticosteroid hormones, can cause this disease. Symptoms include weakness, muscle loss, high blood sugar, decreased resistance to infection, and thin, wrinkled skin. Cushing's disease is usually treated with medical therapy.

Heart Disease

Heart problems can show up in previously healthy dogs as they age, just as older humans can develop similar disorders. If your dog seems weak, won't eat, coughs, and cannot tolerate his normal amount of exercise, take him to the vet to check for possible heart problems. While heart disease can rarely be completely cured, it can often be treated with medication, allowing your Boxer to lead a longer, healthier life.

Deafness

Many older dogs develop hearing loss. If lately your dog seems to ignore you or to startle easily when you come up behind him, he may be going deaf. First, ask your vet to check his ears to rule out infection or an excessive buildup of wax. If his ears are clear, you'll have to accept that your dog is hard of hearing and make certain adjustments to better communicate with him and to keep him safe (see the section to follow, How to Keep Your Older Dog Comfortable).

Eye Disorders

The most common eye problems in older dogs are glaucoma and cataracts. Glaucoma is caused by increased pressure in the eye due to a physiological malfunction. The first sign of glaucoma is usually a mild reddening of the white of the eye. If left untreated, the eye(s) may begin to bulge. At this advanced stage, the dog will likely go blind. If you notice any abnormality in your Boxer's eyes, don't risk permanent damage by taking a wait-and-see approach—take your dog to your vet right away.

Cataracts appear as a cloudiness in a dog's eye(s). They are actually a clouding of the lens of the eye, which prevents a dog from having normal vision. Your vet may prescribe a topical medication. Topical medications allow the eye to dilate, so the dog can see around the clouded lens, but they do not treat the cataract itself. Surgery is highly successful and can prevent blindness. Many owners opt to do nothing, however, since most dogs have little trouble coping with a gradual loss of sight (see How to Keep Your Older Dog Comfortable to follow).

> If you notice any abnormality in your Boxer's eyes, don't risk permanent damage by taking a wait-and-see approach—take your dog to your vet right away.

Lenticular sclerosis, a natural aging and clouding of the lens, may appear to be cataracts to the untrained eye. It is different from a cataract, however, because it does not cause blindness, just a mild clouding that the dog sees through well. Although the two conditions may appear similar to you, your vet can tell the difference.

Urinary Incontinence

Owners who are unaware of this potential old-age condition may wonder why their house-trained dog suddenly starts to have accidents. A number of medical conditions can cause incontinence, including a bladder infection or a weakened bladder sphincter muscle. If your dog becomes incontinent, take him to a vet for a thorough examination and to obtain treatment for any medical problems detected.

Even relatively healthy elderly dogs commonly leak urine occasionally, especially while sleeping. Inexpensive medication, phenopropanolamine, can usually minimize or stop this leakage altogether. If medication doesn't solve the problem, you may need to take your Boxer outside to eliminate during the night. In addition, you may want to place a rubber-backed mat or a plastic tarp covered by an old quilt in your dog's sleeping area to protect your floor and carpet. Doggie diapers can also provide somewhat of a solution. Most important, don't punish your dog for behaviors he can't control. He most likely is as upset as you are. At this stage of his life, he needs love and understanding, not scolding and disapproval.

How to Keep Your Older Dog Comfortable

You can do a number of things to keep your dog content and comfortable in her older years. The most important thing is to pay close attention to and to understand your dog's needs. If she seems sore, massage her aching muscles. If she shivers, cover her with a blanket. If she wakes up one day and seems to have forgotten where she is, reassure her with your voice and touch that she is home and she is loved.

Exercise

Being a Boxer, your dog most likely will resist the notion of growing old. There may be days when she seems to think she's a pup again, dashing around the yard with pep and vigor. Then, there may be days when she lies in her bed and doesn't seem to want to get up. If your dog shows a sudden decrease in energy, make an appointment with your vet right away. If the vet rules out medical problems, your pet may just need a little extra attention and some incentive to get moving. Although older dogs naturally slow down, they still need daily exercise. Modify your Boxer's exercise to fit her age and physical condition. Frequent but short, leisurely walks will get your dog's blood pumping and lift her spirits. A game of hide-and-seek or find the hidden toy can also work your dog's mind and body without overtaxing her.

All dogs love routine, but older dogs especially rely on set patterns during their day. Try to pick certain times to exercise

> Frequent but short, leisurely walks will get your dog's blood pumping and lift her spirits.

your pet and stick with the schedule. Your dog will naturally want to spend more time with you as she senses advancing age, and will look forward to these special moments of one-on-one companionship. Keep in mind that older dogs, especially, must warm up before and cool down after any exercise more strenuous than a stroll around the block.

Although routine is important, a little excitement now and then can add spice to your Boxer's day. Take an impromptu ride to the park or a trip to the beach or a lake. Your dog might even enjoy a dip in calm, soothing waters. If you are at the beach, however, don't let her romp any farther than the water's edge; she may swim out into the surf only to find she's not strong enough to swim back. Swimming in a lake or pond (not a flowing river) provides great, low-stress exercise for your dog. Remember to thoroughly dry her off when she comes out of the water, so she doesn't get chilled.

Boxers are naturally vulnerable to extreme heat and cold, and older Boxers are even more so. If you take her out on a warm day, allow your dog plenty of rest in shaded areas and bring along a canteen of cool water. Remember that your pet will need more frequent stops to catch her breath than she did as a youngster.

Your Boxer may always have enjoyed a cozy fleece sweater and booties when accompanying you on a wintery walk in the woods. But if he's never been introduced to doggie apparel, now may be the time to do some clothes shopping, or you can even use one of your old sweaters with the sleeves cut short.

Bedding/Sleeping Area

If your dog has always slept on the floor or on a thin blanket, now is the time to get something a little cushier. Even normal weight can put a lot of strain and pressure on your Boxer's elbows and hips. You can purchase a special orthopedic dog bed or buy egg-carton foam and cover it with blankets or fake sheepskin for a do-it-yourself doggie de-stressor. If your dog has trouble walking up stairs, you may need to move her bed from an upstairs room to a downstairs area.

While your dog will continue to enjoy some time in the yard, she most likely will spend more and more time lounging in the house by your side. Her extra sensitivity to hot and cold weather make the climate-controlled atmosphere of your home even more appealing. Enjoy this extra time with your pet. You will treasure these memories in the years to come.

Grooming

As mentioned earlier, checking your dog from head to toe is even more important as she ages. Look for any signs of odd lumps or bumps and brush your Boxer thoroughly to keep her looking and feeling her best. Older dogs can experience dry skin. Frequent brushing distributes natural oils over the coat and helps keep this problem in check.

Since your dog now gets less intense exercise than she used to, chances are her nails will need more frequent trimming. Don't neglect this important grooming ritual, or your dog's mobility may suffer.

If you traditionally used a grooming table, you may want to switch to grooming your Boxer on the floor. She probably will feel more comfortable there, and you won't have to worry about her losing her balance and falling.

Dental health is also essential as your dog ages. If you've faithfully brushed your pet's teeth and taken her to the vet for regular teeth cleanings over the years, your Boxer's teeth should remain in pretty good shape. If you notice that your dog has difficulty crunching her dry kibble, you may want to soak it in water to soften it or switch to a canned variety. If she still seems to experience pain when she eats, she may need some dental work.

Putting a dog under anesthesia is always an anxious decision for owners, regardless of the dog's age. You may harbor special concerns about your senior Boxer undergoing anesthesia. Your vet can run a battery of tests beforehand to rule out any potential complications. It is also important that you follow any pre-procedure instructions to the letter. For example, feeding a dog before anesthesia can result in your dog choking while she is under. If

Did You Know?

The old rule of multiplying a dog's age by seven to find the equivalent human age is inaccurate. A better measure is to count the first year as 15, the second year as 10, and each year after that as 5.

you have any questions about the instructions, talk about them with your vet, so you can give your dog the best care possible.

Veterinary Visits

Your vet might recommend that you switch your dog to semi-annual veterinary visits, rather than just coming in once a year. The more often your vet sees your dog, the more likely he or she will be able to spot any problems early on. As your dog ages, discuss preventive care with your veterinarian. He or she may want to run a number of tests on your dog to establish a baseline that will provide a comparison should your dog become sick. A typical senior exam will include a urinalysis, stool exam, and complete blood count. Your veterinarian may also run liver and kidney function tests, chest x rays, and an electrocardiogram.

Nutrition

As discussed previously, obesity can pose serious complications in the older dog. Monitor your dog's weight to keep her trim and fit. Feed a balanced diet and keep your treat-giving in check. If your dog seems to be eating too little and has lost interest in her food, try mixing some canned food with her kibble or stir in some water or unsalted chicken broth and slightly heat the mixture to make a gravy. Make sure the mixture cools down sufficiently before giving it to your dog.

Dehydration in an older dog can be disastrous. If your dog seems to "forget" to drink, you may want to add extra water bowls around the house, so he happens upon fresh water frequently. With a particularly forgetful Boxer, you might also want to issue an occasional command to "get a drink."

If your dog's food and water bowls have always rested on the ground, now would be a good time to invest in elevated bowl stands. This will ease stress on your dog's back and also aid in digestion.

What about supplements? Dogs with reduced kidney function tend to lose B vitamins in their excess urine and might benefit from a supplement. Adding calcium and phosphorus can help prevent softening of bones, but this practice can be dangerous if your dog is experiencing kidney failure. Remember to guard against oversupplementation, which also can be dangerous. Talk to your vet to determine which supplements, if any, he or she recommends for your dog.

Communication

You can help a dog who is losing her sight and/or hearing in several ways. If your dog's eyesight starts to wane, she will actually memorize where things are placed in your home. She may get around so well that you occasionally forget she can't see. Avoid rearranging the furniture, as this may result in your dog bumping into things, which can throw off her confidence and cause her to panic. Also, talk to your Boxer when you approach her, so you don't startle your pet. Never let your dog off-leash in an unfenced area; she could easily wander into a dangerous situation that she couldn't see coming.

If your Boxer is losing her hearing, you'll also want to make some adjustments. If she knows obedience hand signals for commands such as Sit or Down, make sure to use those now. But

Did You Know?

The oldest dog ever documented was an Australian cattle dog named Bluey, who was put to sleep at the age of 29 years and 5 months.

if she doesn't know hand signals, don't despair; you can teach an old dog new tricks. Hand signals come in handy in a number of situations, such as when you are trying to call your hard-of-hearing dog back into the house from across the yard. As with a vision-impaired dog, never let a deaf dog off-leash in an unenclosed area.

Older dogs tend to get forgetful, irritable, and cranky. Practice patience and communicate to your dog how much you care about her with daily petting and nightly hugs.

Getting Your Dog a Companion

As their dog ages, many people entertain the idea of getting a puppy. They think it will put some spark in their older dog's life, and they also secretly hope it will ease their pain when their elder dog passes. Before rushing out to buy a pup, however, you should think long and hard about it. Some older dogs, especially those who are still relatively healthy and active and have socialized well with other dogs throughout their lives, will love a new companion. They may rise to the challenge of keeping up with a youngster and the experience may even add years to their life. On the other hand, an infirm senior or a dog who has had little contact with other canines may resent a newcomer and withdraw. Her health may even fade more quickly. Before adding a new pet to the family, carefully consider your dog's disposition and all aspects of the situation.

Saying Goodbye

As with all meaningful relationships in our lives, saying goodbye to our cherished Boxer is the most difficult part of being a dog owner. It is important that we accept this duty with courage and compassion, and make parting as easy as possible for our loyal companions.

How to Know When to Let Go

It's never easy to decide when to end your best friend's time on this earth. The decision is made for some lucky owners, whose dogs die peacefully in their sleep. Unfortunately for the rest of us, a time may come when we'll have to decide when our dog's life is no longer worth living. This is an extremely personal decision that you and you alone must make. Some owners will do anything to extend their dog's life by a few months or even a few weeks, no matter what the cost. Others, whether due to financial considerations or their personal belief against extending their dogs' suffering, will not go to extreme measures to treat their dogs. Many owners decide that when their pet loses his appetite for food, water, and for life itself, it is time to let go. Again, no one can make that decision but you.

What to Expect

When you decide it is time to alleviate your dog's suffering, call your vet. Some vets will make house calls for euthanasia, whereas others will ask you to bring in your dog. Make sure the clinic staff knows the reason for your visit. Most veterinary practices will let you move immediately into an exam room upon your arrival, where you can be alone with your dog, rather than spending your last moments together in a crowded waiting room.

Your vet will describe the procedure to you and will answer any questions you have. Don't feel you need to hold back your tears. Your vet realizes what a difficult time this is and will understand the flood of emotions that comes with the death of a beloved pet. Talk to your Boxer. Stroke his head and tell him how much you love him. We don't know what animals can understand in a situation like this, but your pet surely will feel comforted by your soothing voice and your presence.

If you feel you absolutely cannot be in the room with your dog during his last moments, don't feel guilty. Each person handles saying good-bye to a pet differently. There is no right or wrong way to face death. Know that your need to distance yourself from your dog's final passing will not wipe away or diminish years of loving care.

After your vet has explained the procedure and answered any questions, he or she may sedate your pet. The vet then injects a drug into your dog's bloodstream that causes unconsciousness and heart failure. Your dog may appear to gasp for breath and may lose control of his bladder. Remember, these are physiological reactions to the drug—your dog will experience no pain.

Remembering Your Pet

Once you say good-bye, you can ask your veterinarian to take care of your dog's remains or you can have your dog cremated and request the ashes. A burial, in your backyard (if local ordinances allow) or in a pet cemetery, is another option. For some, a favorite toy buried under a backyard tree provides the perfect memorial, while others choose to give a donation to an animal charity in their dog's honor. Whatever you choose, make sure you do what feels right for you and your family. The most important thing to remember is that emo-

Leaving Your Pet in Your Will

Who will care for your pet if you die before he does? Many people neglect to think about this, with the result being their beloved pet is placed in an animal shelter after their death. Talk with family and friends and find someone who is truly willing and able to take care of your dog if you should pass. Then speak with your lawyer and include your pet in your will. You may also want to specify a certain amount of money to go to the person caring for your Boxer to offset the costs of food, veterinary care, and other pet-related expenses.

tional pain and grief are natural and must be experienced before the healing can begin.

Stages of Grief

Immediately after losing a pet, you'll probably feel numb; this often accompanies shock and denial. This first stage usually lasts longer for those whose pet's death was unexpected. The death of a senior dog who seemed fine one day, then rapidly declined, may leave his owner feeling that this couldn't possibly have happened.

During the middle stage of grief, you'll likely be filled with depression and anger. You may wake up in the morning expecting to find your Boxer at your feet, only to be hit with a rush of emotion as you remember your dog is no longer with you. You may think you hear the sound of clicking nails in the kitchen or the jingle of dog tags down the hall. You may feel guilty for not trying an experimental medical procedure, or you may feel angry with the veterinarian for not being able to cure your dog. You may find it difficult to make it through the day without crying, and you may

Veterinary Teaching Hospital Grief Hotlines

○ University of California, Davis, California, (916) 752-4200, 6:30-9:30 P.M. PST, Monday through Friday

○ Colorado State University, Fort Collins, Colorado, (970) 491-1242, 9:00 A.M.-5:00 P.M., MT, Monday through Friday

○ University of Florida, Gainesville, Florida, (352) 392-4700 (ext. 4080), takes messages 24 hours a day; someone will call back between 7:00-9:00 P.M. EST

○ Michigan State University, East Lansing, Michigan, (517) 432-2696, 6:30-9:30 P.M. EST, Tuesday, Wednesday, and Thursday

○ Ohio State University, Columbus, Ohio, (614) 292-1823, takes messages 6:30-9:30 P.M. EST, Monday, Wednesday, and Friday

○ University of Pennsylvania, Philadelphia, Pennsylvania, (215) 898-4529

○ Tufts University, North Grafton, Massachusetts, (508) 839-7966, 6:00-9:00 P.M. EST, Monday through Friday

○ Virginia-Maryland Regional College of Veterinary Medicine, Blacksburg, Virginia, (540) 231-8038, 6:00-9:00 P.M. EST, Tuesday and Thursday

○ Washington State University, Pullman, Washington, (509) 335-4569, 6:30-9:00 P.M. PST, Monday, Wednesday, Thursday, 1:00-3:00 P.M. PST, Saturday

have a hard time concentrating at work. It is important at this time to surround yourself with other pet lovers who will understand your grief and not criticize, wondering how you can be so upset over the death of an animal.

The final stage of grief is acceptance. At this point, you'll believe and understand the death of your pet, and the pain may begin to fade. Still, a tug at your heart may accompany memories of your Boxer.

If you experience difficulty reaching this final stage, you may need to seek outside help. Veterinary schools across the nation offer grief-counseling hotlines (see sidebar). You also can check with your veterinarian for local pet-loss counseling services, which humane societies often offer. Books and Internet sites on dealing with the death of a pet can also offer some solace.

Many owners feel they need time to grieve before they can think of getting another pet, while others rush out to buy a puppy to help ease the pain. Whatever you do, realize that a new pet is an individual and can never fully replace your lost Boxer. Appreciate your new pet for the wonderful dog he is and remember your pet for what he was—the Boxer love of your life.

Appendix: Resources

Boarding, Pet Sitting, Traveling

Books

Dog Lover's Companion series
Guides on traveling with dogs
   for several states and cities
Foghorn Press
P.O. Box 2036
Santa Rosa, CA 95405-0036
(800) FOGHORN

*Take Your Pet Too!: Fun
   Things to Do!,* Heather
   MacLean Walters
M.C.E. Publishing
P.O. Box 84
Chester, NJ 07930-0084

Take Your Pet USA, Arthur
   Frank
Artco Publishing
12 Channel St.
Boston, MA 02210

*Traveling with Your Pet 1999:
   The AAA Petbook,* Greg
   Weeks, Editor
Guide to pet-friendly lodging
   in the U.S. and Canada

Vacationing With Your Pet!,
   Eileen Barish
Pet-Friendly Publications
P.O. Box 8459
Scottsdale, AZ 85252
(800) 496-2665

Other resources

The American Boarding Kennels Association
4575 Galley Road, Suite 400-A
Colorado Springs, CO 80915
(719) 591-1113
www.abka.com

Independent Pet and Animal Transportation Association
5521 Greenville Ave., Ste 104-310
Dallas, TX 75206
(903) 769-2267
www.ipata.com

National Association of Professional Pet Sitters
1200 G St. N.W., Suite 760
Washington, DC 20005
(800) 296-PETS
www.petsitters.org

Pet Sitters International
418 East King Street
King, NC 27021-9163
(336)-983-9222
www.petsit.com

Breed Information, Clubs, Registries

American Boxer Club
www.akc.org/breeds/recbreeds/boxer.cfm

American Kennel Club
5580 Centerview Drive
Raleigh, NC 27606-3390
(919) 233-9767
www.akc.org/

Canadian Kennel Club
Commerce Park
89 Skyway Ave., Suite 100
Etobicoke, Ontario, Canada M9W 6R4
(416) 675-5511
www.ckc.ca

InfoPet
P.O. Box 716
Agoura Hills, CA 91376
(800) 858-0248

The Kennel Club
(British equivalent to the American Kennel Club)
1-5 Clarges Street
Piccadilly
London W1Y 8AB
ENGLAND
http://www.the-kennel-club.org.uk/

National Dog Registry
Box 116
Woodstock, NY 12498
(800) 637-3647
www.natldogregistry.com/

Tatoo-A-Pet
6571 S.W. 20th Court
Ft. Lauderdale, FL 33317
(800) 828-8667
www.tattoo-a-pet.com

United Kennel Club
100 East Kilgore Rd.
Kalamazoo, MI 49001-5598
(616) 343-9020
http://ukcdogs.com

United States Boxer Association
http://members.aol.com/Usabox/index.html

Dog Publications

AKC Gazette and AKC Events Calendar
51 Madison Avenue
New York, NY 10010
Subscriptions: (919) 233-9767
www.akc.org/gazet.htm
www.akc.org/event.htm

ARK, quarterly newsletter of the American Rottweiler Club
Marilyn Piusz
339 County Highway 106
Johnston, N.Y. 12095

Direct Book Service
(800) 776-2665
www2.dogandcatbooks.com/direct-book

Dog Fancy
P.O. Box 6050
Mission Viejo, CA 92690
(949) 855-8822
www.dogfancy.com

Dog World
500 N. Dearborn, Suite 1100
Chicago, IL 60610
(312) 396-0600
www.dogworldmag.com/

Fun, Grooming, Obedience, Training

American Dog Trainers Network
161 W. 4th Street
New York, NY 10014
www.inch.com/~dogs/index.html
(212) 727-7257

American Grooming Shop Association
(719) 570-7788

American Herding Breed Association
1548 Victoria Way
Pacifica, CA 94044
www.globalcenter.com/~joell/abba/main.htm

American Kennel Club (tracking, agility, obedience, herding)
Performance Events Dept.
5580 Centerview Drive
Raleigh, NC 27606
(919) 854-0199
www.akc.org/

American Pet Dog Trainers
P.O. Box 385
Davis, CA 95617
(800) PET-DOGS

Animal Behavior Society
Susan Foster
Department of Biology
Clark University
950 Main Street
Worcester, MA 01610-1477

Association of Pet Dog Trainers
P.O. Box 385
Davis, CA 95617
(800) PET-DOGS
www.apdt.com/

The Dog Agility Page
http://www.dogpatch.org/agility/

Grooming supplies
Pet Warehouse
P.O. Box 752138
Dayton, OH 45475-2138
(800) 443-1160

Intergroom
76 Carol Drive
Dedham, MA 02026
www.intergroom.com

National Association of Dog Obedience Instructors
PMB #369
729 Grapevine Highway
Hurst, TX 76054-2085
http://www.nadoi.org/

National Dog Groomers Association
of America
P.O. Box 101
Clark, PA 16113
(724) 962-2711

North American Dog Agility Council
HCR 2 Box 277
St. Maries, ID 83861
www.nadac.com

North American Flyball Association
1400 W. Devon Ave, #512
Chicago, IL 60660
(309) 688-9840
http://muskie.fishnet.com/~flyball
/flyball.html

Schutzund
Landesverband DVG America
113 Vickie Drive
Del City, OK 73115
http://webusers.anet-
stl.com/~dvgamer/

United Schutzhund Clubs of America
3704 Lemay Ferry Road
St. Louis, MO 63125

United States Dog Agility Association, Inc.
P.O. Box 850955
Richardson, Texas 75085-0955
(972) 231-9700
www.usdaa.com/

United States Canine Combined Training Association
2755 Old Thompson Mill Road
Buford, GA 30519
(770) 932-8604
http://www.siriusweb.com/USCCTA/

Grief Hotlines

Chicago Veterinary Medical Association
(630) 603-3994

Cornell University
(607) 253-3932

Michigan State University
College of Veterinary Medicine
(517) 432-2696

Tufts University (Massachusetts)
School of Veterinary Medicine
(508) 839-7966

University of California, Davis
(530) 752-4200

University of Florida at Gainesville
College of Veterinary Medicine
(352) 392- 4700

Virginia-Maryland Regional College of Veterinary Medicine
(540) 231-8038

Washington State University
College of Veterinary Medicine
(509) 335-5704

Humane Organizations and Rescue Groups

American Humane Association
63 Inverness Drive E
Englewood CO   80112-5117
(800) 227-4645
www.americanhumane.org

American Society for the Prevention of Cruelty to Animals (ASPCA)
424 East 92nd Street
New York, NY 10128-6804
(212) 876-7700
www.aspca.org

Animal Protection Institute of America
P.O. Box 22505
Sacramento, CA 95822
(916) 731-5521

Humane Society of the United States
2100 : Street. NW
Washington, DC 20037
(301) 258-3072, (202) 452-1100
www.hsus.org/

Massachusetts Society for the Pre-
    vention of Cruelty to Animals
350 South Huntington Avenue
Boston, MA 02130
(617) 522-7400
http://www.mspca.org/

SPAY/USA
14 Vanderventer Avenue
Port Washington, NY 11050
(516) 944-5025, (203) 377-1116 in
    Connecticut
(800) 248-SPAY
www.spayusa.org/

Medical and Emergency Information

American Animal Hospital Associa-
    tion
P.O. Box 150899
Denver, CO 80215-0899
(800) 252-2242
www.healthypet.com

American Holistic Veterinary Medi-
    cine Association
2214 Old Emmorton Road
Bel Air, MD 21015
(410) 569-2346
www.altvetmed.com

American Kennel Club Canine
    Health Foundation
251 West Garfield Road, Suite 160
Aurora, OH 44202
(888) 682-9696

American Veterinary Medical
    Association
1931 North Meacham Road, Suite
    100
Schaumburg, IL 60173-4360
(847) 925-8070
http://www.avma.org/

Canine Eye Registration Inc.
    (CERF)
Veterinary Medical Data Program
South Campus Courts, Building C
Purdue University
West Lafayette, IN 47907
(765) 494-8179
www.vet.purdue.edu/~yshen/cerf.html

Centers for Disease Control and
  Prevention
1600 Clifton Road NE
Atlanta, GA 30333
(404) 639-3311 (CEC Operator)
(800) 311-3435 (CEC Public In-
  quiries)
www.cdc.gov

National Animal Poison Control
  Center
1717 S. Philo, Suite 36
Urbana, IL 61802
(888) 426-4435, $45 per case, with as
  many follow-up calls as necessary
  included. Have name, address,
  phone number, dog's breed, age,
  sex, and type of poison ingested, if
  known, available
www.napcc.aspca.org

Orthopedic Foundation for Animals
  (OFA)
2300 E. Nifong Blvd.
Columbia, MO 65201-3856.
(573) 442-0418
www.offa.org/

PennHip
c/o Synbiotics
11011 Via Frontera
San Diego, CA 92127
(800) 228-4305

Pet First Aid: Cats and Dogs, by
  Bobbi Mammato, DVM
Mosby Year Book

*Skin Diseases of Dogs and Cats: A
  Guide for Pet Owners and Profes-
  sionals,* Dr. Steven A. Melman
Dermapet, Inc.
P.O. Box 59713
Potomac, MD 20859

U.S. Pharmacopeia
vaccine reactions: (800) 487-7776
customer service: (800) 227-8772
www.usp.org

Veterinary Medical Database/Canine
  Eye Registration Foundation
Department of Veterinary Clinical
  Science
School of Veterinary Medicine
Purdue University
West Lafayette, IN 47907
(765) 494-8179
http://www.vet.purdue.edu/~yshen/

Veterinary Pet Insurance (VPI)
4175 E. La Palma Ave., #100
Anaheim, CA 92807-1846
(714) 996-2311
(800) USA PETS, (877) PET
  HEALTH in Texas
www.petplan.net/home.htm

Nutrition and Natural Foods

California Natural, Natural Pet
Products
PO Box 271
Santa Clara, CA 95052
(800) 532-7261
www.naturapet.com

Home Prepared Dog and Cat Diets,
Donald R. Strombeck
Iowa State University Press
(515) 292-0140

*Infectious Diseases of the Dog and
Cat*, Craig E. Greene, Editor
W B Saunders Company

PHD Products Inc.
PO Box 8313
White Plains, NY 10602
(800) 863-3403
www.phdproducts.net/

Sensible Choice, Pet Products Plus
5600 Mexico Road
St. Peters, MO 63376
(800) 592-6687
www.sensiblechoice.com/

Search and Rescue Dogs

National Association for Search and
Rescue
4500 Southgate Place, Suite 100
Chantilly, VA 20151-1714
(703) 222-6277
http://www.nasar.org/

National Disaster Search Dog Foundation
323 East Matilija Avenue, #110-245
Ojai, CA 93023-2740
http://www.west.net/~rescue/

Service and Working Dogs

Canine Companions for Indepen-
dence
P.O. Box 446
Santa Rosa, CA 95402-0446
(800) 572-2275
http://www.caninecompanions.org/

Delta Society National Service Dog
Center
289 Perimeter Road East
Renton, WA 98055-1329
(800) 869-6898
http://petsforum.com/deltasociety/ds
b000.htm

Guiding Eyes for the Blind
611 Granite Springs Road
Yorktown Heights, NY 10598
http://www.guiding-eyes.org/

North American Working Dog
   Association
Southeast Kreisgruppe
P.O .Box 833
Brunswick, GA 31521

The Seeing Eye
P.O. Box 375
Morristown, NJ 07963-0375
(973) 539-4425
http://www.seeingeye.org/

Therapy Dogs Incorporated
2416 E. Fox Farm Road
Cheyenne, WY 82007
(877) 843-7364
www.therapydogs.com

Therapy Dogs International
6 Hilltop Road
Mendham, NJ 07945
(973) 252-9800
http://www.tdi-dog.org/

United Schutzhund Clubs of
   America
3704 Lemay Ferry Road
St. Louis, MO 63125

Index

for leptospirosis, 115–116
for Lyme disease, 116, 137
for parainfluenza, 115
for parvovirus, 114–115
of pet shop puppies, 27
for rabies, 67, 114, 115
Vegetarian diets, 81
Veterinarians/clinics. *See also* Emergencies; First
     aid; Health concerns; *specific symptoms*
  for aging Boxers, 276
  annual visits, 111–112, 276
  costs, 106, 125–129
  first visit to, 108–111
  flea control and, 134, 135
  food allergies and, 92
  food preparation consultation, 90
  insurance, 126, 127, 128
  prescription diets and, 92
  questions asked by, 111
  questions to ask, 104–105, 107, 110
  savings plans, 127, 129
  selecting, 103–108
  sick calls and emergencies, 121–125
  supplements and, 100, 101, 277
  vaccinations, 27, 67, 112–117, 137
  when to call, 122–124
Vinegar in squirt bottle for training, 191–192
Virginia-Maryland Regional College of Veterinary
     Medicine grief hotline, 282
Vision. *See* Eyes
Vitamins
  C and E as preservatives for fats, 83
  need for, 83–84
  supplements, 99–101, 277
VMDs (doctors of veterinary medicine). *See* Vet-
     erinarians/clinics
Voice tones for training, 177–178
Vomiting
  blood in, 124
  choking from, 146–147
  from coronavirus, 116
  from distemper, 114

first aid for, 144–145
from hepatitis, 114
from leptospirosis, 115
overview, 144–145
from parvovirus, 115
from poisoning, 154
from rabies, 115
removing stains and odors, 72
from roundworms, 139–140
when to call the vet, 123

W, X

Walking. *See also* Exercise and activities
  Canine Good Citizen (CGC) Test, 232
  difficulties from ear mites, 138
  need for, 16, 229–230
  neighborhood etiquette, 251
  nicely on a leash, 169, 205–207
  responsibility for, 50
Walking dandruff (mange), 138
Washing. *See* Cleanliness; Grooming
Washington State University grief hotline, 282
Water
  for aging Boxers, 276–277
  dishes, 62
  giardia in, 143
  need in diet, 84–85
  other drinks, 98
  swimming, 230
Weakness. *See also* Fatigue; Lethargy
  from Cushing's disease, 270
  from distemper, 115
  from heart disease, 270
  from leptospirosis, 115
  from Lyme disease, 116
Weight
  maintenance diet, 159–160
  obesity, 83, 92, 159–161, 267–268
  of puppies, 37, 160–161
  rib-check test, 159
  signs of overweight, 95, 159
  world's heaviest dog, 91

Meet Your Boxer Care Experts

Author   Kim D.R. Dearth is a native New Yorker who graduated from the University of North Carolina at Chapel Hill. A frequent contributor to *Dog World* magazine, Kim is a member of both the Dog Writers Association of America (DWAA) and the Cat Writers' Association (CWA). In 1999, Kim won the DWAA special award for excellence in writing on the topic of grooming. Kim teaches classes in puppy preschool, puppy kindergarten, companion obedience, and agility with her able assistant, Rio, a Shetland Sheepdog. In addition, she is the editor of five local special-interest newspapers in Madison, Wisconsin, where she lives with her husband, her Sheltie Rio, and two cats.

Trainer   Liz Palika has been teaching classes for dogs and their owners for over twenty years. Her goal is to help people understand why their dogs do what they do so that dogs and owners can live together successfully. Liz says, "If, in each training class, I can increase understanding and ease frustration so that the dog doesn't end up in the local shelter because the owner has given up, then I have accomplished my goal!" She is the author of 23 books and has won awards from both the Dog Writers Association of America and the ASPCA. Liz and her husband, Paul, share their home with three Australian Shepherds: Dax, Kes, and Riker.

Series Editor   Joanne Howl, D.V.M., is a graduate of the University of Tennessee College of Veterinary Medicine and has practiced animal medicine for over 10 years. She currently serves as president of the Maryland Veterinary Medical Association and secretary/treasurer of the American Academy on Veterinary Disaster Medicine, and her columns and articles have appeared in a variety of animal-related publications. Dr. Howl presently divides her time between family, small animal medicine, writing, and the company of her two dogs and six cats.